RUSSIAN
PHILOSOPHY

EDITED BY

JAMES · M · EDIE
Northwestern University

JAMES · P · SCANLAN
Ohio State University

MARY-BARBARA · ZELDIN
Hollins College

WITH THE COLLABORATION OF

GEORGE · L · KLINE
Bryn Mawr College

RUSSIAN
PHILOSOPHY

VOLUME II

The Nihilists

The Populists

Critics of Religion and Culture

THE UNIVERSITY OF TENNESSEE PRESS

Acknowledgments

THE EDITORS WISH to thank the publishers who have granted permission to reprint material from the following books:

Alexander Radishchev, *A Journey from Saint Petersburg to Moscow*, Cambridge, Mass., Harvard University Press, 1958.

Alexander Herzen, *From the Other Shore*, New York, George Braziller Inc.; London, Weidenfeld & Nicolson Ltd., 1956.

Fyodor Dostoevsky, *Notes from Underground*, London, William Heinemann Ltd.

Fyodor Dostoevsky, *Summer Impressions*, London, John Calder Ltd., 1955.

Fyodor Dostoevsky, *The Brothers Karamazov*, New York, Random House, 1943.

Fyodor Dostoevsky, *Diary of a Writer*, New York, Charles Scribner's Sons, 1954.

V. V. Rozanov, *Solitaria*, London, Wishart & Co., 1927.

V. V. Rozanov, *L'Apocalypse de notre temps*, Paris, Plon, 1930.

Vladimir Solovyov, *A Solovyov Anthology*, London, Student Christian Movement Press Ltd., 1950.

Nicholas Berdyaev, "Marx versus Man" from *Religion in Life*, Nashville, The Abingdon Press, Inc., 1938.

Nicholas Berdyaev, *Dream and Reality*, London, Geoffrey Bles; New York, The Macmillan Co., 1950.

Nicholas Berdyaev, *Slavery and Freedom*, London, Geoffrey Bles, 1939; New York, Charles Scribner's Sons, 1944.

Nicholas Berdyaev, *The Beginning and the End*, London, Geoffrey Bles; New York, Harper and Brothers, 1952.

Nicholas Berdyaev, *Solitude and Society*, London, Geoffrey Bles, 1938.

Nicholas Berdyaev, *The Destiny of Man*, London, Geoffrey Bles; New York, Harper and Brothers, 1937.

Nicholas Berdyaev, *The End of Our Time*, London and New York, Sheed and Ward, 1933.

Nicholas Berdyaev, *The Divine and the Human*, London, Geoffrey Bles, 1949.

Leon Shestov, *Kierkegaard et la philosophie existentielle*, Paris, J. Vrin, 1936.

George Plekhanov, *The Role of the Individual in History*, New York, International Publishers, 1940.

George Plekhanov, *Fundamental Problems of Marxism*, New York, International Publishers, n.d.

We also wish to thank Professor Peter K. Christoff and Mouton & Co. of The Hague for permission to publish Professor Christoff's translation of Ivan Kireyevsky's "On the Necessity and Possibility of New Principles in Philosophy" prior to its appearance in the series of "Slavistic Printings and Reprintings" being published by Mouton & Co. We wish to thank Philip Rahv and the *Partisan Review* for permission to reprint Mr. Rahv's translation of Vissarion Belinsky's "Letters to V. P. Botkin" which appeared in the *Partisan Review* in the Fall issue of 1960 (pp. 728-736); Professor Marvin Farber, editor of *Philosophy and Phenomenological Research*, for permission to reprint George L. Kline's translation of Leon Shestov's "In Memory of a Great Philosopher: Edmund Husserl," which appeared in that journal in June, 1962 (pp. 449-471); Donald A. Lowrie for permission to use his translation of Nicholas Berdyaev's "Marx versus Man"; Mrs. Tatiana Frank and Victor Frank for permission to use selections from Simon Frank's *Reality and Man* prior to its publication in English, and Mrs. Natalie Duddington for permission to publish her translation of Simon Frank's "Of the Two Natures in Man" and Nicholas O. Lossky's "Intuitivism."

We thank the officials of the Northwestern University Graduate School, Goucher College, the Hollins College Faculty Research and Travel Fund, and the Ford Foundation for grants to the editors for research and the preparation of this work.

We wish to recognize the following libraries for special assistance given in research on this work: The Library of Congress, The New York Public Library, The Newberry Library, The University of Chicago Library, The Fishburn Library of Hollins College, The Columbia University Library, The Widener Library at Harvard University, The Library of the United States Information Service in Calcutta, The National Library of Calcutta, The Goucher College Library, and The Northwestern University Library.

Our special thanks go to Professor Jesse Zeldin of Hollins College for his substantial editorial advice on the work as a whole, to Professor Wallace Cayard of West Liberty State College for his help in making the Berdyaev selections, and to Leo Werneke for his help in preparing the index, as well as to Miss Dorothy A. Doerr, Librarian of the Fishburn Library, and Mrs. Sue Deaton Ross and Mrs. Marilyn Scanlan for their help in preparing the manuscript.

Finally, we are particularly indebted to Professor George L. Kline for his assistance in the preparation of this work. He not only contributed a number of original translations but also gave substantial help by revising several other translations, by suggesting selections to be included, by putting at our disposal his vast fund of general and specific knowledge in the field of Russian thought and Russian philosophy, and by giving us invaluable aid and advice in the preparation of this work as a whole and of each of its parts. Without his help and inspiration the publication of this historical anthology of Russian philosophy could have been neither successfully planned nor achieved.

J. M. E.

J. P. S.

M.-B. Z.

Preface

Russian speculation has always been decidedly *man-centered*. From the beginnings of philosophy in the seventeenth and eighteenth centuries, and into the post-Revolutionary emigration, certain themes have remained constant: the problem of good and evil in individual and social life, the meaning of individual existence, the nature of history. Russian thinkers turned late, and hesitantly, to such technical disciplines as logic, theory of knowledge, and philosophy of science. Even metaphysics and philosophical theology, as practiced in Russia, were intimately linked to ethics, social philosophy, and the philosophy of history. Indeed, the small group of Russian religious thinkers who might be called "theocentric" rather than "anthropocentric" made their most striking *philosophical* contributions in these same man-centered disciplines.

Furthermore, Russian philosophical thought has been uniquely non-academic and non-institutional. One could scarcely write a history of philosophy in Germany without including such professional academics as Kant, Fichte, Schelling, and Hegel; nor could one discuss philosophy in the twentieth century without reference to Professors Heidegger, Whitehead, Wittgenstein, and Carnap.

In Russia the situation was quite different: the original and influential thinkers (and originality of thought has not always coincided with influence) have almost without exception been non-academic. The professors of philosophy in the universities and theological academies, though competent, tended to be faithful disciples of one or another Western master rather than

independent thinkers. Vladimir Solovyov is an exception, but
even he left the academic world fairly early, as a result of
differences with university and governmental authorities.

Thus the major Russian thinkers—until the twentieth century
—were not university professors but, in a large sense, "critics."
Their counterparts in Western Europe would be thinkers like
Kierkegaard, John Stuart Mill, Nietzsche and Sartre (both of
whom *began* as professors), the later Santayana and the later
Wittgenstein. Most of these Russians made their living by writing
book reviews; professionally they were literary critics. But "literature" in Russia has always been conceived very broadly—to
include not just poetry, the novel, and the short story, but also
political and philosophical commentary. In the current English
sense of the terms, these Russians were political, social, and
cultural critics as well as literary critics. (The untranslatable
Russian word for such wide-ranging "literary" activity is
publitsistika.)

In Russia, more than elsewhere, the major literary figures have
been concerned with philosophical problems, or, more precisely,
with philosophical formulations of the perennial "problems of
men." Tolstoy, Dostoevsky, and Pasternak are the obvious examples; less well known in this regard are Gogol and, among the
poets, Fet (who translated Schopenhauer), and the Symbolists,
particularly Blok and Bely. At the same time, many Russian
thinkers best known as literary, philosophical, and religious critics
have been gifted and productive poets: for example, Skovoroda,
Radishchev, Khomyakov, and, of course, Vladimir Solovyov.

Related both to its non-academic character and to its involve-
ment with *belles lettres* is the fact that Russian philosophical
thought has been marked by a special intensity and an impatience
with moderation. A kind of personal risk, an "existential" decision or commitment, was involved in being an intellectual in
Russia, a commitment to oppose the repressive aspects of "Russian
reality" (and sometimes of Western theory) in the name of
human freedom and dignity. This in turn is related to the almost
monastic isolation of the nineteenth-century Russian *intelligentsia*,
and the exclusion (after the Decembrist uprising of 1825) of free
and creative thinkers from academic life. University instruction
in philosophy was formally proscribed in Russian universities

from 1850 until 1863. From 1884 to 1889, permitted instruction was officially limited to lecture-commentaries on selected texts of Plato and Aristotle.

From the 1830's on, the informal philosophical discussion group or "circle" (*kruzhok*, pl. *kruzhki*) was a major instrument of philosophical education among the most gifted of Russian university students, as well as a major channel for the penetration of German metaphysics and French socialist theory into Russian intellectual life.

For the reasons sketched above, philosophy in Russia was seldom "pure"—in the sense of non-committed or non-instrumental. Ideas, for the Russian intellectuals of the nineteenth century, were weapons. Most Russians viewed "pure" philosophy, in the Platonic sense of the "passion to know the truth," not merely as an abstruse exercise but also as an evasion of pressing moral and socio-political concerns. This attitude can be expressed in Russian by saying that they subordinated *istina*—theoretical truth—to *pravda*—practical "truth-justice." Russian thinkers conceived their central task as the *iskaniye pravdy*—the quest for truth-justice.

On this question it is possible to distinguish a "rationalist" and an "irrationalist" tradition in Russian thought. The rationalists (e.g., the "Men of the Sixties," Tolstoy, Solovyov, the Marxists) assumed that theoretical truth (*pravda-istina*) can and should serve as a support for practical justice (*pravda-spravedlivost*) in individual and social life. The irrationalists—inconsistently and hesitantly in the nineteenth century (e.g., Herzen and the Populists)—consistently and unhesitatingly in the twentieth century (Shestov)—assumed the priority of *pravda-spravedlivost*, in the sense of moral value, and were willing to bracket, or reject outright, the claims of *pravda-istina*, understood as theoretical truth. In Shestov's formulation: one must either absolutize theoretical truth and thus relativize moral values, or else relativize theoretical truth in order to absolutize moral values, thus "redeeming" the life of the existing individual.

This "either-or" echoes Kierkegaard's, although Shestov formulated it—under the influence of Dostoevsky and Nietzsche—long before he had read Kierkegaard. However, Shestov's "revolt against reason" is also in part a revolt against Kant's terminological assimilation (perpetuated by Hegel) of speculation to action, of "theoretical reason" to "practical reason." For Shestov the common term is a fraud: what the German philosophers, up to but not including Schopenhauer and Nietzsche, had called "practical reason" is not *reason* at all—is not cognitive, but instinctive, intuitive, emotive—a mode of value-appropriation, of decision, and action. In this sense, Shestov's "existentialism," even more than Berdyaev's, represents the culmination of one major tradition in Russian philosophy. The other major tradition—that of the "rationalists"—is today represented chiefly by the epigoni of Marxism-Leninism, who are, needless to say, unalterably opposed to every form of existential philosophy.

Russian Philosophical Terminology

Russian philosophical terminology was largely stabilized during the 1830's and 1840's, partly under the influence of Bakunin and Belinsky, partly under the influence of such Slavophiles as Kireyevsky and Khomyakov—all of them drawing heavily upon Hegelian models. Russian is the only European language that has a precise technical equivalent of Hegel's notorious *Aufhebung,* i.e., *snyatiye.* The term is sometimes (inadequately) rendered in English by the exotic "sublation." (The Russian *snyatiye* preserves the threefold sense—not suggested by the English—of "cancellation," "raising to a higher level," and "preservation.")

The Hegelian coloring of Russian philosophical terminology— fixed long before Marxism had appeared on the Russian scene— was doubtless a mixed blessing. It made possible distinctions which were often invidious and sometimes careless, e.g., the Slavophile opposition of "Reason"—*razum (Vernunft)*—to mere "Understanding"—*rassudok (Verstand).* And it preserved ambiguities which might better have been dissolved, e.g., *pravo (Recht):* meaning both "law" and "right"; *samosoznaniye (Selbstbewusstsein):* meaning both consciousness *of* self and consciousness *by* self, i.e., the self as, respectively, object and subject of awareness; *nauka (Wissenschaft),* in the broad sense which includes philosophy and scholarship as well as science. But this Hegelian terminology had the marked advantage of bringing Russian philosophical discourse into contact with a lively and powerful philosophical tradition.

The present work is intended as a comprehensive anthology of Russian philosophical writings, arranged in generally chronological order. It is designed for use by the student of Russian philosophy and intellectual history, as well as the general reader with an interest in Russian culture. Fortunately, there is almost nothing in Russian philosophical writing so technical as to be beyond the grasp of such a reader.

The selected bibliographies consist primarily of works in English, occasionally supplemented by French or German titles, and very occasionally (in the absence of appropriate non-Russian works) by Russian titles. This applies to primary as well as secondary sources.

The development of Russian philosophy through its various schools and "isms" is traced in the general introductions to each of the nine parts of the work. Detailed discussion of individual thinkers is to be found in the special introductions which precede selections from their work.

SELECTED GENERAL BIBLIOGRAPHY OF WORKS ON RUSSIAN AND SOVIET PHILOSOPHY

Acton, Harry B., *The Illusion of the Epoch: Marxism-Leninism as a Philosophical Creed*, London, 1955; Boston, 1957.

Berdyaev, Nicholas, *The Russian Idea*, trans. R. M. French, New York, 1948; paperback edition: Boston, 1962.

Bochenski, J. M., *Soviet Russian Dialectical Materialism*, trans. from the 3rd German edition by Nicolas Sollohub, Dordrecht, 1963.

Bubnoff, Nikolai von, ed., *Russische Religionsphilosophen. Dokumente*, Heidelberg, 1956.

Chyzhevski, Dmytro, "Hegel in Russland," in *Hegel bei den Slaven*, Bad Homburg vor der Hohe, 1961, pp. 145-396 (reprint of the 1934 edition).

Fedotov, George P., *The Russian Religious Mind*, Cambridge, Mass., 1946.

———, *A Treasury of Russian Spirituality*, New York, 1948.

Jakowenko, Boris V., *Filosofi russi: saggio di storia della filosofia russa*, trans. from the Russian, Florence, 1925.

Koyré, Alexandre, *Etudes sur l'histoire de la pensée philosophique en Russie*, Paris, 1950.

———, *La philosophie et le problème national en Russie au début du XIX* siècle*, Paris, 1929.

Lossky, Nicholas O., *History of Russian Philosophy*, London and New York, 1951.

Marcuse, Herbert, *Soviet Marxism: A Critical Analysis*, New York, 1958; paperback edition with new preface: New York, 1961.

Masaryk, Thomas G., *The Spirit of Russia: Studies in History, Literature and Philosophy*, trans. E. and C. Paul, 2 vols., New York, 1955.

Pascal, Pierre, "Les grands courants de la pensée russe contemporaine," in *Les grands courants de la pensée mondiale contemporaine*, ed. M. F. Sciacca, Milan, 1959, Pt. 1, Vol. 2.

Raeff, Marc, ed., *Russian Intellectual History: An Anthology*, New York, 1966.

Scheibert, Peter, *Von Bakunin zu Lenin: Geschichte der russischen revolutionären Ideologien, 1840-1895*. Vol. 1: *Die Formung des radikalen Denkens in der Auseinandersetzung mit deutschem Idealismus und französischem Bürgertum*, Leiden, 1956.

Schmemann, Alexander, ed., *Ultimate Questions: An Anthology of Modern Russian Religious Thought*, New York, 1965.

Simmons, Ernest J., ed., *Continuity and Change in Russian and Soviet Thought*, Cambridge, Mass., 1955. Especially Pt. IV: "Rationality and Nonrationality," pp. 283-377, with contributions by Theodosius Dobzhansky, Fr. Georges Florovsky, Waldemar Gurian, George L. Kline, and Herbert Marcuse, and a summary and review by Geroid T. Robinson.

Utechin, S. V., *Russian Political Thought: A Concise History*, New York, 1964.

Weidlé, Wladimir, *Russia Absent and Present*, trans. A. Gordon Smith, London and New York, 1952.

Wetter, Gustav A., *Dialectical Materialism: A Historical and Systematic Survey of Philosophy in the Soviet Union*, trans. from the 4th German edition by Peter Heath, London and New York, 1958.

Zenkovsky, V. V., *A History of Russian Philosophy*, trans. George L. Kline, 2 vols., London and New York, 1953.

Contents

VOLUME II

VOLUME III

Book Seven: PRE-REVOLUTIONARY PHILOSOPHY AND
THEOLOGY

NICHOLAS FYODOROV
   The Question of Brotherhood or Relatedness, and of
the Reasons for the Unbrotherly, Dis-Related, or
Unpeaceful State of the World, and of the Means for
the Restoration of Relatedness

VLADIMIR SOLOVYOV
   Lectures on Godmanhood
   The Meaning of Love
   Foundations of Theoretical Philosophy

Book Four

THE NIHILISTS

WHEN MICHAEL BAKUNIN CLOSED HIS ESSAY, "The Reaction in Germany," in 1842 with a celebration of "the passion for destruction," he was in effect anticipating the men of the 1860's—Russian thinkers who went much further in intellectual and social iconoclasm than the Westernizers of the 1840's. On a positive foundation of utilitarianism and materialism in philosophy, the men of this later generation mounted an all-out attack on prevailing Russian social institutions and habits of thought. They were the Russian "Nihilists," led by NICHOLAS CHERNYSHEVSKY (1828-1889), Nicholas Dobrolyubov (1836-1861), and DMITRY PISAREV (1840-1868).

Bakunin himself was a Westernizer whose long and active career as writer and revolutionary spanned both periods, and he accepted the later, Nihilist outlook almost as completely as the younger men did. But on the whole the Westernizers were an obsolete older generation in the eyes of the Nihilists—a situation forcefully dramatized in Ivan Turgenev's *Fathers and Sons* (1862), which gave the very word "Nihilist" to Russian literature and thence to the world. The "fathers" of the novel are full of humanitarian, progressive sentiments; like Belinsky and Herzen, they extol "personality" and individual dignity. But to the "sons," typified by the brusque, scientifically minded Bazarov, the "fathers" were concerned too much with generalities, not enough with the specific material evils of the day. They tended to look at things aesthetically and abstractly rather than scientifically and concretely. "Nature," Bazarov says, "is not a temple but a workshop." Science and its direct practical application alone will benefit man, and no accepted principles or moral rules, no established social institutions, no useless cultural frills like music or painting must be allowed to distract man from them. In one of their direct confrontations, an incredulous "father" questions the Nihilist "sons":

> "I do not understand how you can avoid recognizing principles, rules. What is the motive of your actions?"
>
> "I have already told you, uncle, that we don't recognize any authorities," Arkady intervened.
>
> "We act by the force of what we recognize as beneficial," Bazarov declared. "At the present time rejection is the most beneficial of all things, and so we reject."
>
> "Everything?"
>
> "Everything."
>
> "How? Not only art, poetry—but also—it is a terrible thing to say—"
>
> "Everything!" Bazarov repeated with complete imperturbability.[1]

To the "fathers" they seemed a strange new breed.

The flesh and blood Nihilist leaders bore greater resemblance to human beings and were less alienated from their intellectual forebears than Turgenev suggests, but they *were* men of a somewhat different sort. For one thing, they came chiefly from a lower social stratum. Among the Westernizers only Belinsky was not a member of the gentry; the others were cultivated gentlemen who never completely lost the aura of aristocracy. Among the Nihilists, on the other hand, only Pisarev was of gentry origin. Both Chernyshevsky and Dobrolyubov were sons of provincial Russian Orthodox priests, and in general the Nihilists represented a new class on the Russian intellectual scene— the *raznochintsy*, or men of miscellaneous rank below the gentry: they came from the families of clerics, professional men, minor officials, merchants. Many of them supported themselves by writing for literary journals when they were not in prison or in Siberia. Deeply, even fanatically, dedicated to the cause of freedom and justice, they were the first true members of the non-

1. *The Vintage Turgenev*, New York, 1960, I, 207-208.

aristocratic Russian *"intelligentsia"* (another word given to the world by these mid-nineteenth-century currents of Russian intellectual life).

Furthermore, the Nihilists of the 1860's and the Westernizers of the 1840's lived in different social climates. The men of the forties pleaded for reforms which could scarcely be anything but distant dreams at the height of Nicholas' absolutism. Both Herzen and Bakunin emigrated, and Belinsky died young in 1848. But even while they lived in Russia they were more spectators than hopeful activists, always somewhat removed from the possibility of genuine change. The men of the sixties, on the other hand, had had their appetites whetted for reform. A liberal spirit swept over Russia with the accession of Alexander II in 1855. Restrictions on admittance to the universities were eased, control of the press was reduced, and broad social reforms were promised—above all the abolition of serfdom. When emancipation finally came in 1861, however, it was a bitter disappointment to the men of the sixties, for its terms gave the serfs little chance of economic self-sufficiency or genuine freedom. There were peasant uprisings and student disturbances. Nationalist disorders in Poland added to the agitation of both the government and the *intelligentsia*. Repressive measures against the universities and the press were reintroduced, and the upsurge of hope dating from 1855 began another decline. Chernyshevsky was arrested in 1862 and banished to Siberia in 1864. Pisarev was also arrested in 1862, was imprisoned in the Peter and Paul fortress in Saint Petersburg until 1866, and died near Riga, Latvia, in 1868. The Nihilists, closer to the immediate social evils of Russian life and to the possibility of reform, had greater reason to grow frustrated and take to extremes as this possibility was removed.

A final difference between the Westernizers and the Nihilists lay in their intellectual ancestry. The Westernizers were reared on German idealism, progressing from its romantic extremes to Hegel, who at least temporarily had a great attraction for them. The Nihilists were never enthusiastic idealists if they were idealists at all. Their intellectual pabulum was Feuerbach, the French socialists, and the German "vulgar materialists." Büchner, Moleschott, and Vogt were favorites. Comte's positivism appealed to them. John Stuart Mill came to have great influence among them: they detested his bourgeois liberalism but accepted whole-heartedly the utilitarian pleasure-principle and its ruthless appli-cation to hoary traditions and institutions. Later they read Dar-win, who appealed to them because he brought man out of the clouds and into the mud of animal life—though Chernyshevsky preferred the Lamarckian version of the mechanics of evolution. Unlike the Westernizers, they never passed through a stage of spiritualizing man or advocating a "reconciliation with reality."

It is hardly surprising, then, that the Nihilists should surpass the Westernizers in debunking and rejecting. All these influ-ences conspired to give them a naturalistic outlook in philosophy and a horror of the social *status quo;* their attention was directed to temporal man, encumbered by "irrational" institutions that had, they thought, no right to exist. No doubt they found it not only an intellectual duty but a pleasure to prick the balloons of pompous conventionalism and "aestheticism" in Russian thought and life. Not a little sheer perverse satisfaction is in evidence when Pisarev puts chefs and billiards players on an artistic level with Beethoven and Raphael, or enjoins writers to "hate with a great and holy hatred the enormous mass of petty and rotten stupidities" in Russian life. Among the Nihilist leaders' less scholarly disciples and among the Russian students who used the name "Nihilism" to dignify youthful rebelliousness, this rejection of traditional standards went still further, expressing itself in everything from harmless crudities of dress and behavior to the lethal fanaticism of a revolutionary like Sergey Nechayev.[2] And it was a "Nihilist student," Dmitry Karakozov, whose attempt on the Tsar's life in 1866 completed the return of Russian society to the dark repression of the era of Nicholas I.

It would be a mistake, however, to regard the intellectual leaders of Nihilism as bomb-throwing negativists devoid of posi-tive interests or ideals—a misinterpretation unfortunately fos-tered by the term "Nihilism" itself. Actually a coherent positive doctrine lay behind the harsh slogans; the rejections had a pur-

2. For a discussion of the ideas and activities of Nechayev and other revolutionary activists of the period, see Avrahm Yarmolinsky, *Road to Revolution*, New York, 1962, pp. 114-168.

pose. The "great and holy hatred" Pisarev recommended was needed, he maintained, because existing practices prevented "the ideas of the good, the true, and the beautiful from clothing themselves in flesh and blood and becoming living actuality." [3] Indeed, the philosophical message of Nihilism suffered more from dogmatism than from negativism: the Nihilists were cocksure of their ideas, and they formulated them in a blunt, simplistic fashion foreign to the more measured reflections of the older generation of Westernizers. Chernyshevsky maintains, for example, that "the moral sciences already have theoretical answers to nearly all the problems that are important for life," [4] and as he presents them these answers are by no means complex. Oversimplified and dogmatic, a philosophical system is nonetheless offered by the Nihilists which can be summarized briefly under traditional headings.

Metaphysically, the Nihilists adopted a broadly materialistic position. Both Chernyshevsky and Pisarev explicitly regarded themselves as materialists. To the philosophical critic of today, however, the materialism of the Nihilists, like that of the present-day Dialectical Materialists, may seem extremely capacious, if not vague. Pisarev, in "Nineteenth-Century Scholasticism," identifies materialism simply with the view that only what is perceptible exists, and a similar conception is adopted by Chernyshevsky in "The Anthropological Principle in Philosophy." Pisarev himself provided a revealing commentary on the broad use of "materialism" and related philosophical terms by Russian thinkers: "Since we ourselves," he writes, "have hitherto not been party to any philosophical school, we have contrived to give our own meaning to all the philosophical terms which have come to us in accordance with the level of our own intellectual processes. The results have been most unexpected: anyone who eats, drinks, and sleeps to excess we call a materialist, while to utter fools who cannot do anything practical we give the name of romantic or idealist." [5] But under whatever name, the Nihilists were concerned to view man as a unitary animal organism, to deny the

3. See below, p. 91.
4. See below, p. 40.
5. *Sochineniya D. I. Pisareva*, St. Petersburg, 1894-1897, IV, 39.

existence of "spirits" of any sort, embodied or disembodied—
in short, to acknowledge the world of the natural sciences as
the world of reality. Man, says Chernyshevsky, is a complex
chemical compound, governed strictly by the law of causality.

On this "scientific" basis, Chernyshevsky and Pisarev advanced
a hedonistic ethics of "rational egoism" or egoistic utilitarianism
in which man is viewed as acting, inevitably and properly, to
promote his own self-interest. Their objection to what Pisarev
called "moral twaddle" was, like Nietzsche's after them, not an
objection to the realm of the ethical as such but to an unrealistic and sentimental emphasis on altruism or benevolence—
impulses by which men are never really moved. In this connection, despite their exposure to the writing of John Stuart Mill,
they more closely resembled the earlier British utilitarians, Jer-
emy Bentham and James Mill. But while the Nihilists emphasize
man's selfishness they also insist that only in an ill-constructed
society does egoism yield socially undesirable consequences. In
a properly ordered society the most egoistic behavior will also
be the behavior most productive of the public good. Fundamentally and naturally, the interests of society and the interests of
the individual are identical.

As for the social philosophy in which this proper ordering of
society is depicted, however, there is again considerable loose-
ness in the Nihilists' doctrine—owing at least in part to the fact
that censorship prevented the frank expression of radical convictions. They were, of course, democrats and socialists. In his
famous novel, *What Is To Be Done?*, the most influential literary
vehicle of Nihilism, Chernyshevsky addressed himself to the socialist order of the future in which cooperation rather than competition would prevail. But aside from idealized pictures of a seam-
stresses' cooperative, the book contains little specific discussion
of how this order is to come about or precisely what it will consist in. In other writings Chernyshevsky took up the idea, first
stated by Herzen, that the commune and the *artel* gave Russia
a "special path" to socialism; but it was left to the Populists
of the 1870's to construct a comprehensive social philosophy
incorporating this idea.

In many respects the most significant area of Nihilist philosophical activity was the sphere of aesthetics, literary criticism,

and art. Here again censorship played an important role: literary criticism was permissible where social or religious criticism was not. As a result, much of what is most interesting in the writings of these as well as of other nineteenth-century Russian thinkers comes in the guise of literary criticism or theory of art. But there was also a substantive reason for the Nihilists' attention to aesthetics: it was the stronghold of everything they opposed philosophically. Existing conceptions of aesthetics and art were the bulwark of sentimentalism, emotionalism, irrationalism, spiritualism, and, most of all, of the expenditure of valuable social resources on "useless frills." When Pisarev calls for "the annihilation of aesthetics" it is these conceptions, survivals from the heyday of German romanticism and idealism, that he is attacking. For the Nihilists art *can* be justifiable and valuable, but only if it is *socially useful*. Literature, in particular, can perform an important function in awakening and educating men, stimulating them to improve themselves and ultimately to improve society; to do so it must be hortatory and didactic. On this ground the Russian tradition of "civic criticism," inaugurated by Belinsky in his later years, flourished at the hands first of Dobrolyubov and then of Pisarev among the Nihilists.

But while the major Nihilists gave art a significant role in society, and devoted their own energies largely to the service of art in the form of literature, it was *science* that they saw as man's single most potent intellectual tool. More than anything else it is the worship of natural science that characterized Nihilism as a positive philosophical attitude in the Russia of the 1860's. The Nihilists rejected art when it lay completely outside the realm of science or did not serve science. They rejected history as a study because its content and methods were scientifically dubious. Pisarev observes somewhat petulantly in "The Realists" that if Belinsky had had a proper education in mathematics and the natural sciences, he would have done Russia ten times more good, given his enormous talent, than he did with the "semi-literary, semi-philosophical" education he received.[6] Study the natural sciences and follow no authority but that of your own scientific intellect—such in brief was the positive message of Nihilism.

As a movement Nihilism did not outlast the sixties. By the end

6. *Ibid.,* IV, 33.

of that decade the major figures were either dead or banished, and most of the minor figures had emigrated, many to join the Bakuninist party of revolutionary anarchists.[7] Never a numerous movement, Nihilism nonetheless spawned much discussion, not only among its supporters but also among its critics.[8] Dostoevsky, for example, whose novel *The Possessed* portrays Nihilist leaders in a severely critical light, was strongly affected by Nihilism and returned to the subject repeatedly in other works. Through the Nihilist movement the secularization and radicalization of the Russian *intelligentsia* was completed and a major step was taken toward the more fully developed materialism and socialism of the Russian Marxists. As forerunners of Marxism-Leninism in Russia, the Nihilist leaders are highly regarded by present-day Soviet thinkers.

7. Franco Venturi, *Roots of Revolution*, trans. Francis Haskell, New York, 1960, pp. 328-330.
8. See Charles A. Moser, *Antinihilism in the Russian Novel of the 1860's*, The Hague, 1964.

NICHOLAS GAVRILOVICH
CHERNYSHEVSKY
[1828–1889]

Sometimes called "the first man of the sixties," Nicholas Chernyshevsky gave Russian Nihilism its initial philosophical formulation and became the chief spokesman of revolutionary socialist thought in his day. And through his imprisonment and exile he became, like Alexander Radishchev before him, a symbol of martyrdom to subsequent generations of Russian radicals.

Chernyshevsky was born in the town of Saratov on the lower Volga in 1828. His father, a Russian Orthodox priest, gave him an intensive home education like that of his British contemporary and subsequent mentor, John Stuart Mill; when Nicholas was sent to the local theological seminary in 1842 he was already well versed in the major modern and ancient languages. When he completed the seminary program in 1846, he decided against further theological study and received his parents' consent to enroll in the Faculty of History and Philology at the University of Saint Petersburg. After his graduation from the University in 1850, he returned to Saratov and taught literature in a secondary school. In 1853, he married and again left Saratov for Saint Petersburg to work for a Master's degree in Russian literature. Concurrently he began to write for some of the leading literary journals, soon becoming principal editor of *Sovremennik* (The Contemporary). With his friend and disciple Nicholas Dobrolyubov, Chernyshevsky gave *The Contemporary* its character as the foremost organ of radical opinion in the sixties.

From his early days at the University Chernyshevsky read

widely in the philosophical and political literature which came
to Russia from Western Europe. He first read the German
idealist philosophers, Schelling and Hegel, but an initial attraction
to Hegel soon waned—as did the strong Orthodox religious faith
he brought to the University. When he read Feuerbach's *Essence
of Christianity* in 1849 it impressed him powerfully, and by
1850 he had abandoned idealism completely and become a dedicated Feuerbachian—an allegiance he avowed to the end of his
life. With this development toward philosophical materialism and
atheism went a rapid conversion to socialism. Chernyshevsky
had close contacts with members of the Petrashevsky Circle in
1848 and 1849, and largely through them he was introduced
to the writings of Fourier, Considérant, Proudhon, and Louis
Blanc. He came to admire Russia's older critics, Herzen and
Belinsky—though by the late fifties his radicalism had so far
outstripped theirs that he disagreed vehemently with Herzen
over the tactics of social reconstruction in the homeland. Convinced that salvation could come to Russia only through a violent struggle for socialism and democracy, Chernyshevsky
consciously devoted himself to the revolutionary cause, warning
his bride-to-be that forced labor or hanging would almost surely
be his fate.[1]

Chernyshevsky's first major work, begun in 1853 and published
in 1855, was his Master's dissertation, entitled *The Aesthetic
Relations of Art to Reality*. The main body of the work is a
vigorous if somewhat diffuse critique of the reigning Hegelian
aesthetics. According to Chernyshevsky, the idealistic system errs
by placing art above reality: it sees art as originating in an
irresistible striving for beauty which, unsatisfied by anything
in objective reality, leads man to create artificial embodiments of
true beauty. To counter this separation of art from life, Chernyshevsky advances, in the concluding portions of the essay which
are reprinted here, a position he later identified as "an attempt
to apply Feuerbach's ideas to the solution of the fundamental
problems of aesthetics."[2] Chernyshevsky agrees that art is a sub-

1. Venturi, *op. cit.*, p. 140.
2. Nicholas Chernyshevsky, *Selected Philosophical Essays*, Moscow, 1953,
p. 416.

stitute for concrete reality, but maintains that it is an aesthetically inferior one. True beauty resides in life, and the primary purpose of art is to reproduce living beauty as a compensation for man's frequent lack of opportunity to experience the reality itself. But the artist is not simply a passive recorder; in his selection and creation he explains and passes judgment on the reality he portrays, and this gives his art a moral dimension as well. Art is then justified as being derivative from and subservient to life: such is Chernyshevsky's "realistic," utilitarian message in the realm of aesthetics.

This subordination of aesthetic values to moral and social values is strongly characteristic of Chernyshevsky's contributions to *The Contemporary*, particularly the major essays written in 1855 and 1856 and later collected under the general title, *Essays on the Gogol Period of Russian Literature*. Criticism of this sort was Dobrolyubov's special talent, however, and with the easing of conditions that surrounded the accession of Alexander II, Chernyshevsky turned increasingly to political and economic topics. He was alone among the leading Nihilists in being well equipped to discuss economic issues, having studied some of the major economists such as Adam Smith, Ricardo, Malthus, and J. S. Mill. He addressed himself particularly to the economic questions concerning the Russian peasantry which were raised by the proposed emancipation. In one of his chief works of the period, "A Criticism of Philosophical Prejudices Against the *Obshchina*" (1858), he defended the peasant village commune as the nucleus of socialism in Russia. In 1860, he published an annotated Russian translation of J. S. Mill's *Principles of Political Economy*.

Dating from the same period is Chernyshevsky's chief philosophical work, "The Anthropological Principle in Philosophy" (1860)—a long, rambling essay which begins as a critique of a philosophical work by Peter Lavrov, proceeds to the condition of political thought in Europe, and finally concentrates, in the sections reprinted below, on expounding what Chernyshevsky views as the proper "scientific" approach to all the questions of "the moral sciences." This is the approach, clearly related to Feuerbach's "anthropologism," dictated by what Chernyshevsky calls "the anthropological principle"—the conception of man as a unitary biological organism, no more possessing a dual, spiritual-material nature than a plant or a chemical compound does. In fact, Chernyshevsky maintains that from the scientific point of view man *is* a chemical compound, albeit a highly complex one, and thus is subject to the same laws and necessities as govern all chemical processes. Consequently the methods of the natural sciences are alone applicable to the study of man. Indeed the most fundamental and significant truths about man have already been garnered by the sciences, according to Chernyshevsky. It has been proved, he contends, that men always act egoistically to attain their own good, which ultimately means their own pleasure; that work is natural to man, a prime source of pleasure, while idleness breeds unhappiness; and that a man's character is determined by his environment.

The ethical and social implications of these principles were spelled out by Chernyshevsky in the novel, *What Is To Be Done?*, written when he was already a political prisoner in 1863. Despite its shortcomings from a literary standpoint, this book was Chernyshevsky's single most influential work. In it he attempts to portray in both a credible and an appealing fashion the lives and loves of the "new men"—their contempt for everything traditional, their naturalness, their simplicity, their love of socially useful labor, the "rational" relationships they establish between man and woman. His efforts were accepted without reservation by the young radicals, many of whom had found Turgenev's Bazarov a caricature, and the book became a veritable gospel of Nihilism. Described in less detail by Chernyshevsky were the economic and political features of the new order: the sewing cooperatives established in the novel assumed the character of Fourierist phalansteries, but there is little further discussion of specific features of social organization. Chernyshevsky was interested in economics and politics, but he was more interested in the psychological and moral features of the new order.

Chernyshevsky's arrest in 1862 was less the result of any overt revolutionary activity on his part than of his acknowledged position as leader of the radical forces. After two years in the Peter and Paul fortress he was banished to Siberia. In exile he wrote sporadically, but his situation was onerous and he produced nothing as significant or influential as his earlier works. Besides another novel, entitled *Prologue*, his noteworthy writings of this period include several letters and an essay, "The Character of Human Knowledge" (1885), devoted to questions of epistemology—a subject otherwise largely neglected by the Nihilists. In the essay he adopts a realistic position, condemning neo-Kantian phenomenalism. In 1889, Chernyshevsky was finally permitted to return to his native Saratov, but his health was broken and he died a few months later, after twenty-five years of forced exile.

For more than half of his adult life Chernyshevsky was little more than a symbol of intellectual resistance and of dedication to the cause of justice and freedom. But in this respect his moral influence on the radical Russian *intelligentsia*, added to that of his earlier writings, was enormous and far-reaching. Lenin admired him and was much influenced by *What Is To Be Done?* Nicholas Ishutin, one of the first and most dedicated of the revolutionary activists reared on the novel, declared: "There have been three great men in the world—Jesus Christ, Paul the Apostle, and Chernyshevsky." [3] From a philosophical point of view, Chernyshevsky's significance was not great, but he is important as the first and fullest expounder of the materialistic, utilitarian attitude toward aesthetics, metaphysics, and ethics that Nihilism represents.

SELECTED BIBLIOGRAPHY

Works:
Nicholas G. Chernyshevsky, *Selected Philosophical Essays*, Moscow, 1953.
—————, *What Is To Be Done?*, introd. E. H. Carr, the Benjamin R. Tucker translation revised and abridged by Ludmilla B. Turkevich, New York, 1961.

Secondary Sources:
V. V. Zenkovsky, *A History of Russian Philosophy*, trans. George L. Kline, 2 vols., London and New York, 1953, pp. 320-326.
Franco Venturi, *Roots of Revolution*, trans. Francis Haskell, New York, 1960, pp. 129-186.
E. Lampert, *Sons Against Fathers: Studies in Russian Radicalism and Revolution*, Oxford, 1965.
Francis B. Randall, *Chernyshevskii*, New York, 1967.

3. Quoted in Venturi, *op. cit.*, p. 331.

[NICHOLAS CHERNYSHEVSKY]

The Aesthetic Relations of
Art to Reality *

The sea is beautiful; looking at it, we never think of being
dissatisfied with it, aesthetically. But not everyone lives near the
sea; many people never in their lives get a chance to see it. Yet
they would very much like to see it, and consequently seascapes
please and interest them. Of course, it would be much better
to see the sea itself rather than pictures of it; but when a good
thing is not available, a man is satisfied with an inferior one.
When the genuine article is not present, a substitute will do.
Even the people who can admire the real sea cannot always
do so when they want to, and so they call up memories of it.
But man's imagination is weak; it needs support and prompting.
So to revive their memories of the sea, to see it more vividly
in their imagination, they look at seascapes. This is the sole aim
and object of very many (the majority of) works of art: to give
those people who have not been able to enjoy beauty in reality
the opportunity to acquaint themselves with it at least to some
degree; to serve as a reminder, to prompt and revive memories
of beauty in reality in the minds of those people who are
acquainted with it by experience and love to recall it. . . .

Thus, the first purpose of art is to reproduce nature and life,
and this applies to all works of art without exception. Their
relation to the corresponding aspects and phenomena of reality is
the same as the relation of an engraving to the picture from
which it was copied, or the relation of a portrait to the person
it represents. An engraving is made of a picture not because
the latter is bad, but because it is good. Similarly, reality is

* Reprinted, with extensive revisions and corrections for this volume by
James P. Scanlan, from Nicholas G. Chernyshevsky, *Selected Philosophical
Essays*, Moscow, 1953, pp. 364-377, 379. The revisions and corrections were
made by reference to the Russian text in Nicholas G. Chernyshevsky,
Esteticheskiye otnosheniya iskusstva k deystvitelnosti, Moscow, 1955, pp.
108-125, 128-129.

reproduced in art not in order to eliminate flaws, not because reality as such is not sufficiently beautiful, but precisely because it is beautiful. Artistically an engraving is not superior to the picture from which it is copied, but much inferior to it; similarly, works of art never attain the beauty and grandeur of reality. But the picture is unique; it can be admired only by those who go to the picture gallery which it adorns. The engraving, however, is sold in hundreds of copies all over the world; everyone can admire it whenever he pleases without leaving his room, without getting up from his couch, without throwing off his dressing gown. Similarly, a beautiful object in reality is not always accessible to everyone; reproductions of it (feeble, crude, pale, it is true, but reproductions all the same) in works of art make it always accessible to everybody. A portrait is made of a person we love and cherish not in order to eliminate the flaws in his features—what do we care about these flaws? we do not notice them, or if we do we like them—but in order to give us the opportunity to admire that face even when it is not actually in front of us. Such also is the aim and object of works of art; they do not correct reality, do not embellish it, but reproduce it, serve as a substitute for it. . . .

While not claiming in the least that these words express something entirely new in the history of aesthetic ideas, we think nonetheless that the pseudo-classical "imitation of nature" theory that prevailed in the seventeenth and eighteenth centuries demanded of art something different from the formal principle implied by the definition: "Art is the reproduction of reality." In support of our statement that there is an essential difference between our view of art and that contained in the imitation of nature theory, we shall quote here a criticism of that theory taken from the best textbook on the now prevailing system of aesthetics. This criticism will, on the one hand, show the difference between the conceptions it refutes and our view, and, on the other, will reveal what is lacking in our initial definition of art as reproducing reality, and will thus enable us to proceed to a more exact development of concepts of art.

The definition of art as imitation of nature reveals only

its formal object; according to this definition art should strive as far as possible to repeat what already exists in the external world. Such repetition must be regarded as superfluous, for nature and life already present us with what, according to this conception, art should present to us. What is more, the imitation of nature is a vain effort which falls far short of its object because in imitating nature, art, owing to its restricted means, gives us only deception instead of truth and only a lifeless mask instead of a really living being.[1]

Here we shall observe, first of all, that the words, "Art is the reproduction of reality," as well as the sentence, "Art is the imitation of nature," define only the formal principle of art; to define the content of art we must supplement the first conclusion we have drawn concerning its aim, and this we shall do subsequently. The other objection does not in the least apply to the view we have expounded; from the preceding exposition it is evident that the reproduction or "repetition" of the objects and phenomena of nature by art is by no means superfluous; on the contrary, it is necessary. Turning to the observation that repetition is a vain effort which falls far short of its object, it must be said that this argument is valid only when it is assumed that art wishes to compete with reality and not simply serve as a substitute for it. We, however, assert that art cannot stand comparison with living reality and completely lacks the vitality that reality possesses; we regard this as beyond doubt. . . .

Let us see whether further objections to the imitation theory apply to our view:

> Since it is impossible to achieve complete success in imitating nature, all that remains is to take smug pleasure in the relative success of this hocus-pocus; but the more the copy bears an external resemblance to the original, the colder this pleasure becomes, and it even grows into satiety or revulsion. There are portraits which, as the saying goes, are awfully like the originals. An excellent imitation of the song of the

1. Loosely quoted by Chernyshevsky from Part III of Hegel's Introduction to his *Vorlesungen über die Aesthetik* (pages 54-55 in the Berlin, 1842, edition).—TRANS.

nightingale begins to bore and disgust us as soon as we learn that it is not a real nightingale singing, but some skillful imitator of the nightingale's trilling; this is because we have a right to expect different music from a human being. Such tricks in the extremely skillful imitation of nature may be compared with the art of the conjurer who without a miss threw lentils through an aperture no bigger than a lentil, and whom Alexander the Great rewarded with a medimnos of lentils.[2]

These observations are perfectly just, but they apply to the useless and senseless copying of what does not deserve attention, or to the depiction of mere externals devoid of content. (How many vaunted works of art earn this biting, but deserved, ridicule!) Content worthy of the attention of a thinking person is alone able to shield art from the reproach that it is merely a pastime, which it all too often is. Artistic form does not save a work of art from contempt or from a pitying smile if, by the importance of its idea, the work cannot answer the question: Was it worth the trouble? A useless thing has no right to respect. "Man is an end in himself"; but the things man makes must have their end in the satisfaction of man's needs and not in themselves. That is precisely why the more perfectly a useless imitation bears external resemblance to the original, the more disgust it arouses. "Why were so much time and labor wasted on it?" we ask ourselves when looking at it. "And what a pity that such lack of content can go hand in hand with such perfection of workmanship!" The boredom and disgust aroused by the conjurer who imitates the song of the nightingale are explained by the very remarks contained in the above criticism: a man who fails to understand that he ought to sing human songs and not make the trills that have meaning only in the song of the nightingale is deserving only of pity.

As regards portraits which are awfully like the originals, this must be understood as follows: to be faithful, every copy must convey the essential features of its original. A portrait that fails to convey the chief, the most expressive, features of a face is not

2. Another loose quotation from the same work (pp. 56-57).—TRANS.

a faithful portrait; and when, at the same time, the petty details of the face are distinctly shown, the portrait is rendered ugly, senseless, lifeless—how can it be anything but awful? Objection is often raised to what is called the "photographic copying" of reality; would it not be better to say that copying, like everything man does, calls for understanding, for the ability to distinguish essential from inessential features? "Lifeless copying"— such is the usual phrase; but a man cannot make a faithful copy if the lifeless mechanism is not guided by living meaning. It is not even possible to make a faithful facsimile of an ordinary manuscript if the meaning of the letters that are being copied is not understood. . . .

We must now supplement the definition of art presented above, and from the examination of the formal principle of art proceed to the definition of its content.

Usually it is said that the content of art is the beautiful; but this restricts the sphere of art too much. Even if we grant that the sublime and the comic are moments of the beautiful, the content of many works of art will not come under the three headings of the beautiful, the sublime, and the comic. In painting, these subdivisions do not apply to pictures of domestic life in which there is not a single beautiful or ridiculous person, to pictures of old men or old women not distinguished for exceptional beauty of age, and so forth. In music it is still more difficult to introduce the usual subdivisions; if we put marches, pathetic pieces, and so forth, under the heading of the sublime, if we put pieces that breathe the spirit of love or gaiety under the heading of the beautiful, and if we find numerous comic songs, there still remain an enormous number of works the content of which cannot be put under any of these headings without stretching a point. Under what heading are we to put sad melodies—under the sublime, as suffering, or under the beautiful, as tender dreams?

But of all the arts, the one that is most difficult to squeeze into the tight compartments of beauty and its moments, with respect to content, is poetry. Its sphere is the whole realm of life and nature. The poet's views on life in all its manifestations are as diverse as the thinker's conceptions of these diverse phenomena; and the thinker finds in reality much more than the beautiful, the sublime, and the comic. Not all grief reaches the point of tragedy; not all joy is graceful or comical. That the content of poetry is not exhausted by the well-known three elements can easily be seen from the fact that poetical works no longer fit into the frame of the old subdivisions. That dramatic poetry depicts not only the tragic or the comic is proved by the fact that besides comedies and tragedies the drama also had to appear. The epic, which belongs chiefly to the sublime, has been replaced by the novel, with its innumerable categories. For most lyrical poems today it is impossible to find among the old subdivisions any heading that would indicate the character of their content; hundreds of headings would not suffice, so three are certainly not enough to embrace them all (we are speaking of the character of the content and not of the form, which must always be beautiful).

The simplest way to solve this riddle would be to say that the sphere of art is not limited only to beauty and its so-called moments, but embraces everything in reality (in nature and in life) that is of interest to man not as a scholar but as an ordinary human being; that which is of common interest in life—such is the content of art. The beautiful, the tragic, and the comic are only the three most determinate of the thousands of elements upon which vital interests depend, and to enumerate them all would mean enumerating all the feelings and aspirations that stir man's heart.

It is scarcely necessary to adduce more detailed proof of the correctness of our conception of the content of art, since although another, narrower definition of content is usually offered in aesthetics, our view predominates in actual fact, i.e., among artists and poets themselves. It constantly finds expression in literature and in life. If it is thought necessary to define the beautiful as the main or, to be more exact, the sole essential content of art, the real reason for this is that the distinction between beauty as the object of art and beauty of form, which is indeed an essential quality of every work of art, is only vaguely seen. But this formal beauty, or unity of idea and image, of content and form, is not the special feature that distinguishes art from all other branches of human activity. In acting, a man always has an aim, which constitutes the essence of his action. The worth of the act itself is judged by the degree to which it conforms to the aim we wished to realize by it. All man's works are judged by the degree of perfection attained in their execution. This is a general law for handicraft, for industry, for scientific activity, etc. It also applies to works of art: the artist (consciously or unconsciously, it makes no difference) tries to reproduce for us a certain aspect of life; it goes without saying that the merits of his work will depend upon how he has done his job. "A work of art strives for the harmony of idea and image" no more and no less than does the shoemaker's craft, the jeweler's craft, calligraphy, engineering, moral resolve. "All work should be done well"—such is the meaning of the phrase "harmony between idea and image.". . .

We have already observed that the important word in this phrase is "image"—it tells us that art expresses an idea not through abstract concepts, but through a living, individual fact. When we say that art is the reproduction of nature and life, we are saying the same thing: in nature and in life there are no abstract beings; everything in them is concrete. A reproduction must as far as possible preserve the essence of the thing reproduced; therefore, a work of art must contain as little of the abstract as possible; everything in it must be, as far as possible, expressed concretely in living scenes and in individual images. . . .

Confusion of beauty of form as an essential quality of a work of art, and beauty as one of the numerous objects of art, has been one of the causes of the sad abuses in art. "The object of art is beauty," beauty at all costs, art has no other content. What is the most beautiful thing [prekrasnoye] in the world? In human life—beauty [krasota] and love; in nature—it is difficult to decide—there is so much beauty in it. Thus it is necessary, appropriately and inappropriately, to fill poetical works with descriptions of nature: the more there is of this, the more beauty there is in our work. . . .

Inappropriate dilation on the beauty of nature is not so harmful in a work of art; it can be skipped, for it is tacked on in an external way; but what is to be done with a love plot? It cannot be ignored, for it is the base to which everything else is tied with Gordian knots; without it everything loses coherence and meaning. Apart from the fact that a loving couple, suffering or triumphant, makes thousands of works frightfully monotonous, apart from the fact that the vicissitudes of their love and the author's descriptions of beauty leave no room for essential details, this habit of depicting love, love, eternally love makes poets forget that life has other aspects much more interesting for man in general. All poetry, and all life depicted in it, assumes a sort of sentimental, rosy hue; instead of seriously depicting human life a great many works of art represent an excessively youthful (to refrain from using more exact epithets) view of life, and the poet usually appears to be a very young lad whose stories are interesting only for people of the same moral or physiological age as himself. Lastly, this degrades art in the eyes of people who have emerged from the blissful period of early youth. Art seems to be a pastime too sickly sentimental for adults and not without its dangers for young people. We certainly do not think that the poet ought to be prohibited from describing love; but aesthetics must demand that he describe love only when he really wants to do so. . . .

Love, appropriately or inappropriately—this is the first harm inflicted on art by the idea that the content of art is beauty. The second, closely connected with the first, is artificiality. In our times people laugh at Racine and Madame Deshoulières, but it is doubtful whether modern art has left them far behind as regards simplicity, naturalness of the springs of action, and genuine naturalness of dialogue. The division of *dramatis personae* into heroes and villains may to this day be applied to works of art in the pathetic category. How coherently, smoothly, and eloquently these people speak! Monologues and dialogues in modern novels are not much less stilted than the monologues in classical tragedies. "Everything in works of art must be clothed in beauty," and one of the conditions of beauty is that all the details must develop out of the plot: so the characters in novels and plays are given such profoundly thought-out plans of action as persons in real life scarcely ever draw up. And if one of the characters takes an instinctive, thoughtless step, the author deems it necessary to justify it on the grounds of the essence of the character's personality, and the critics are displeased with the fact that "the action is unmotivated"—as if an action is always motivated by individual character and not by circumstances and by general traits of the human heart. . . . Let us, however, return to the question of the essential purpose of art.

The first and general purpose of all works of art, we have said, is to reproduce phenomena of real life that are of interest to man. By real life we mean, of course, not only man's relation to the objects and beings of the objective world, but also his inner life. Sometimes a man lives in a dream—in that case the dream has for him (to a certain degree and for a certain time) the significance of something objective. Still more often a man lives in the world of his emotions. These states, if they become interesting, are also reproduced by art. We mention this in order to show that our definition also takes in the imaginative content of art.

But we have said above that art has another purpose besides reproduction, namely, to explain life. This can be done to some degree by all the arts: often it is sufficient to call attention to an object (which art always does) in order to explain its significance, or to enable people to understand life better. In this sense, art differs in no way from a discourse about an object; the only difference here is that art achieves its purpose much better than a discourse, particularly a learned discourse; it is much easier for us to acquaint ourselves with an object, we begin to take an interest in it much more quickly when it is presented to us in living form than when we get a dry reference to it. Fenimore Cooper's novels have done more to acquaint society with the life of savages than ethnographic narratives and arguments on the importance of studying this subject.

But while all the arts can point to new and interesting objects, poetry always of necessity points sharply and clearly to the essential features of an object. Painting reproduces an object in all its details; so does sculpture. But poetry cannot take in an excessive amount of detail; of necessity leaving a great deal out of the picture, it focuses our attention on the features retained. This is viewed as an advantage that poetic scenes have over reality; but every single word does the same to the object it denotes. In the word (concept), too, everything incidental is left out and only the essential features of the object are retained. For the inexperienced mind the word denoting the object may be clearer than the object itself, but this clarity is only an impoverishment. . . . An object or event may be more intelligible in a poetical work than in reality, but the only merit we recognize in that is the clear and vivid allusion to reality; we do not attach independent significance to it as something that could compete with the fullness of real life. We cannot refrain from adding that every prose narrative does the same thing poetry does. The concentration of attention upon the essential features of an object is not the distinguishing feature of poetry, but the common feature of all rational speech.

The essential purpose of art is to reproduce what is of interest to man in real life. But, being interested in the phenomena of life, man cannot but pronounce judgment on them, consciously or unconsciously. The poet or artist cannot cease to be a man and thus he cannot, even if he wants to, refrain from pronouncing judgment on the phenomena he depicts. This judgment is expressed in his work—this is another purpose of art, which places it among the moral activities of man.

There are men whose judgment on the phenomena of life consists almost exclusively in that they betray an inclination for some aspects of reality and avoid others: these are men whose mental activity is weak. The work of such a man—poet or artist —has no other purpose than that of reproducing his favorite side of life. But if a man whose mental activity is powerfully stimulated by questions engendered by observing life is gifted with artistic talent, he will, in his works, consciously or unconsciously strive to pronounce a living judgment on the phenomena that interest him (and interest his contemporaries, for a thinking man cannot think about insignificant problems that interest nobody but himself). His painting or his novels, poems, and plays will present or solve problems that arise out of life for the thinking man; his works will be, as it were, essays on subjects presented by life. This trend may find expression in all the arts (in painting, for example, we can point to pictures of social life and historical scenes), but it is developing chiefly in poetry, which provides the fullest opportunity to express a definite idea. In such a case the artist becomes a thinker, and works of art, while remaining in the sphere of art, acquire scientific significance. It goes without saying that in this respect there is nothing corresponding to the work of art in reality—but this applies only to its form. As regards content, as regards the problems presented or solved by art, they are all to be found in real life, only without premeditation, without *arrière-pensée*.

Let us suppose that a work of art develops the idea that straying temporarily from the true path will not doom a strong nature, or that one extreme leads to another; or that it depicts a man in conflict with himself; or depicts, if you will, the conflict between passions and lofty aspirations (we are pointing to different fundamental ideas we have discerned in *Faust*)—does not real life provide cases where the same situations develop? Is not high wisdom obtained from the observation of life? Is not science simply an abstraction from life, the placing of life within a formula? Everything science and art express is to be found in life, and found in its fullest and most perfect form, with all its living details—the details which usually contain the true meaning of the matter, and which are often not understood by science and art, and still more often cannot be embraced by them. In the events of real life everything is true, nothing is overlooked, there is not that one-sided, narrow view from which all the works of man suffer. As instruction, as learning, life is fuller, truer, and even more artistic than all the works of scholars and poets. But life does not think of explaining its phenomena to us; it is not concerned with deducing axioms. This is done in works of science and art. True, the deductions are incomplete, the ideas are one-sided compared with what life presents; but they have been made for us by geniuses; without their aid our deductions would be still more one-sided and meager.

Science and art (poetry) are manuals for those beginning the study of life; their purpose is to prepare the student to read the original sources, and later to serve as reference books from time to time. It never occurs to science to conceal this; nor does it occur to poets to conceal it in their offhand remarks about the point of their works. Aesthetics alone persists in asserting that art is superior to life and reality.

Connecting everything that has been said, we get the following view of art: the essential purpose of art is to reproduce everything in life that is of interest to man. Very often, especially in poetical works, the explanation of life, judgment of its phenomena, also comes to the fore.

The relation of art to life is the same as that of history; the only difference in content is that history, in its account of the life of mankind, is concerned mainly with factual truth, whereas art gives us stories about the lives of men in which the place of factual truth is taken by faithfulness to psychological and moral truth. The first function of history is to reproduce life; the second, which is not performed by all historians, is to explain it. By failing to perform the second function the historian remains a mere chronicler and his work serves merely as material for the true historian, or as reading matter to satisfy curiosity. By performing this second function the historian becomes a thinker, and as a consequence his work acquires scientific merit. Exactly the same must be said about art. History does not set out to compete with real historical life; it admits that the pictures it paints are pale, incomplete, more or less incorrect, or at all events one-sided. Aesthetics must admit that art, too, and for the same reasons, must not even think of comparing itself with reality, much less of surpassing it in beauty. . . .

Defense of reality as against fantasy, the attempt to prove that works of art cannot possibly stand comparison with living reality—such is the essence of this essay. But does not what the author says degrade art? Yes, if showing that art stands lower than real life in the artistic perfection of its works means degrading art. But protesting against panegyrics does not mean disparagement. Science does not claim to stand higher than reality, but that gives it nothing to be ashamed of. Art, too, must not claim to stand higher than reality; that would not degrade it. Science is not ashamed to say that its aim is to understand and explain reality, and then to use its explanation for man's benefit. Let not art be ashamed to admit that its aim is to compensate man, in case he lacks the opportunity to enjoy the full aesthetic pleasure afforded by reality, by reproducing this precious reality as far as possible, and by explaining it for his benefit.

Let art be content with its fine and lofty mission of being a substitute for reality in the event of its absence, and of being a manual of life for man.

Reality stands higher than dreams, and essential purpose stands higher than fantastic claims.

[NICHOLAS CHERNYSHEVSKY]

The Anthropological Principle in Philosophy *

That part of philosophy which deals with questions of man, just like the other part which deals with questions of external nature, is based on the natural sciences. The principle underlying the philosophical view of human life and all its phenomena is the idea, worked out by the natural sciences, of the unity of the human organism; the observations of physiologists, zoologists, and medical men have driven away all thought of dualism in man. Philosophy sees in him what medicine, physiology, and chemistry see. These sciences prove that no dualism is evident in man, and philosophy adds that if man possessed another nature, in addition to his real nature, this other nature would surely reveal itself in some way; but since it does not, since everything that takes place and manifests itself in man originates solely from his real nature, he cannot have another nature.

This proof is completely beyond doubt. It is as convincing as the grounds on which you, dear reader, are convinced, for example, that at the moment you are reading this book there is no lion in the room in which you are sitting. You think that this is so because you do not see a lion or hear one growl. But is this alone a sufficient guarantee that there is no lion in your room? No, you have a second guarantee—the fact that you are alive. Were there a lion in your room it would have sprung upon you and torn you to bits. The inevitable consequences of the presence of a lion are absent, and therefore you know that there is no lion. . . .

But while there is unity in man's nature, we see in him two

* Reprinted, with minor corrections and revisions for this volume, from Nicholas G. Chernyshevsky, *Selected Philosophical Essays*, Moscow, 1953, pp. 70-73, 88-89, 91-109, 120-126, 128-134. The corrections and revisions were made by reference to the original Russian text in Nicholas G. Chernyshevsky, *Antropologichesky printsip v filosofii*, Moscow, 1948, pp. 31-34, 52-75, 88-104.

different orders of phenomena: phenomena of what is called a material order (a man eats, walks), and phenomena of what is called a moral order (a man thinks, feels, desires). In what relation do these two orders of phenomena stand to one another? Does not the difference between them contradict the unity of man's nature that is demonstrated by the natural sciences? The natural sciences answer that there are no grounds for such a hypothesis, for there is no object that possesses only one quality. On the contrary, every object displays an incalculable number of different phenomena which, for convenience, we place in different categories, calling each category a quality, so that every object has numerous qualities of different kinds. For example, wood grows and it burns; we say that it possesses two qualities: vegetative power and combustibility. Is there any resemblance between these two qualities? They are entirely different; there is no concept that can cover both these qualities except the general concept of quality. There is no concept to cover both categories of phenomena corresponding to these qualities except the concept of phenomenon. Or, for example, ice is hard and shiny. What is there in common between hardness and shininess? The logical distance between these two qualities is immeasurable, or it would be more correct to say that there is no logical distance between them, great or small, because there is no logical relation between them. This shows that the combination of completely heterogeneous properties in one object is the general law of things.

But in this diversity the natural sciences also discover connection—not in the forms of manifestation, not in the phenomena, which are totally unlike each other, but in the way the diverse phenomena originate from the same element when the energy with which it acts is increased or diminished. For example, water has the property of having temperature—a property common to all bodies. No matter what the property we call heat may consist in, under different circumstances it reveals itself in extremely diverse degrees. Sometimes a given object is cold—that is to say, it displays very little heat. Sometimes it is very hot—that is to say, it displays a great deal of heat. When water, no matter under what circumstances, displays very little heat, it is a solid—

ice. When it displays somewhat more heat, it is a liquid. And when there is a great deal of heat in it, it becomes steam. In these three states, the same quality reveals itself in three orders of totally different phenomena, so that one quality assumes the forms of three different qualities, branches out into three qualities simply according to the different quantities in which it is displayed: quantitative difference passes into qualitative difference. . . .

Among the English, the word "science" does not by any means cover all the branches of knowledge it covers among us and the other continental nations. By science the English mean mathematics, astronomy, physics, chemistry, botany, zoology, geography—the branches of knowledge we call the "exact" sciences and those closely allied to them in character. But they do not apply this term to history, psychology, moral philosophy, or metaphysics. It must be said that there is, indeed, a tremendous difference between these two halves of learning as regards the quality of the concepts that prevail in each of them. From one half, every man who is in the least enlightened has already expelled all groundless prejudices, and all rationally minded people already adhere to the same fundamental conceptions in these fields. Our knowledge about these departments of existence is very incomplete, but, at all events, everybody agrees as to what we know definitely in these departments, what we do not yet know, and, lastly, what has been definitely refuted by exact research.

For example, if you say that the human organism needs food or needs air nobody will dispute it. If you say that we do not yet know whether the substances that now serve as man's food are the only things that can nourish man and that other substances may, perhaps, be found that will be useful for this purpose, no enlightened person will dispute it. He will only add that although new foodstuffs may be found, and in all probability will be found, they have not been found yet; and that for the time being man can only use the known substances, such as cereals, meat, milk, or fish. You, in your turn, will fully agree with this observation, and no dispute can possibly arise. The only point of dispute you can raise is whether the probability of the speedy discovery of new nutritive substances is great or small, and to what category of things these new, as yet undiscovered, substances are likely to belong. But in this dispute, you and your opponent will both know and admit that you are merely expressing assumptions which lack full validity, which may be more or less useful to science in the future (for assumptions, hypotheses, give direction to scientific research and lead to the discovery of truths which confirm or refute them), but are not yet scientific truths. If, finally, you say that man cannot live without food, here again everybody will agree with you and understand that this negative statement has an inseparable logical connection with the positive statement: "The human organism needs food." Everybody will understand that if one of these two statements is accepted, the other must also be accepted.

It is entirely different in moral philosophy, for example. No matter what you say, some clever and educated men will always come forward and say the opposite. If, for example, you say that poverty has a bad effect upon the mind and heart of man, many clever people will object and say: "No, poverty sharpens thinking, it forces the mind to seek means to avert it; it ennobles the heart by turning our thoughts away from the vanities of pleasure to the virtues of patience, self-sacrifice, and sympathy for the needs and misfortunes of others." Very well. But if, on the contrary, you say that poverty has a beneficial effect upon man, there will also be many clever people, perhaps even more than in the first case, who will object and say: "No, poverty deprives a man of the means for intellectual development, hinders the development of an independent character, leads to unscrupulousness in the choice of means for averting poverty, or simply of sustaining life; it is the chief source of ignorance, vice, and crime." In short, no matter what conclusion you might think of drawing in the moral sciences, you will find that it, and the opposite one, and many others which are inconsistent both with your conclusion and with the opposite one, or with one another, have earnest champions among clever and enlightened people. The same applies to metaphysics, and to history, with which neither the moral sciences nor metaphysics can dispense. . . .

The union of the exact sciences, under the government of mathematics—that is, counting, weighing, and measuring—is year after year spreading to new spheres of knowledge, is growing by the inclusion of newcomers. Chemistry was gradually followed by all the sciences concerned with plant and animal organisms: physiology, comparative anatomy, various branches of botany and zoology. Now the moral sciences are joining them. What is happening to the moral sciences is what happens to proud but poverty-stricken people when a distant relative—not, like themselves, proud and boastful of their ancient lineage and incomparable virtues, but a plain, honest man—acquires wealth. For a long time they live off his charity, considering it beneath their dignity to turn, with his aid, to the honest work which made him a success. But gradually, eating better and dressing better, they become more reasonable, their empty boastfulness subsides, they become respectable, and at last they understand that not work but pride is shameful. Finally they adopt the habits that enabled their relative to succeed. Then, with his assistance, they quickly attain a good position and begin to enjoy the respect of rational people, not for the imaginary virtues they had boasted of in the past, but for their new and real qualities which are useful to society, for the work they do.

Not so long ago the moral sciences could not have had the content to justify the title of science they bore, and the English were quite right then in depriving them of a title they did not deserve. The situation today has changed considerably. The natural sciences have already developed to such an extent that they provide much material for the exact solution of moral problems, too. All the progressive thinkers among those who are studying the moral sciences have begun to work out these problems with the aid of precise methods similar to those by which the problems of the natural sciences are being worked out. When we spoke about the controversies among different people on every moral problem, we were referring only to the old and very widespread but now obsolete conceptions and methods of investigation, and not to the character the moral sciences are now acquiring among progressive thinkers. We were referring to the former routine character of these branches of science and not to their present form. In their present form, the moral sciences differ from the so-called natural sciences only in that they began to be worked out in a truly scientific way later, and therefore have not yet been developed to the same degree of perfection as the latter.

The difference here is only one of degree: chemistry is younger than astronomy and has not yet attained the same degree of perfection; physiology is still younger than chemistry and is still further removed from perfection; psychology, as an exact science, is still younger than physiology and has been worked out even less. But, while differing from each other in the amount of exact knowledge acquired, chemistry and astronomy do not differ either as regards the validity of what has been learned, or in the methods employed to arrive at exact knowledge in the particular subjects. The facts and laws discovered by chemistry are as authentic as the facts and laws discovered by astronomy. The same must be said about the results achieved by present-day exact research in the moral sciences. . . .

The first result of the entry of the moral sciences into the sphere of the exact sciences is that a strict distinction has been drawn between what we know and what we do not know. The astronomer knows that he knows the dimensions of Mars, and he knows just as positively that he does not know the geological composition of that planet, the character of the plant and animal life on it, or whether there *is* any plant or animal life on it. If someone took it into his head to claim that clay, granite, birds, or mollusks existed on Mars, the astronomer would reply: you are asserting something you do not know. If the fantast were to go even further in his assumptions and assert, for example, that the birds that inhabit Mars are not subject to disease and that the mollusks do not need food, the astronomer, assisted by the chemist and physiologist, would prove to him that this is impossible. Likewise, in the moral sciences a strict distinction has been drawn between what is known and what is not known, and on the basis of what is known the unsoundness of some of the previous assumptions concerning what still remains unknown has been proved.

It is definitely known, for example, that all the phenomena of the moral world originate from one another and from external circumstances in conformity with the law of causality, and on this basis all assumptions that there can be any phenomena that do not arise from preceding phenomena and from external circumstances are regarded as false. Hence, present-day psychology does not accept, for example, the assumptions that in one case a man performs a bad action because he wanted to perform a bad action, while in another case he performs a good action because he wanted to perform a good action. It says that the bad action, or the good action, was certainly prompted by some moral or material fact, or combination of facts, and that the "wanting" is only the subjective impression which accompanies, in our consciousness, the genesis of thoughts or actions from preceding thoughts, actions, or external facts.

The example most often given of an action based on nothing but our will is this: I get out of bed. Which foot do I put out first? Whichever one I want to. But this only appears to be so at a superficial glance. Actually, facts and impressions determine which foot a man puts out of bed first. If there are no special circumstances or thoughts he will put out the foot that is most convenient for the anatomical position of his body in the bed. If there are special motives that outweigh this physiological convenience, the result will change according to the circumstances. If, for example, the thought occurs to the man: "I shall put out my left foot rather than my right," he will do so. Here, however, one cause (physiological convenience) was simply displaced by another (the thought of displaying independence), or it would be more correct to say that the second cause, being the stronger, triumphed over the first. But how did the second cause arise? Whence came the thought of displaying independence of external conditions? It could not have arisen without a cause. It was created either by something said in conversation with someone, or by the recollection of a previous dispute, or something like that. Thus, the fact that a man can, if he wants to, put out the foot that is not convenient for the anatomical position of his body in the bed does not prove that he can put out this foot or that foot without any cause. It only proves that the manner of getting out of bed can be determined by causes that are stronger than the anatomical position of the body before getting out of bed.

The phenomenon that we call "will" is itself a link in a series of phenomena and facts joined together by causal connection. Very often, the immediate cause of the manifestation of our will to perform a certain action is thought. But the definite inclination of the will is also due solely to a definite thought: whatever the thought is, so is the will. If the thought were different the will would be different. But why did a particular thought arise and not a different one? Because it, too, arose from some thought, some fact—in short, from some cause. In this case, psychology says the same thing that physics and chemistry say in similar cases: if a certain phenomenon occurs, we must seek the cause of it and not be satisfied with the vapid statement: it occurred of its own accord without any special cause— "I did this because I wanted to." That's all very well, but why did you want to? If you answer: "Simply because I wanted to," it will be the same as saying: "The plate broke because it broke; the house was burned down because it was burned down." These are not answers at all; they are only a cloak to cover up laziness in seeking the real cause, lack of desire to know the truth. . . .

But if the moral sciences are still obliged to say "We do not know" in answer to very many questions, we shall be mistaken if we assume that among the problems they have not yet solved are those which, according to one of the prevailing opinions, are insoluble. No, the ignorance in these sciences is not of this kind. What, for example, does chemistry not know? It does not at present know what hydrogen will be when it passes from the gaseous to the solid state—a metal or a nonmetal. There are strong grounds for assuming that it will be a metal, but we do not yet know whether this assumption is correct. Chemistry also does not know whether phosphorus and sulphur are simple substances or whether they will in time be resolved into the simplest elements. These are cases of theoretical ignorance. Another category of problems that chemistry cannot solve at present consists of the numerous cases of inability to satisfy practical demands. Chemistry can make prussic acid and acetic acid, but it cannot yet make fibrin. As we can see, these and other problems it cannot at present solve are of a very special character, a character so special that they occur to the minds only of people who are fairly well acquainted with chemistry.

The problems the moral sciences have not yet solved are of exactly the same kind. Psychology, for example, discovers the following fact: a man of low mental development is unable to understand a life different from his own; the more his mind develops, the easier it is for him to picture another sort of life. How is this fact to be explained? In the present state of science, a strictly scientific answer to this question has not yet been found; all we have are various surmises. Now tell us, would this question arise in the mind of anyone not familiar with the present state of psychology? Scarcely anybody but a scientist has even noticed the fact to which this question applies. It is like the question as to whether hydrogen is or is not a metal; people unacquainted with chemistry are not only unaware of this question, they are unaware of the existence of hydrogen. For chemistry, however, this hydrogen, the existence of which would not have been noticed had it not been for chemistry, is extremely important. Similarly, the fact that a man of low mental development is unable to understand a life different from his own, whereas a mentally developed man is able to do so, is extremely important for psychology. Just as the discovery of hydrogen led to an improvement in the theory of chemistry, so the discovery of this psychological fact led to the formation of the theory of anthropomorphism, without which not a step can now be taken in metaphysics.

Here is another psychological problem, which also cannot be definitely solved in the present state of science: children have a propensity for breaking their toys; why is this? Should it be regarded only as a clumsy form of the desire to adapt things to one's requirements, a clumsy form of what is called man's creative activity, or is it a trace of the sheer urge to destroy which some writers ascribe to men? . . .

Thus, the theoretical problems that are still unsolved in the present state of the moral sciences are, in general, of such a character that they arise in hardly anybody's mind except the specialist's. The layman even finds it hard to understand how learned people can spend their time investigating such petty things. On the other hand, the theoretical problems that usually seem to be important and difficult to the layman have, in general, ceased to be problems for present-day thinkers, because they are solved beyond doubt with extreme ease at the very first application of the powerful means of scientific analysis. It is found that half of these problems arise simply from the fact that people are unaccustomed to think, and the other half find answers in phenomena with which everybody is familiar.

What becomes of the flame of a burning candle when we extinguish the candle? Would a chemist agree to call this question a problem? He would say that it is simply a jumble of words arising from ignorance of the most fundamental, the simplest facts of science. He would say: the burning of a candle is a chemical process; flame is one of the phenomena of this process, one of its aspects, one of its qualities, to express it in ordinary language. When we extinguish the candle we put a stop to the chemical process; naturally, with its cessation its qualities vanish. To ask what becomes of the flame when we extinguish a candle is like asking what becomes of the figure 2 in the figure 25 when we strike out the whole figure—nothing is left of either the 2 or the 5; both have been struck out. Such a question can be asked only by someone who does not understand what writing a figure and then striking it out means. To all the questions of such people there is one answer: friend, you are totally ignorant of arithmetic and you had better begin to learn it.

For example, the following baffling question is asked: Is man a good or an evil being? Lots of people rack their brains attempting to solve this problem. Nearly half of them decide that man is by nature good; others, also constituting nearly half of the brain-rackers, decide otherwise; they say man is by nature bad. Outside these two opposed dogmatic parties are several skeptics who jeer at both sides and say that the problem is insoluble.

But at the very first application of scientific analysis the whole thing turns out to be as clear as can be. A man likes what is pleasant and dislikes what is unpleasant—this, one would think, is beyond doubt, because the predicate simply repeats the subject: A is A, what is pleasant to a man is pleasant to a man; what is unpleasant to him is unpleasant to him. Good is he who does good to others, bad is he who is bad to others—this, too, is clear and simple, one would think. Let us now combine the simple truths; we will get the following deductions: a man is good when, in order to obtain pleasure for himself, he must give pleasure to others. A man is bad when, in order to obtain pleasure for himself, he is obliged to cause displeasure to others. Here human nature cannot be blamed for one thing or praised for the other; everything depends on circumstances, relationships (institutions). If certain relations are constant, the man whose character is molded by them is found to have acquired the habit of acting in conformity with them.

Therefore, we may think that John is good, while Peter is bad; but these opinions apply only to individual men, not to man in general, just as we attribute to individual men and not to man in general the habits involved in sawing planks and forging iron. John is a carpenter, but we cannot say that man in general is or is not a carpenter. Peter can forge iron, but we cannot say that man in general is or is not a blacksmith. The fact that John became a carpenter and Peter a blacksmith merely shows that under certain circumstances, which existed in John's life, a man becomes a carpenter; while under other circumstances, which existed in Peter's life, a man becomes a blacksmith. In exactly the same way, under certain circumstances a man becomes good, under others he becomes bad.

Thus from the theoretical side the problem of the good and bad qualities of human nature is solved so easily that it cannot even be called a problem: it contains its own complete solution.

It is quite another matter, however, when you take the practical side; when, for example, it seems to you that it is much better for a man himself, and for all those around him, to be good rather than bad; and when you want to make everybody good. From this aspect the matter presents many difficulties. As the reader will observe, however, these difficulties relate not to science but to the practical application of the means indicated by science. In this respect psychology and moral philosophy are in exactly the same position as the natural sciences. The climate in North Siberia is too cold. If you were to ask how it could be made warmer, the natural sciences would have no difficulty in finding an answer: Siberia is closed to the warm atmosphere of the South by mountains, and its northern slope is open to the cold atmosphere of the North. If there were mountains on the northern border and none on the southern, that part of the country would be much warmer than it is now. But we as yet lack the means with which to put this theoretical solution of the problem into practice.

Similarly, the moral sciences already have theoretical answers to nearly all the problems that are important for life, but in many cases man lacks the means to put into practice what is indicated by theory. Incidentally, in this respect the moral sciences have an advantage over the natural sciences. In the natural sciences, all the means belong to the sphere of so-called external nature; in the moral sciences, only half the means belong to this category, while the other half are contained in man himself. Consequently, half the matter depends entirely upon man feeling strongly enough the need for a certain improvement. This feeling in itself provides him with a very considerable part of the conditions necessary for the improvement. We have seen, however, that the conditions that depend upon the state of man's own impressions are not enough; material means are also needed. In respect to this half of the conditions, in respect to material means, the practical problems of the moral sciences are in a much more favorable position than they are in respect to the conditions which lie within man himself. Formerly, when the natural sciences were still undeveloped, insurmountable difficulties could be met with in external nature that prevented the satisfaction of man's moral requirements. This is not the case now: the natural sciences already offer man such powerful means of command over external nature that no difficulties arise in this respect.

Let us return, as an example, to the practical question of how people could become good, so that bad people should become an extreme rarity in the world, and that bad qualities should lose all perceptible importance in life because of the extreme rarity of the cases in which they were displayed. Psychology tells us that the most abundant source of the display of bad qualities is inadequacy of means for satisfying requirements; that a man commits a bad action—that is, harms others—almost only when he is obliged to deprive them of things so as not to remain himself without the things he needs. For example, when crops are poor and there is not enough food for everybody, there is a great increase in crime and of all sorts of evil deeds; people rob and cheat one another for a crust of bread.

Psychology also adds that human needs differ greatly in degree of intensity. The most urgent need of every human organism is to breathe; but sufficient means for satisfying this need are available to people in practically all situations, so that evil deeds due to the want of air are hardly ever committed. But if an extraordinary situation arises, when there is not sufficient air for everybody, then such quarrels and wrongdoing do arise. For example, if a large number of people are locked in a stifling room with one window, quarrels and strife nearly always arise and even murder may be committed for a place near the window. Next to the need to breathe (continues psychology), a man's most urgent requirement is food and drink. Very often very many people suffer from a shortage of the articles needed to satisfy these requirements properly, and this is the cause of the largest number of bad actions of all kinds, of nearly all the situations and institutions that are the constant causes of bad actions. If this one cause of evil were abolished, at least nine tenths of all that is bad in human society would quickly disappear. Crime would be reduced to one tenth. In the course of one generation coarse manners and conceptions would yield to humane manners and conceptions. The restrictive institutions that are based on coarseness and ignorance would be robbed of their foundation, and soon nearly all restriction would be abolished.

We are told that this theoretical conclusion could not be put into practice before because of the imperfection of the technical arts. We are not sure whether this is true in respect to the past, but it is beyond dispute that in the present state of mechanics and chemistry, with the means with which these sciences provide agriculture, the land in every country in the Temperate

Zone could provide a great deal more food than is needed for an abundant supply of provisions for populations ten and twenty times larger than the present populations of these countries.[1] Thus, external nature creates no obstacles to supplying the entire population of every civilized country with an abundance of food; the only task that remains is to make people conscious of the possibility and necessity of energetically pursuing this goal.

Rhetorically, it may be said that they are already concerning themselves with this matter sufficiently, but exact and cold scientific analysis reveals the hollowness of the pompous phrases we so often hear on this subject. Actually, not a single human society has as yet adopted on any extensive scale the means indicated by the natural sciences and the science of public welfare for the promotion of agriculture. Why this is so, why there is such unconcern in human societies for the application of scientific advice to the satisfaction of such an urgent need as the need for food, what circumstances and attitudes generate and foster this bad state of economy, and how circumstances and attitudes must be changed in order that the state of economy may be improved—these are again new problems, the theoretical solution of which is very easy; and again, the practical application of the scientific solutions depends upon man becoming imbued with certain impressions.

We shall not, however, deal here with either the theoretical solution or the practical difficulties of these problems; this would lead us too far afield, and we think that our foregoing remarks are already sufficient to explain the present position of the moral sciences. We wanted to say that the working out of the moral sciences on precise scientific lines is just beginning and that, therefore, exact theoretical solutions for very many extremely important moral problems have not yet been found. But these problems for which theoretical solutions have not yet been

1. In England, the land could feed at least 150,000,000 people. The panegyrics sung in praise of the astonishing perfection of English agriculture are justified insofar as rapid improvements are taking place there, but it would be a mistake to think that the resources of science are already being employed on a sufficiently wide scale. This is just beginning, and nine tenths of the cultivated land in England is still tilled by routine methods that in no way correspond to the present state of agricultural knowledge.

found are of a purely technical character and are of interest only to specialists, while, on the other hand, the psychological and moral problems that are extremely interesting, and seem to the layman to be extremely difficult, have already been precisely solved, and, moreover, have been solved very easily and simply with the very first application of exact scientific analysis; theoretical answers to them have already been found.

We added that from these indubitable theoretical solutions arise very important and useful scientific indications as to what means must be employed to improve the conditions of human life, and that some of these means must be taken from external nature whereas others must be provided by the reasoning faculty of man himself. Concerning the former means, external nature no longer creates any obstacles in the present state of development of the natural sciences, and concerning the latter, the only obstacles that are to be met with today are obstacles to the awakening of man's reasoning faculty arising from the apathy and ignorance of some people and the deliberate opposition of others, and in general from the power that prejudice exercises over the vast majority of people in every society. . . .

The next subject to be dealt with in our essays is man as an individual. . . .

We shall put aside for a time the psychological and moral-philosophical problems concerning man and deal with the physiological, medical, or any other problems you please, but not with man as a moral being, and try first of all to say what we know about him as a being that possesses a stomach, a head, bones, veins, muscles, and nerves. We shall examine him only from the side that the natural sciences find in him; the other aspects of life we shall examine later, if time allows.

Physiology and medicine find that the human organism is an extremely complex combination of chemicals that undergoes an extremely complex chemical process we call life. This process is so complex and so important to us that the branch of chemistry engaged in research in it has been awarded the title of a special science and is called physiology. . . .

Physiology is only a variety of chemistry, and its subject is only a variety of the subjects dealt with in chemistry. Physiology itself has not kept all its departments in strict unity under a common name; some of the aspects of the subjects it investigates, i.e., the chemical processes that take place in the human organism, are of such special interest for man that investigations into them, which are part of physiology, have been awarded the name of separate sciences. Of these aspects we shall mention one: investigation of the phenomena that cause and accompany the various deviations of this chemical process from its normal form. This part of physiology bears the special name of medicine. Medicine, in its turn, branches out into numerous sciences with special names. . . .

When a subject under investigation is very complex, it is useful, for the sake of convenience, to divide it into parts. Hence, physiology divides the complex process that goes on in the living human organism into several parts, the most marked of which are: respiration, digestion, circulation of the blood, motor phenomena, sensation. Like every other chemical process, this entire system of phenomena has its birth, growth, decline, and end. Therefore, physiology regards the processes of respiration, nutrition, blood circulation, motor activity, sensation, and so forth, and conception or fertilization, growth, senility, and death, as if they were special subjects. But here again it must be borne in mind that these different segments and aspects of the process are divided only in theory, to facilitate theoretical analysis; actually, they constitute one indivisible whole. . . .

Some parts of physiology have already been elaborated very well. Such, for example, are the researches into the processes of respiration, digestion, blood circulation, conception, growth, and senility. Motor phenomena have not been explained in such detail, and the process of sensation still less. . . .

We have said that some parts of the process of life have not been explained in as great detail as others; but this does not mean that we have not already positively learned a great deal about those parts, the investigation of which is at present in a very imperfect state. First, even supposing that some special aspect of the vital process were still totally inaccessible to exact analysis on the lines of mathematics and the natural sciences, its character would be approximately known to us from the character of other parts that have already been fairly well investigated. This would be a case like that of determining the shape of the head of a mammal from the bones of its leg. We know that merely from an animal's shoulder blade or collarbone science can fairly precisely reproduce its entire figure, including its head—so much so that when, later on, a whole skeleton is found, it confirms the scientific inference concerning the whole which was arrived at from one of its parts. We know, for example, what digestion is. From this we already know approximately what sensation is: digestion and sensation are so closely interconnected that the character of one determines the character of the other.

Above we said that such deductions concerning unknown parts drawn from known parts are particularly valid and particularly important when they are presented in a negative form: A is closely connected with X; A is B; from this it follows that X cannot be either C, D, or E. For example, supposing the shoulder blade of some antediluvian animal is found; perhaps we shall not be able unerringly to determine to what particular category of mammals it belonged, or perhaps we shall mistakenly put it in the cat or the horse category. But from this shoulder blade alone we can determine without error that it was neither a bird, a fish, nor a testacean.

We have said that these negative deductions are important in all sciences, but they are particularly important in the moral sciences and in metaphysics, because the errors which they have removed did exceptional practical harm to these sciences. In the olden days, when the natural sciences were still undeveloped, the whale was mistakenly regarded as a fish and the bat was regarded as a bird; but in all probability not a single person suffered as a result. Owing to the same cause, however, i.e., inability to subject a thing to exact analysis, mistaken opinions arose in metaphysics and in the moral sciences which caused people much more harm than cholera, plague, and all infectious diseases.

Let us suppose, for example, that idleness is pleasant and that work is unpleasant. If this hypothesis becomes the prevailing opinion, every man will take every opportunity to ensure for himself a life of idleness and compel others to work for him. This will give rise to every kind of enslavement and thievery, from so-called slavery proper and wars of conquest to the present more refined forms of these phenomena. This supposition has actually been made by people; it actually became the prevailing opinion and has prevailed to this day, causing incalculable suffering.

Let us now try to apply to the concept of pleasure or enjoyment the deduction drawn from an exact analysis of the vital process. The phenomenon of pleasure or enjoyment belongs to that part of the vital process which is called sensation. Let us suppose for the moment that we have not yet had exact investigation of this part of the vital process, as a separate part. Let us see whether anything about it can be deduced from the exact information that science has acquired about nutrition, respiration, and blood circulation. We see that each of these phenomena constitutes the activity of certain parts of our organism. We know what parts operate in the phenomena of respiration, nutrition, and blood circulation, and we know how they operate. Perhaps we would err if from this information we drew any conclusion about what particular parts of the organism operate in the phenomenon of pleasant sensation, and about how they operate; but we have clearly seen that only the action of some part of the organism gives rise to what are called the phenomena of life. We see that when there is action there is a phenomenon, and that when there is no action there is no phenomenon. From this we see that in order to obtain a pleasant sensation there must be some kind of action on the part of the organism.

Let us now analyze the concept of action. Action calls for the existence of two things, something that acts and something that is acted upon, and it consists in the former exerting effort to alter the latter. For example, the chest and lungs move and decompose air in the process of respiration; the stomach digests food in the process of nutrition. Thus, a pleasant sensation must also consist in the alteration of some external object by the human organism. We do not yet know exactly what object is altered, or exactly how it is altered, but we already see that the source of pleasure must be some kind of action by the human organism upon external objects.

Let us now try to draw a negative deduction from this result. Idleness is the absence of action; obviously, it cannot produce the phenomenon that is called pleasant sensation. It now becomes perfectly clear to us why the well-to-do classes of society in all civilized countries complain of constant ennui, complain that life is unpleasant. This complaint is quite justified. For the rich, life is as unpleasant as it is for the poor, because owing to the custom introduced in society by a mistaken hypothesis, wealth is associated with idleness, that is, the thing that should have served as a source of pleasure is deprived by this hypothesis of the possibility of affording pleasure. Whoever is accustomed to abstract thinking will be convinced in advance that observation of everyday relationships will not contradict the results of scientific analysis. But even those who are unaccustomed to abstract thinking will be led to the same conclusion by pondering the meaning of the facts that constitute so-called high society life. In it there is no normal activity—i.e., activity, the objective side of which corresponds to its subjective role; there is no activity that deserves the name of serious activity.

To avoid a subjective disturbance in the organism, to avoid sicknesses that are the result of inaction, to avoid ennui, the society man must create fictitious activity in place of normal activity. He lacks motion that has an objective rational purpose, so he "takes a constitutional," i.e., spends as much time putting one foot in front of the other as he ought to do in walking to work. He has no physical work to do, so he spends as much time doing gymnastics for the benefit of his health, i.e., waving his arms and bending his body (if not in the gymnasium, then at the billiard table, or at a turning lathe for a hobby) as he ought to spend on physical work. He has no practical cares concerning himself or his family, so he engages in scandal and intrigue, i.e., spends as much mental effort on nonsense as he ought to spend on practical affairs. But none of these artificial means can afford the human organism the satisfaction that is required for good health.

The life of the rich man of the present day is like that of the Chinese opium eater: unnatural excitement is followed by lethargy, intense satiety by purposeless activity, which leaves him in the very state of ennui from which he tried to escape by indulging in it. . . .

When one speaks without a plan, one never knows where one's

words will lead. We see now that we have got to the point of speaking about moral or exalted feelings. On the question of these feelings, practical deductions from ordinary, everyday experience have absolutely contradicted the old hypotheses which ascribed to man a multitude of diverse altruistic strivings. People learned from experience that every man thinks only of himself, is more concerned about his own interests than he is about the interests of others, that he nearly always sacrifices the interests, honor, and life of others to his own. In short, everybody learned that all men are egoists. In practical affairs, all prudent people have always been guided by the conviction that egoism is the only motive that governs the actions of everybody they have dealings with. If this opinion, daily confirmed by the experience of every one of us, were not countered by a fairly large number of other facts of everyday life, it would, of course, soon gain the upper hand in theory, too, over the hypotheses that egoism is only a corrupted heart, and that a man who is not corrupted is guided by motives antithetical to egoism: that he thinks of others' good rather than his own, that he is prepared to sacrifice himself for others, and so forth.

But the difficulty arose precisely from the fact that the hypothesis that man is prompted in his strivings by the interests of others, a hypothesis refuted by hundreds of experiences in everyone's daily life, seemed to be confirmed by fairly numerous cases of altruism, self-sacrifice, and so forth. For example, Curtius throws himself into the abyss to save his native city; Empedocles jumps into a crater to make a scientific discovery; Damon offers to die in order to save Pythias; Lucretia stabs herself in order to vindicate her honor.

Until recent times there were no scientific means of precisely deducing these two categories of phenomena from one principle, of bringing opposite facts under one law. A stone falls to the ground, steam rises. In the olden days people thought that the law of gravity which operates in a stone does not operate in steam. It is now known that both these opposite movements, the falling of the stone and the rising of steam, are due to the same cause, are governed by the same law. It is now known that under certain circumstances the force of gravity, which generally tends to make things fall, manifests itself by compelling some bodies to rise. We have repeated many times that the moral sciences have not yet been worked out as fully as the natural sciences, but even in their present, by no means brilliant state the problem of bringing all, often contradictory, human actions and feelings under one principle has already been solved, as have nearly all the moral and metaphysical problems which had puzzled people before the moral sciences and metaphysics began to be elaborated according to strictly scientific method. As in all aspects of man's life, human motives are not prompted by two natures, two fundamental laws which differ from or contradict one another. As in human life as a whole, all the diverse phenomena in the sphere of human motives and conduct spring from one nature, are governed by one law.

We shall not discuss these actions and feelings which everybody recognizes as being egoistic, selfish, prompted by selfish interest. We shall turn our attention only to those feelings and actions which seem to bear an opposite character. In general, it is necessary only to examine more closely an action or a feeling that seems to be altruistic to see that all of them are based on the thought of personal interest, personal gratification, personal benefit; they are based on the feeling that is called egoism. There will be very few cases where this basis will not be apparent even to a man who is not accustomed to make psychological analyses.

If a husband and wife have lived in harmony together, the wife will quite sincerely and very deeply grieve over the death of her husband; but listen to the words in which she expresses her grief: "Who will care for me now? What shall I do without you? Life will be impossible for me without you!" Underscore the words *me, I, for me:* they express the meaning of her lamentation, they are the basis of her grief.

Let us take a feeling that is far loftier, purer than the greatest connubial love: a mother's love for her child. Her lamentation over its death is exactly the same: "My angel! How I loved you! What a joy you were to me! How I nursed you! How much suffering, how many sleepless nights you cost me! I have been robbed of all my hopes in you, I have been robbed of all my joy!" Here again we have the same *my, I, to me.*

The egoistic basis is just as easily discovered in the most sincere and tenderest friendship.

Not much more difficulty is presented by those cases in which a man makes sacrifices for the object of his love. Even though he sacrifices his life, the basis of the sacrifice is personal calculation or an intense burst of egoistic passion. Most cases of so-called self-sacrifice do not deserve that name. The inhabitants of Saguntum committed suicide to avoid falling alive into the hands of Hannibal. Such heroism may rouse wonder, but it was entirely prompted by egoistic interest. These people had been accustomed to live as free citizens, to suffer no wrong, to respect themselves and to be respected by others; the Carthaginian general would have sold them into slavery and their lives would have been a constant torment. They acted in the same way as a man with a toothache who goes to have the bad tooth pulled. They preferred an instant of mortal pain to endless years of torment. In the Middle Ages, heretics burnt at the stake at a slow fire of damp logs would try to break their chains in order to throw themselves into the flames: better to suffocate in an instant than choke for hours. Such indeed was the position of the inhabitants of Saguntum. We were wrong in assuming that Hannibal would have merely sold them into slavery. Had they not exterminated themselves, the Carthaginians would have exterminated them, but they would have first subjected them to barbarous torture, and common sense prompted them to prefer a quick death to a slow and painful one.

Lucretia stabbed herself after Tarquinius Sextus had raped her, but she too was prompted by self-interest. What awaited her in the future? Her husband might have spoken words of consolation and endearment to her, but such words would have been sheer nonsense, testifying to the nobility of the one who uttered them, but by no means averting the inevitable consequences of the incident. Collatinus might have said to his wife: "I regard you as pure and love you as before." With the conceptions prevailing at that time, however, and prevailing with but little alteration today, he could not have proved his words by deeds; willy-nilly, he had already lost considerable respect and love for his wife. He might have attempted to conceal this loss by deliberately exaggerated tenderness toward her, but such tenderness is more offensive than coldness, more bitter than beating and abuse. Lucretia was right in thinking that suicide was preferable to living in a state that was degrading compared to the life she had been accustomed to. A fastidious person would prefer to go hungry rather than touch food that had been in any way polluted. A self-respecting person would prefer death to degradation.

The reader will understand that we are not saying all this with the object of belittling the great praise of which Lucretia and the inhabitants of Saguntum are worthy. To argue that a heroic action was at the same time a wise one, that a noble deed was not a reckless one, does not, in our opinion, mean belittling heroism and nobility.

From these heroic deeds let us pass to a kind of action which is more ordinary, though still only too rare. Let us examine cases like the devotion of a man who gives up all his pleasure and the free disposal of his time in order to look after another man who needs his care. A man who spends weeks at the bedside of a sick friend makes a far greater sacrifice than if he were to give him all his money. But why does he makes such a sacrifice? What feeling prompts him to do it? He sacrifices his time, his freedom, to his feeling of friendship—we emphasize, *his* feeling. This feeling is so strong that gratifying it gives him greater pleasure than he would obtain from any other occupation, even from his freedom. Were he to ignore it, refrain from gratifying it, he would feel greater discomfort than he would from refraining to gratify all other needs. Of exactly the same kind are the cases when a man forgoes all pleasure and gain for the sake of science or some conviction. Newton and Leibniz, who denied themselves all love for women in order to devote all their time and thoughts to scientific research, were, of course, heroes all their lives. The same must be said of those political figures who are usually called fanatics. Here again we see that a certain need becomes so strong in a man that it gives him pleasure to satisfy it even at the expense of other very strong needs. By their nature, these cases differ very sharply from the motive that prompts a man to sacrifice a very large sum of money in order to gratify some base passion, but in their theoretical formula they all come under the same law: the strongest passion gains the upper hand over those that are less strong, which are sacrificed to the former.

A careful examination of the motives that prompt men's actions shows that all deeds, good and bad, noble and base, heroic and craven, are prompted by one cause: a man acts in the way that gives him the most pleasure. He is guided by self-interest, which causes him to abstain from a smaller gain or a lesser pleasure in order to obtain a larger gain or a greater pleasure. The fact that good and bad actions are prompted by the same cause does not, of course, diminish the difference between them. We know that diamond and coal are both pure carbon; nevertheless a diamond is a diamond, a very costly article, while coal is coal, a very cheap article. The great difference between good and evil fully deserves our attention. We shall begin with an analysis of these concepts in order to ascertain what circumstances develop or weaken good in human life.

It has been noted that different people in the same society regard quite different and even opposite things as good. For example, if a man bequeaths his property to people outside his family, these people regard it as a good action, while the relatives who lose the legacy regard it as a very bad one. The same difference in the conception of good is observed in different societies and in different epochs in the same society. For a long time, the conclusion drawn from this was that there is nothing constant, nothing independent in the concept "good" that could be subject to a common definition, that it is a purely conventional concept, dependent upon the arbitrary opinion of men.

But when we examine more closely the relation of the actions that are called good to the people who call them that, we find that this relation always has one common, invariable feature which causes an action to be placed in the category of good. Why do the people outside the testator's family regard the action by which they came into possession of the property as good? Because that action was beneficial to them. On the other hand, it was detrimental to the testator's relatives who lost the legacy, and that is why they regard it as a bad action. War against infidels for the spread of Mohammedanism seemed to the Mohammedans to be a good cause because it benefited them, it brought them booty. This opinion was fostered among them particularly by the higher clergy, whose power grew with new conquests. Individuals regard as good the actions of other people that are beneficial to them; society holds as good what is useful to the whole of society, or to the majority of its members. Lastly, people in general, irrespective of nation or class, describe as good that which is useful to mankind in general.

[There are frequent cases when the interests of different nations and classes clash either with one another or with the interests of mankind in general.]Equally frequent are cases when the interests of a given class clash with the interests of the nation. In all these cases a controversy arises over the character of the action, institution, or connection that is beneficial for some and detrimental to other interests. The adherents of the side to which it is detrimental say that it is bad; the advocates of the side that benefits from it say that it is good. In such cases it is very easy to decide on which side theoretical truth lies. The interests of mankind as a whole stand higher than the interests of an individual nation; the common interests of a whole nation are higher than the interests of an individual class; the interests of a large class are higher than the interests of a small one. In theory, this gradation is beyond doubt; it is merely the application to social problems of the geometrical axioms: "the whole is greater than the part," "the larger quantity is greater than the smaller quantity."

Theoretical fallacy inevitably leads to practical harm. In those cases when, for its own advantage, an individual nation tramples upon the interests of mankind, or when an individual class tramples upon the interests of the nation, the result is always detrimental not only to the side whose interest has been encroached upon, but also to the side that has hoped to gain by this. It always turns out that a nation which enslaves mankind ruins itself; an individual class that sacrifices the whole nation to its own interest comes to a bad end itself. From this we see that when national interests clash with class interests, the class which thinks of turning national misfortune to its own advantage is mistaken from the very outset; it is blinded by false calculations.

The illusion that entices it sometimes bears the form of a very sound calculation, but we shall cite two or three cases of this kind to show how fallacious such calculations can be. Manufacturers think that prohibitive tariffs are to their advantage; but in the end it is found that with prohibitive tariffs the nation remains poor and, because of its poverty, cannot maintain an extensive manufacturing industry. Thus, the manufacturing class itself remains not nearly as rich as that class is under free trade. All the mill owners in all the countries that have prohibitive tariffs taken together do not possess half the wealth that has been acquired by the mill owners of Manchester. Landowners in general hope to gain from slavery (serfdom) and from other forms of forced labor; but in the end it is found that the landowning class in all countries where forced labor exists is ruined. Bureaucracy sometimes deems it necessary for its own good to hinder the intellectual and social development of the nation, but here too the result is always that it finds its own affairs disturbed and it becomes impotent.

We have cited cases in which the calculations of a class which harms the interests of the nation in pursuit of its own advantage appear to be extremely well grounded; but here too the result shows that this was only apparent, that the calculations were wrong, that the class which had acted to the detriment of the nation had deceived itself with respect to its own interests. Nor can it be otherwise: the French or Austrian manufacturer is, after all, a Frenchman or an inhabitant of Austria, and everything that is detrimental to the country to which he belongs, the strength of which is the basis of his own strength, the wealth of which is the basis of his own wealth, is detrimental to him too, for it dries up the source of his own strength and wealth.

Exactly the same must be said about the cases where the interests of an individual nation clash with the interests of mankind in general. Here too it is always found that the calculations of the nation which sets out to further its interests by damaging those of mankind were totally mistaken. Conquering nations have always ended by being exterminated or enslaved themselves. . . .

We have said all this in order to *show* that the concept good is not impaired but, on the contrary, is strengthened, is most sharply and precisely defined, when we discover its real nature, when we find that good means utility. Only if we interpret it in this way are we able to eliminate all the difficulties that arise out of the contradictory conceptions of good and evil prevailing in different epochs and civilizations, among different classes and nations. Science deals with nations, not with an individual man; with man, but not with a Frenchman or Englishman, not with the merchant or the bureaucrat. Only what enters into human nature is recognized as a truth in science. Only that which is useful to man in general is regarded as true good. All deviations from this norm in the conceptions of a given nation or class are a mistake, a hallucination, which may cause much harm to other people, but most of all to that nation or class which falls into this error by adopting through its own fault, or that of others, a position among other nations or classes that makes it think that what is detrimental to mankind in general is beneficial for itself. "Perished like the Avers"—history repeats these words over every nation and every class that is overcome by the fatal hallucination that its interests clash with the interests of mankind in general.

If there is any difference between good and utility, it is only that the concept of good brings out very strongly the feature of constancy, durability, fertility, abundance of lasting and beneficial results, which, however, is also possessed by the concept of utility. It is precisely this feature that distinguishes it from the concepts of pleasure and enjoyment.

The object of all human desires is pleasure, but there are two kinds of sources from which we derive pleasure. One kind is associated with transient circumstances over which we have no control, or if we have, they pass off without any lasting result. The other kind is associated with facts and circumstances which are firmly embedded within us or—if they are outside of us— are present constantly for a long time. A sunny day in Saint Petersburg is a great relief, a source of innumerable pleasant sensations for the inhabitants of that city. But this sunny day is a transient phenomenon, having no foundation and leaving no lasting results in the lives of the inhabitants of Saint Petersburg. It cannot be said that that day provided utility; it provided only pleasure. Good weather in Saint Petersburg is a useful phenomenon only in those few cases, and only for a few people, when it is fairly prolonged and as a consequence creates a lasting improvement in the health of a few invalids. But whoever leaves Saint Petersburg for some place with a good climate acquires something useful with respect to his health and the enjoyment of nature, because he acquires a durable source of lasting pleasure. When a man receives an invitation to a good dinner he receives only pleasure, not something useful (and, of course, he does not even receive pleasure unless he is a gourmet). But if the man with gourmet proclivities comes into a large sum of money, he receives something useful, that is to say, the opportunity to enjoy good dinners for a long time to come.

Thus by useful things we mean the durable principles of enjoyment, so to speak. If this fundamental feature of the concept "utility" were always borne firmly in mind when that term is used, there would be absolutely no difference between utility and good. But, first, the term "utility" is sometimes applied in what might be called a frivolous manner to principles of pleasure which, while not exactly transient, are not very durable either. And second, these durable principles of enjoyment can be divided into two categories according to degree of durability: not very durable and very durable. It is this latter category that is designated by the term "good." Good is, as it were, the superlative of utility, very useful utility. A doctor has restored to health a man who had been suffering from a chronic illness—what did the doctor bring his patient, good or utility? Here it would be equally convenient to use either term, because the doctor brought his patient the most durable principle of enjoyment.

Our thinking tends constantly to recall external nature, which is supposed to be the only thing that comes within the purview of the natural sciences, which are supposed to embrace only one part of our knowledge and not the whole of it. We have observed, moreover, that these essays of ours indicate that we have a very cold heart, and a vulgar and low mind, which seeks in all things only utility, which pollutes everything with the quest for material grounds, which understands nothing lofty and lacks all poetic feeling. We want to mask this shameful lack of poetry in our heart. We shall look for something poetic with which to ornament our essay. Influenced by the thought of the importance of the natural sciences, we set out in search of poetry in the sphere of material nature, and there we find flowers. Let us then decorate one of our dry pages with a poetic comparison. Flowers, those enchanting sources of fragrance, those exquisite but fleeting fountains of delight to our eyes, are pleasure or enjoyment. The plant on which they grow is utility. On one plant there are many flowers; some fade, others bloom in their place. Hence, that from which many flowers grow is called a useful thing. But there are numerous annual flowering plants, and there are also rose trees and oleanders which live many years, and each year bring forth many flowers. Likewise it is by its lasting nature that good excels the other sources of pleasure that are simply called useful things and are not vouchsafed the name "good," just as a violet is not vouchsafed the name "tree." They belong to the same category of things, but they are not all as great and long-lasting.

The fact that the term "good" is applied to very durable sources of lasting, constant, and very numerous pleasures, of itself explains the importance that all thinking people ascribe to the good when discussing human affairs. If we think that "good is higher than utility," we are only saying "very great utility is higher than not very great utility"; we are only expressing a mathematical truism, such as that 100 is more than 2, that an oleander bears more flowers than a violet.

The reader sees that the method of analyzing moral concepts in the spirit of the natural sciences, divesting the object of all pomposity and transferring it to the sphere of very simple and natural phenomena, places moral concepts on an unshakable foundation. If by useful we mean that which serves as a source of numerous pleasures, and by good, simply that which is very useful, no doubt whatever remains concerning the aim that is ascribed to man—not by extraneous motives or promptings, not by problematical assumptions, or by mysterious relationships to something which is still very uncertain—but simply by reason, by common sense, by the need for pleasure. That aim is—the good. Only good actions are prudent; only he who is good is rational, and he is rational only to the degree that he is good. When a man is not good he is merely an imprudent wastrel who pays thousands of rubles for things that are worth kopeks, spends as much material and moral strength in acquiring little pleasure as could have enabled him to acquire ever so much more pleasure.

But in this same conception of good as very durable utility we find still another important feature, which helps us to discover precisely what phenomena and actions chiefly constitute the good. External objects, no matter how closely they may be bound to a man, nevertheless are only too often parted from him: sometimes he abandons them, sometimes they desert him. Country, kinsmen, wealth—all these things can be abandoned by man, or they can abandon him. But there is one thing he cannot possibly part from as long as he lives; there is one thing that is inseparable from him—himself. If a man can be useful to people because of his wealth, he can also cease to be useful if he loses his wealth. If, however, he is useful to other people because of his own virtues—because of his own spiritual qualities, as it is usually expressed—all he can do is commit suicide; but as long as he refrains from doing that he cannot cease to be useful to other people: not to be so is beyond his strength, beyond his power. He may say to himself: I shall be wicked, I shall harm people; but he will not be able to do it, any more than a clever man could be a fool even if he wanted to.

Not only is the good done by the qualities of the man himself much more constant and lasting than the good done merely because he owns certain external objects, but the results are far greater. The good or bad use to which external objects are put is casual; all material means are as easily, and as often, used to people's detriment as to their benefit. The rich man who uses his wealth to benefit some people in some cases, harms others, or even the same people, in other cases. For example, a rich man can give his children a good upbringing, develop their health and their minds, and impart much knowledge to them. All this would be useful to the children. But whether these things will actually be accomplished is uncertain; often they are not. On the contrary, the children of the rich often receive an upbringing that makes them weak, sickly, feeble-minded, vacuous, and pitiful; in general they acquire habits and ideas that are harmful to them. If such is the influence of wealth upon those whom the rich man cherishes most, then, of course, still more notable is the harm it does to other people who are not so dear to the rich man's heart. Thus it must be supposed that the rich man's wealth does more harm than good to the people who have direct relations with him.

But while it is possible to harbor some doubt as to whether the harmful influence wealth exercises upon these individuals is equal to the benefit they derive from it or, as in all probability is the case, greatly exceeds it, it is a totally indisputable fact that the wealth of individuals does far more harm than good to society as a whole. This is revealed with mathematical precision by that section of the moral sciences which began earlier than the others to be elaborated in conformity with an exact scientific system, and some of the departments of which have already been fairly well elaborated by the science of social material welfare that is usually called political economy. What we find in relation to the great ascendancy that material wealth gives some people over others, applies in an even greater degree to the concentration in the hands of individuals of another means of influencing the fate of other people which is external to the human organism —namely, power or authority. It too, in all probability, does much more harm than good even to the people who come into direct contact with it, and the influence it exercises upon society as a whole is incomparably more harmful than beneficial.

Thus, the only remaining real source of perfectly durable benefit for people from the actions of other people are the useful qualities that lie within the human organism itself. That is why it is these qualities which are designated as good, and that is why the term "good" properly applies only to man. His actions are based on feeling, on the heart, and they are directly prompted by that side of organic activity which is called "will." Therefore, when discussing good, a special study must be made of the laws that govern the action of the heart and will. But the will is given means of gratifying the feelings of the heart by the conceptions formed by the mind, and therefore it is also necessary to pay attention to that aspect of thinking that relates to means of influencing the fate of other people. . . .

But we had almost forgotten that the term "anthropological" in the title of our essay still remains unexplained. What is this "anthropological principle in the moral sciences"? The reader has seen what this principle is from the very character of these essays. It is that a man must be regarded as a single being having only one nature, that a human life must not be cut into two halves, each belonging to a different nature; that every aspect of a man's activity must be regarded as the activity of his whole organism, from head to foot inclusively, or if it is the special function of some particular organ of the human organism we are dealing with, that organ must be regarded in its natural connection with the entire organism. . . .

As for the word "anthropology," it comes from the word "anthropos," which means "man"—but the reader knows that without our telling him. Anthropology is a science which, no matter what part of the human vital process it may deal with, always remembers that the process as a whole, and every part of it, takes place in a human organism, that this organism is the material which produces the phenomena under examination, that the qualities of the phenomena are conditioned by the properties of the material, and that the laws by which the phenomena arise are only special cases of the operation of the laws of nature.

DMITRY IVANOVICH PISAREV
[1840–1868]

I<small>F</small> CHERNYSHEVSKY WAS THE ORIGINATOR of Nihilist philosophy in Russia, Dmitry Pisarev was its most militant champion. In a series of brilliant polemical essays written in the last decade of a tragically short life, Pisarev gave extreme expression to both the positive and the negative features of the Nihilist creed.

Dmitry Ivanovich Pisarev was born in 1840 into the family of a nobleman whose fortunes had fallen. His early childhood was spent on the family estate in the province of Oryol, south of Moscow, where he received a rigorously correct upbringing supervised by his mother. From 1851 to 1856 he attended a Saint Petersburg *gymnasium*. As a youth he was particularly. pious and had strong ascetic inclinations. He was much impressed by a reading of Gogol's *Selected Passages from a Correspondence with Friends*, the politically conservative, devoutly religious work which provoked Belinsky's famous *Letter to Gogol*.

In 1856, Pisarev entered Saint Petersburg University, but his studies were interrupted by a mental breakdown (1859-1860) which led him twice to attempt suicide. Only after four months in an asylum was he able to resume his work. In 1858, he began to write for *Rassvet* (Dawn), a women's liberal journal of the day; the current literature he read in preparing his articles, he says, "forced me out of my confined cell into the fresh air." [1] He discovered the world of radical opinion, and by the time he left the University in 1861 he was not only thoroughly acquainted

1. Quoted in editor's introduction to Dmitry Pisarev, *Selected Philosophical, Social, and Political Essays*, Moscow, 1958, p. 9.

with the writings of Chernyshevsky, Dobrolyubov, their intellectual ancestors, and their current disciples, but he had made
the Nihilist outlook his own, completely abandoning his Orthodox
religious creed. In the same year he began to write for the
journal *Russkoye Slovo* (Russian World), which from 1862—with
Dobrolyubov dead and Chernyshevsky in prison—gradually assumed, under Pisarev's leadership, the mantle of *The Contemporary* as the leading organ of Russian radicalism.

The enthusiasm with which Pisarev expressed his new radical
outlook contributed powerfully to his influence, but it also
proved dangerous. At the end of 1861, the Tsarist authorities had
arranged the publication of a pamphlet aimed at discrediting
Alexander Herzen, then a troublesome voice from abroad. In-
censed by this and by other repressive steps taken by the government, Pisarev in June, 1862, penned a reply castigating the
government and openly advocating revolution: "What is dead
and rotten must of itself fall into the grave. All we still have
to do is to give a last push and cover their stinking corpses with
dirt." [2] For this indiscretion Pisarev was confined in the Peter
and Paul fortress for over four years. In prison his literary activity went on unabated, however, and his articles (now somewhat more circumspect) continued to appear in *Russian Word*
and continued to have a strong impact on the Russian *intelligentsia*. The bulk of Pisarev's literary production dates from
these prison years. He was released at the end of 1866. In the
summer of 1868 he drowned while swimming in the Baltic Sea—
whether by accident or intentionally is not known.

Pisarev's thought, though fundamentally in agreement with
Chernyshevsky's, is marked by significantly different emphases,
and the selections which follow have been chosen to show the
differences as well as the agreement. Chief among these is the
extreme emphasis Pisarev placed, in his early writings, on individual autonomy—a concern clearly related to his interest in the
writings of Max Stirner. Pisarev initially gave less attention than
Chernyshevsky and Dobrolyubov did to constructive social programs, and expressed more insistently the need to destroy—to
break the hold of traditional customs, institutions, and ideas on

2. "Shedo-Ferroti's Pamphlet," in *ibid.*, p. 147.

the individual. Thus in the article "Plato's Idealism" (1861), the concluding portion of which is reprinted here, Pisarev criticizes the society described in Plato's *Republic* for the restraints it places upon the individual. (His readers could not fail to notice that most of what he said applied to Tsarist Russia as well.) And he does not condemn such restraints because they indirectly harm *society;* they are simply "unnatural," "offensive," "humiliating." But even in this essay Pisarev's special concern for individual autonomy is combined with the general Nihilist preference for experience over speculation, the concrete over the abstract, the useful and "practical" over the "ideal."

All these concerns are elaborated in the early article which made Pisarev's reputation, "Nineteenth-Century Scholasticism" (1861). Branding the majority of the existing intellectual productions of Russian literature as arid scholastic exercises, Pisarev in one breath espouses Nihilist "materialism" and calls for "subjectivity" in thought—attention to living problems and a personal commitment on the part of the thinker. In accents clearly anticipating the later demands of Nietzsche and modern-day existentialists, he criticizes the Russian philosopher Peter Lavrov for failing to exhibit such subjective engagement. Accompanying this methodological stress on individuality, moreover, is an extreme statement of free individual development as the goal of all intellectual labor. The chief task of literature, he maintains in an earlier portion of the essay not included below, must be "to emancipate the person from all the trammels imposed on him by the timidity of his own thoughts, by caste prejudices, the authority of tradition, by any striving toward a common ideal, and all the antiquated rubbish that prevents a living man from breathing freely and developing in every direction." [3]

Pisarev's early dedication to individual autonomy was noticeably tempered, however, as he began to devote more attention to constructive programs for achieving the changes he desired. Such a shift is evident in his essay, "The Realists" (1864), a characteristic presentation of both the negative tone and the positive direction of Pisarev's maturing Nihilism. In this essay Pisarev attempts to portray the true Nihilist—or "thinking real-

3. *Ibid.,* p. 79.

ist," as he prefers to call him—by defending the character of Bazarov in *Fathers and Sons*. Advocating what he later called "the annihilation of aesthetics," Pisarev here makes clear the positive social need for this annihilation. Russia's chief ills, he asserts, are poverty and ignorance. Until they are eradicated individuality cannot flower, and they can be eradicated only by concentrating all available intellectual energies on the task. If poetry can aid in this social work, well and good; it is then useful and no longer belongs to the realm of "aesthetics." But what is chiefly needed is the popularization of the natural sciences. Science is the social medicine which must be taken "by the bucket and the barrelful." In this essay the Nihilists' utilitarian, "materialistic" emphasis on science is put in full positive perspective and given a social justification.

In "The Realists" Pisarev adopts a social stance, but a certain uneasiness as to the place of individual autonomy in society is still discernible in his insistence on the distinction between work and leisure: "When you rest you belong to yourself; when you work you belong to society." And in the last analysis the essay's recommendations are not for organized social action but for individual self-improvement, as the final pages of the selections included here indicate. Any lingering uncertainties as to the compatibility of individual and society were soon dispelled, however, and in "Thinking Proletariat" (1865) Pisarev proclaims the complete harmony of society's demands with the needs of the (properly) egoistic individual. This essay, too, defended fictional models of Nihilism—this time Chernyshevsky's "new men" in *What Is To Be Done?* The essay's title itself is indicative of Pisarev's shifting emphasis. In his view the significance of useful work, in a social system based on cooperation rather than competition, is so great as to erase all distinction between the interests of the individual and the interests of society; there is no longer any cause for concern about individual autonomy. The "new men" are enlightened beings who recognize that the strictest selfishness and the broadest altruism work together. They labor for the good of mankind because they passionately enjoy it. On this basis Pisarev paints the ideal of the future in hues more glowing than those of Chernyshevsky himself.

This picture of social well-being was the developed positive ideal of Nhilism, the end which justified the destructive means it advocated. Pisarev in September, 1861, had expressed the destructive motif in strident tones: "What can be smashed should be smashed. What withstands the blow is fit to survive. What flies into pieces is rubbish. In any case, strike out right and left; no harm can come of it." [4] The later Pisarev did not recant these words, but he came, like Chernyshevsky, to focus on the social solidarity of productive individuals rather than on the sheer annihilation of the old obstacles to individual autonomy.

SELECTED BIBLIOGRAPHY

Works:

Dmitry Pisarev, *Selected Philosophical, Social, and Political Essays*, Moscow, 1958.

Secondary Sources:

Armand Coquart, *Dmitri Pisarev (1840-68) et l'idéologie du nihilisme russe*, Paris, 1946.
Eugeni Lampert, *Sons Against Fathers: Studies in Russian Radicalism and Revolution*, Oxford, 1965.
Thomas G. Masaryk, *The Spirit of Russia*, trans. E. and C. Paul, New York, 1955, II, 53-81.
V. V. Zenkovsky, *A History of Russian Philosophy*, trans. George L. Kline, 2 vols., London and New York, 1953, pp. 337-340.

4. Pisarev, "Skholastika XIX veka," *Sochineniya D. I. Pisareva*, 6 vols., St. Petersburg, 1894-1897, I, 375.

[DMITRY PISAREV]

Plato's Idealism*

Plato is unquestionably entitled to our esteem as a powerful mind and a remarkable talent. The colossal mistakes this talent made in the sphere of abstract thought derived not from weakness of mind, shortness of sight, or timidity of thought, but from the predominance of the poetic element, from deliberate contempt of the testimony of experience, and from an overweening desire, common in powerful minds, to extract the truth from the depths of one's own creative spirit instead of examining and studying it in particular phenomena.

Despite his mistakes and the complete untenability of his system, Plato may with all justice be called the father of idealism. Whether this was a signal service to humanity is, of course, a question that will be answered in different ways by representatives of different schools of abstract thought. But whatever the answer, nobody will deny Plato a place of honor in the history of science. Geniuses sometimes make felicitous mistakes that have a stimulating effect on the minds of whole generations. At first highly popular, later they are criticized; the popularity and the subsequent criticism together long serve as a school for mankind, as the ground of an intellectual struggle, as an occasion for the development of capacities, as a guiding and determining principle of historical trends and radical changes.

Plato, however, did not confine himself to the realm of pure thought, and he failed to realize that the true meaning of historical and political life cannot be understood while experience and individual phenomena are neglected. He tried to solve practical problems without even knowing how to pose them properly, so that his efforts in this direction are so feeble and groundless

* Translated by J. Katzer and reprinted, with revisions and corrections for this volume by James Scanlan, from Dmitry Pisarev, *Selected Philosophical, Social, and Political Essays*, Moscow, 1958, pp. 66-71. The revisions and corrections were made by reference to the original Russian text in *Sochineniya D. I. Pisareva*, 6 vols., St. Petersburg, 1894-1897, I, 275-280.

that they collapse completely at the lightest touch of criticism. His efforts show no rational love for mankind, no respect for the individual, no artistic proportion, no unity of purpose, no moral loftiness of ideal.

Imagine a fanciful but ugly edifice—one with arches, pediments, porticoes, belvederes, and colonnades, none of which has any practical purpose—and you will get an idea of the impression produced on the reader by Plato's treatises, the *Republic* and the *Laws*. "The primary aim of the state," Plato thinks, "is to make its citizens virtuous and ensure the material and moral welfare of all." Recent investigators, as for instance Wilhelm Humboldt (*Ideen zu einem Versuch die Grenzen der Wirksamkeit des Staats zu bestimmen*), view the matter in a different light and define the state as a protective institution that safeguards the individual against abuse and attack by internal and external enemies. By this definition they release the adult citizen from the peculiar and unwanted guardianship imposed upon him throughout his life in Plato's republic.

Apart from the erroneousness of the basic view, we find that the aim Plato pursued cannot even be achieved by the means and methods he suggested in his treatises. Virtue is required of the citizen, but Plato places the latter under humiliating restraints, against which moral and aesthetic feeling must rise up. The reader is faced with a dilemma: either the citizens, as self-respecting people, will not put up with this constraint, in which case all of Plato's institutions go by the board; or else they will submit to it and, systematically perverted by it, will lose the capacity to be virtuous. Virtue (even as Plato understands it) and the observance of the laws in his ideal state are two incompatible principles. Wisdom, courage, temperance, and justice are the four cardinal virtues in Plato's moral philosophy. Which of these four virtues denies man the right of free criticism and results in absolute submission? If none of these virtues is fit for the dutiful citizens of the ideal state, then that means that Plato separates the ideal of man from the ideal of the citizen.

Many thinkers of antiquity, among them Aristotle in his *Politics*, say that virtue can be achieved only by the fully enfranchised citizens and does not exist for the slave, the artisan, or the woman. But Plato, who imposes unnatural and offensive restraints upon *all* the citizens of his state, goes much further. He gives society a structure which, by its very existence, makes it impossible not only to attain the ideal but even to strive towards it. Coming from a thinker who believes that there is no salvation apart from an ideal, such an arrangement must seem exceedingly peculiar. If a man's ideal cannot be achieved even theoretically in civil society, the conclusion follows either that man must live and develop outside society, or else that the notorious ideal is a useless plaything of idle imagination. Neither of those conclusions would have pleased Plato, but both can be eliminated only by rejecting utopian theory or revising the ideal.

In Plato's republic there are officials, warriors, artisans, tradesmen, slaves, and females—but there are no human beings, nor can there be any. Each individual is a cog, a pinion, or a wheel of a certain size and shape in the machine of state: aside from this official function he has no significance in any quarter: he is neither son, nor brother, nor husband, nor father, nor friend, nor lover. He is taken from his mother's breast at birth and placed in a home for children; he is not shown to his parents for several years, and his origin is deliberately forgotten. He is brought up in the same way as other children of the same age, and as soon as he begins to remember things and to be aware of himself he feels that he is state property, linked to no one and to nothing in the world around him. When he grows up he is assigned a definite post; he becomes a warrior, and warlike exercises become his chief occupation and amusement. As a good citizen he is obliged to put into these exercises the remnants of energy and soul that have not been dried up by his schooling. When his beard appears and his masculine strength has developed he is examined and certified by a special dignitary, who then brings him a young girl fit, in the dignitary's opinion, to become the young man's wife. The offspring accrue to the advantage of society and are treated in exactly the same fashion as the parents were. When a man grows old, he is made a civic official and appointed to some existing department: he becomes a judge, or a treasurer, or is placed in charge of young people, according to what he has been found suited for. Trade and the handicrafts are considered demeaning to the full-fledged citizen and are forbidden by law.

The external forms in which these political convictions must be embodied are barely sketched in Plato's works. He thinks that the wisest and worthiest must stand at the head of the state, but it is a matter of supreme indifference to him whether it be one sage or several.

As an aristocrat by birth and a man who thought himself immeasurably superior to the masses in intellect and moral dignity, Plato found the democratic form of rule repugnant. . . . According to Plato, rulers have no obligations towards the individuals they rule, so that deceit, violence, and arbitrariness are permitted as tools of government. The laws of morality which are binding on private individuals do not apply to statesmen; the latter must be wise but the right to judge the degree of their wisdom is taken away from the individuals most interested and is, it seems, granted only to the Demiurge. On the one hand, arbitrariness has only the limits he deigns to give it. On the other hand, no limitation is placed on submissiveness, and if it begins to slacken it must be increased artificially, by measures moral or physical, stringent or mild, depending on the patient's constitution and the doctor's discretion. The removal of harmful influences must play an important role in the moral education or medical treatment to be applied to the citizens of the ideal state. Homer is banished as an immoral teller of fairy tales; myths are rewritten and stuffed with exalted ideas; statues of Apollo and Aphrodite are draped in the interests of decency. To prevent citizens of the ideal state from being led into temptation by neighboring peoples, intercourse with foreign lands must be made as difficult and limited as possible. . . . It would be useless to analyze such regulations, for they speak for themselves loudly and eloquently.

I shall permit myself the observation that to mankind's credit, the spirit of Plato's political ideas has never attempted to win a place in real life. The most unbridled despots—men like Xerxes of Persia, Caligula, and Domitian—have never tried to destroy the family or to reduce their nation to the level of a stud farm with a stroke of the pen. Fortunately for their subjects, these

gentlemen were not philosophers; they butchered people as a
pastime, but at least they did not try to remake mankind or
systematically pervert their fellow citizens. Enlightened and intelligent despots like Louis XI, Tiberius, and Ferdinand the Catholic
exerted a conscious influence on their subjects, but their projects
and indeed their wildest dreams never achieved the majesty and
boldness that mark Plato's ideas. They shared the same aspirations,
but Plato, spurred by his poetic genius, pursued these aspirations
with unparalleled energy. The mighty spirit of criticism and
doubt, the element of free thinking and individuality was the
worst enemy of such aspirations and was therefore hateful to
Plato. The slogan of national welfare provided all these men
with a moral support, and Plato, too, employed it. The army was
their material support, and the same force plays an important role
in Plato's republic. Like the sages of the ideal republic, these
rulers thought themselves the worthiest and the best of their
fellow citizens, men called upon to be the instructors and physi-
cians of an underdeveloped and morally sick humanity. Roman
torture and executions, the Spanish Inquisition, the campaigns
against the Albigenses, Cardinal La Balue's cage, the flames that
licked Huss at the stake, the Massacre of Saint Bartholomew, the
Bastille, and so on and so forth may be termed *bitter but useful*
medicines which at various times and in varying doses the
healers of mankind have administered to their patients willy-nilly,
without asking their consent. The principle advanced by Plato
in the *Republic* and the *Laws* is not unknown to latter-day
European civilization.

[DMITRY PISAREV]

Nineteenth-Century Scholasticism *

It is only against theory that materialism is waging a struggle; in practical life we are all materialists and are always at odds with our theories. The whole difference between the idealist and the materialist in practical life is that to the former the ideal is a standing reproach and a constant nightmare, while the latter feels at liberty and in the right so long as he is not doing actual evil to anyone.

Let us suppose that you are an extreme idealist in theory. You sit down at your desk and look for some work you have begun. You look around, search every corner, and if your note pad or book fails to present itself to your senses you decide that it is not there and proceed to search elsewhere, even though your mind tells you that you had put it on the desk. If you take a sip of tea and discover that it has not been sugared, you will immediately rectify the omission even though you were firmly convinced that you had already done what was needed and put as much sugar into the tea as you usually do. Thus you see that the firmest conviction dissolves when it collides with what is manifest, and that you involuntarily attach far greater significance to the evidence of your senses than to the considerations of your intellect.

Employ this principle in all spheres of thought from the lowest to the highest and you will get the most complete materialism: I know only what I see or, in general, what the evidence of my senses can persuade me. I can go to Africa myself and see nature there, and that is why I can believe travelers' stories about tropical vegetation. I myself can verify a historian's work by comparing it with the genuine documents, and therefore I can

* Translated by J. Katzer and reprinted, with revisions and corrections for this volume by James P. Scanlan, from Dmitry Pisarev, *Selected Philosophical, Social, and Political Essays*, Moscow, 1958, pp. 103-114. The revisions and corrections were made by reference to the original Russian text as printed in *Sochineniya D. I. Pisareva*, 6 vols., St. Petersburg, 1894-1897, I, 360-369.

accept the results of his research. On the other hand, the poet gives me no means of convincing myself as to the materiality of the figures and constructions he has created, so that I can boldly assert that they *do not* exist, even though they *could* exist. When I see an object, I need no dialectical proofs of its existence: *manifestness is the best guarantee of reality.* When I am told of an object which I do not see and can never see or perceive with my senses, I say and I believe that it does not exist for me. *Impossibility of evident manifestation excludes any reality of existence.*

Such are the canons of materialism, and philosophers of all ages and nations would have saved much time and effort, and in many cases would have spared their zealous admirers fruitless efforts to understand the non-existent, if in their investigations they had not stepped beyond the sphere of objects which are open to immediate observation.

In the history of mankind there have been several clear heads who have pointed to the limits of cognition, but a dreamy aspiration towards a non-existent infinity has usually gained the upper hand over the cool criticism of the skeptical mind, thus leading to fresh hopes and fresh disappointments and fallacies. The Greek atomists were followed by Socrates and Plato; neo-Platonism lived cheek by jowl with Epicureanism; Bacon and Locke and the eighteenth-century Encyclopaedists were succeeded by Fichte and Hegel. It may well be that after Feuerbach, Vogt, and Moleschott there will again arise some system of idealism which for a time may satisfy the mass of people better than the sober world outlook of the materialists. For the time being, however, there can be no doubt that materialism is gaining the upper hand; all scientific investigations are based on observation, and the logical development of a basic idea, a development that is not grounded on facts, meets with stubborn mistrust in the world of scholarship. . . .

Let us now briefly examine the attitude our critics and scholarly literature have taken towards these contemporary phenomena and problems.

To write competently about philosophy is something new for us. Seminarian philosophy has existed for a long time, but fortunately it finds no readers or admirers outside a certain caste. . . .

During the past four years, articles with philosophical content have begun to appear among us, in certain measure suited to the reading public. True, there is talk in them of some kind of general ideal, and they contain many obscure passages and much useless dialectic, but at least they do not heap coals on the heads of those thinkers who disagree with them, but argue in a moderate tone without using Old Slavonic expressions, falling into sacred horror, or displaying pious indignation. Lavrov's articles on Hegelianism, on the mechanistic theory of the world, on the contemporary German theists, and the like have shown the author's extensive erudition and thorough acquaintance with the external history of philosophical systems. Those two qualities, rather rare in writers of our day, have won Lavrov a journalistic reputation.

Our critics have not been able to find Lavrov's weak sides because they find indefiniteness of conclusions and dialectical subtleties very much to their liking, and that writer's weakness lies precisely in the absence of subjectivity and of clear-cut and integral philosophical convictions. This weakness might have escaped public notice so long as Lavrov wrote historical essays on philosophy and gave expositions of the theories of others; in such work indefiniteness of personal convictions in the author may pass for historical impartiality and objectivity and impress the reader as a positive quality. But the *Annals of the Fatherland* for January of this year published the text of three public lectures delivered by Lavrov under the general title, "Three Talks on the Contemporary Significance of Philosophy." This title itself should have given ground for hope that Lavrov would set forth *his own* ideas on philosophy and openly join with one of the two parties in the grand schism in the world of philosophy today, i.e., either declare that speculative philosophy is impossible, or defend its right to existence. . . .

The result was quite otherwise. The talks failed to touch upon the contemporary significance of philosophy, completely evaded the questions raised in this field by the most recent school of thinkers, and did not represent any definite world outlook. Lavrov was at such pains to conceal his own personality that no efforts will bring it to the fore. While refraining from stating any clear and definite opinion, Lavrov limited himself to the general confines of the elementary logic, psychology, and aesthetics taught at secondary schools under the title of literary theory. Each thought develops from the one before; they are all linked together and they are logically consistent. What remains a mystery is why they develop, what the reason of their developing can be, and, finally, what they lead to.

What, in the final analysis, is this science known as philosophy? Can it be merely medicinal gymnastics for the mind, . . . an occupation that commences at a whim and ceases when we so will it, without leading anywhere, or solving a single problem, or shattering a single delusion, or implanting a single living idea in the mind, or causing the heart to beat more rapidly? Can *that* be philosophy? Was it not philosophy that brought about mass movements, shattered the old idols, and shook antiquated forms of civic and social life in the past? Consider the eighteenth century! The Encyclopaedists! No, say what you please, what Lavrov calls philosophy has no roots, it lacks flesh and blood, and it boils down to mere playing on words. That is scholasticism, an idle game of intellect that can be played with equal facility in England and Algiers, in the Celestial Empire and present-day Italy. What is the contemporary significance of such philosophy? What is its justification in real life? What are its rights to existence?

Lavrov poses the question: what is the *ego?* He wrestles with the problem over a whole page and ends by saying that he finds it scientifically insoluble. Why should he have raised it then? What is the natural and vital need to solve the problem of the *ego?* What consequences in the domain of thought or in private or public life can the solution of this question lead to? To search for such a solution is just like trying to square the circle. Compared to such mental gymnastics, the philosopher's stone, the elixir of life, and *perpetuum mobile* are extremely useful things, which, if unattainable, are at least evidence that the seeker after them aspires towards tangible goods and is following the path of experiment, so that he may stumble upon some unexpected and useful discovery. The very problem of the *ego* and Lavrov's attempts to illuminate it from various angles remain incomprehensible to any man endowed with ordinary common sense and uninitiated in the mysteries of the philosophical schools. This circumstance, I think, is the most striking proof of the illegitimacy, or more precisely the utter uselessness, of such intellectual exercises.

It is not in the spirit of the times to drive the ignorant crowd, the *profanum vulgus*, out of the temple of learning. It is inhumane, and it is dangerous. Lavrov, of course, is not in favor of such things, since he himself delivers *public* lectures. If the generality and not only the select are to study and reflect and wish to do so, it would be good to expel from science everything that can be understood only by the few and can never become common knowledge. It would be strange to call the second part of Goethe's *Faust*, which nobody understands, a work of superlative genius. In exactly the same way, it would be strange to call a cosmic truth or a cosmic question any idea or question that is but vaguely understood by a negligible minority of narrowly developed people. And how can one refrain from calling narrow and distorted the development of minds which are steeped in abstractions all their lives, which juggle forms that are devoid of content, and which deliberately turn away from the alluring diversity of living phenomena, from the practical activities of other men, from the interests of their country, from the joys and sorrows of the world around them? The activities of people such as these are simply an indication of some kind of disproportion in the development of the separate parts of the organism; all their vital forces are concentrated in their heads; for these individuals their cerebral urges, which satisfy themselves and find their aims within themselves, have replaced the variegated and complex process that is called living. To give this phenomenon the force of law would be just as strange as seeing in the ascetic or the castrate the highest phase of man's development.

Abstractions can be interesting and intelligible only to the abnormally developed and insignificant minority. That is why we have full right to take arms against abstractions in science for two reasons: first, in defense of the integrity of man's individ-

uality, and secondly, in defense of that healthy principle which
is gradually penetrating into social consciousness and impercepti-
bly removing the boundary lines between the estates of society
and destroying caste seclusion and exclusiveness. Intellectual
aristocratism is a dangerous thing, just because it operates imper-
ceptibly and does not reveal itself in clear-cut forms. The mon-
opoly of knowledge and humane development is of course one
of the most pernicious of monopolies. What kind of science is it
which by its very essence is inaccessible to the masses? What
kind of art is it whose works can be enjoyed only by the few
specialists? It should always be remembered that people do not
exist for science and art, but science and art have flowed from
man's natural need to enjoy life and adorn it in every possible
way. If science and art impede life, if they disunite men, if
they lay the foundation of caste divisions, then we shall have
no truck with them. That, however, is not the case; true science
leads to tangible knowledge, and what is tangible, what can be
seen with the eyes and felt with the hands will be understood
by a child of ten, a simple peasant, a man of the world, and a
learned scholar.

And so, from whatever angle you look at dialectics and abstract
philosophy, they will be seen as a useless waste of time and
effort. If we are to analyze Lavrov's public lectures, then I think
that in dealing with the first two lectures there is no need to
follow the author step by step, refute his separate statements, or
catch him in particular contradictions. . . . The third talk—on
philosophy in life—differs from the first two in its greater inner
content. Here Lavrov's philosophical convictions are finally stated
in a more definite form and lead to real conclusions in the sphere
of practical life. It is worthwhile saying a few words about
this lecture.

Lavrov says, first, that the purpose of life lies outside its process, which "at each moment is only a transitory fortuitous
expression of something that cannot be fully embodied, something that comprises what is highest, essential, and relatively
unchanging in man—his moral ideal."

Secondly, Lavrov says that a view of life which claims that
we aspire only toward pleasure is the coarsest and most elemen-

tary: "The first rule—seek what brings you pleasure—is open to animals as well as to man, to the savage as well as the man of education, to the child as well as the adult. The last rule— scorn everything but the highest good—is a statement that the most rigorous ascetic will not deny, and it is common knowledge that true ascetics are very rare among men."

I should like to remark in passing that freaks are also a great rarity among men and are even preserved in alcohol!

Thirdly, Lavrov says: "Humanity is the sum of all the principal branches of activity in the life of the individual. It is, however, a sum, not a commixture. Each activity presents its problem, its aim, and its ideal, and is sharply different from another; one of mankind's chief evils consists in the inadequate differentiation of these problems, in the transferral of ideals from one field of activity to another."

But if there were no ideals, then there would be nothing to transfer, and hence there would be no confusion. Why, then, should an ideal be taken as a necessary condition of development?

The excerpts cited show clearly that Lavrov inclines to a world outlook that differs materially from the thoughts I have set forth in the foregoing pages. I base everything on direct sensation; Lavrov builds everything on reflection and system. I demand tangible results from philosophy; Lavrov is satisfied with the aimless movement of thought in the sphere of formal logic. I consider manifestness the fullest and the sole guarantee of reality; Lavrov attaches great importance to dialectical proof, inquires into the essence of things, and says that it is incognizable; consequently he supposes that it somehow exists independently of the phenomenon. Our views are in almost diametrical opposition in the field of moral philosophy. Lavrov demands that the ideal and the purpose of life should lie outside the process of life; I see in life only a process, and I eliminate purpose and ideal. Lavrov has a special respect for the ascetic; I take upon myself the right to pity the ascetic as I would pity the halt, the blind, or the mad. Lavrov sees in humanity a kind of complex product of various moral spices and ingredients; I think that humanity can be fully revealed only in an integral individuality which has developed absolutely naturally and independently, untrammeled by service to various ideals, an individuality that has not wasted its strength in struggling against itself.

I have said that, in my opinion, a critic should express his *own* view of things and give the reader his *own* personal impressions; that is what I have done with respect to Lavrov. I have placed my views next to his and I give my reader the fullest liberty to select or reject any of them. I have not endeavored to convince anyone of the correctness of my thoughts and have not made it my aim to bring the reader over to my point of view at any price. Intellectual and moral propaganda is, in some measure, an encroachment upon another's liberty. What I would like is not so much to make the reader agree with me as to induce him to think independently and provide him with an occasion for an independent discussion of the questions I have raised. . . .

If my article were to evoke some denial, then the discussion would develop in the sphere of real and vital phenomena and would not turn into scholastic *logomachy*.

[DMITRY PISAREV]

The Realists *

It seems to me that a quite autonomous trend of thought is beginning to be elaborated at the present time in Russian society. I do not think that this trend is completely new or entirely original; it is certainly conditioned by what preceded it and by what surrounds it; it certainly borrows what meets its needs from various quarters. In this respect, of course, it is fully subject to the general natural law that in nature nothing comes from nothing. The autonomy of this nascent trend consists rather in the fact that it is inseparably linked with the actual needs of our society. It has been created by those needs, and only thanks to them does it exist and gradually develop.

When our grandfathers amused themselves with Martinism, Masonry, or Voltairism, when our fathers consoled themselves with romanticism, Byronism, or Hegelianism, they were like youths who try desperately to convince themselves that they feel an irresistible need to smoke a strong cigarette after dinner. The youths do in fact have a need to appear to be adults, and this need is perfectly natural and legitimate, but at the same time the smoking as such has not the slightest connection with the real needs of their organism. So it was with our immediate ancestors. They were very bored and had a real need to occupy their minds with reflections of some sort, but why they subscribed to an imported Martinism or Byronism or Hegelianism— you will not find the answer to this in the organic needs of the Russian people. All these *isms* were subscribed to solely because they were the mode among Europeans; none of them had the slightest connection with what was taking place in our society. Now, apparently, things have changed. We are borrowing more than ever; we are translating more books than ever; but now we know what we are doing, and we can render ourselves an

* Translated for this volume by James P. Scanlan, from D. I. Pisarev, "Realisty," *Sochineniya D. I. Pisareva*, 6 vols., St. Petersburg, 1894-1897, IV, 1-8, 26-29, 58-63, 95-97, 112-113, 119-121, 125, 128, 130, 133, 136, 145-146.

account of why we are taking just this and not something else.

Our accusatory literature had its birth at the end of the Crimean War and grew rapidly. It was very feeble and insignificant, even very shortsighted, but its birth was a phenomenon completely natural and entirely organic. The blow provoked a sensation of pain, and subsequently the desire arose to eliminate this pain. The accusations were directed, of course, to those aspects of our life which were eyesores to everyone. . . .

But we saw then and we still see before us two enormous facts, from which all our individual troubles and afflictions flow. In the first place, we are poor, and in the second place, we are stupid. These words, of course, need further elucidation.

We are poor: this means that in comparison with the average person we have little bread, little meat, little wool, little linen, few dresses, few pairs of boots, few undershirts, few human habitations, few comfortable pieces of furniture, few good farm implements—in short, few of the products of labor which are necessary to maintain life and to continue productive activity. *We are stupid:* this means that the brains of the vast majority of us are in almost complete disuse, and that perhaps one ten-thousandth part of the available brains are working in one way or another, producing thoughts that are twenty times less sensible than the thoughts they could produce under normal and certainly not exhausting operation. There is, of course, nothing to take offense at here; when a man is sleeping, he cannot use his mind; when Ivan Sidorovich is winning a pot from Stepan Paramonovich at cards, he cannot use his mind. In short, the only people who are not using their minds are those who in their present situation are unable to do so. Those who can are doing so, but haphazardly, because the demand for such use is small, and the most enthusiastic actor will be cold and uninspired when he has to play before an empty house. It goes without saying that our intellectual poverty is not an incurable ailment. We are not idiots, or constitutionally simian, but we are people of the Caucasian race who have remained sitting in one place, like our dear Ilya Muromets, and finally have weakened our minds by this prolonged and pernicious inactivity. We must begin to stir them, and their true strength will very quickly return to them.

This is certainly necessary, but here is the trouble: we are poor because we are stupid, and we are stupid because we are poor. The snake is biting its own tail, portraying an eternity from which there is no escape. Charles Fourier says with perfect justice that the chief force of all the evils of modern civilization resides in this accursed *cercle vicieux*. To grow rich we must, at least somewhat, improve the antediluvian methods of our agricultural and industrial production—that is, we must become more intelligent; but we have no time to become more intelligent, because the enveloping poverty gives us no rest. So we move in place, as best we can.

It is possible, however, to burst out of this vicious circle at two points. *First,* we know that a large share of the products of labor passes out of the hands of the working population into the hands of unproductive consumers. To increase the amount of products remaining in the hands of the producer means to diminish his poverty and give him the means for further development. To this end were directed the legislative dispositions of the government on the peasant question. In this spot the vicious circle can be broken only through legislative action, and hence we shall not expand on this side of the matter.

Second, we can act on the non-producing consumers, but of course we must act on them not through moral twaddle but through living ideas, and thus we must address ourselves only to those consumers who wish to undertake useful and absorbing work but do not know how to begin or what to apply their strength to. Those people whose situation permits them and whose personal character gives them the desire to use their minds must spend their resources with extreme circumspection and economy; that is, they must undertake only that work which can bring genuine benefit to society. Such economy of intellectual resources is always necessary everywhere, because mankind has never anywhere been so rich in active intellectual resources as to permit itself the slightest extravagance in the expenditure of these resources. Yet there has always been frightful extrava-

gance everywhere, and that is why the results hitherto attained
have been so miserable. With us the extravagance has likewise
been great, even though we have had nothing to squander.
Hitherto we have had in all about ten cents' worth of intellectual capital, but with our notorious bravado we have out-
rageously squandered even this wretched pittance. Strict economy is still more necessary for us than for other, really educated
nations, because in comparison with them we are paupers.

But in order to observe such economy it is necessary above all
to elucidate to ourselves, to the last degree of clarity, what is
useful and what is useless to society. And it is here, on these
elucidations, that literature should work. It seems to me that we
are beginning to feel the need for intellectual economy and are
striving to understand the concept of true advantage or utility.
And in this consists that independent trend of thought which
in my opinion is being worked out in contemporary Russian
society. If this trend grows, the vicious circle will be broken.
Economy of intellectual resources will increase our intellectual
capital, and this increased capital, applied to useful production,
will increase the quantity of bread, meat, clothes, boots, tools,
and all other material products of labor. The obligation to culti-
vate this trend and break through the vicious circle from this
quarter is wholly incumbent on our literature, because in this
sphere literature can operate autonomously.

Economy of intellectual resources is nothing other than a strict
and consistent realism. "Nature is not a temple but a workshop,"
says Bazarov, "and man is a workman in it." Rakhmetov [1] sees
only the people he "needs" to see; reads only the books he
"needs" to read; even eats only the food he "needs" to eat to
maintain his physical strength, while likewise he maintains his
strength only because it seems to him he "needs" it—i.e., it is
connected with the overall goal of his life. Rakhmetov's peculiarity consists solely in the fact that he needs less rest than other
honest and intelligent people do; one may say that he rests only
when he sleeps. The entire remaining part of his life is spent at
work, and all this work has only one objective: to diminish the

1. The paragon of "realism" in Chernyshevsky's *What Is To Be Done?*—
TRANS.

quantity of human pains and increase the quantity of human pleasures. This has always been the aim, consciously or unconsciously, directly or indirectly, of all the efforts of all intelligent and honest men, of all thinkers and innovators. The more consciously and directly the activity of men has been directed toward this aim, the more considerable has been the quantity of good they have brought. . . .

We, however, are ordinary people, and if we decided to exclude rest and purely personal pleasure from our lives we would make martyrs of ourselves and even then would harm the common cause; we would overtax ourselves, and would deprive ourselves of the chance to contribute the small quantity of utility that corresponds to the dimensions of our powers. . . . When you are resting and enjoying yourself, no one has the right to send you to work; the common cause of humanity is not advanced by compulsory labor. . . . But when you have rested and enjoyed yourself to your heart's content, and have undertaken work of your ·own free will, then society, in the person of each of its members, immediately acquires the right to control and criticize you; it pronounces its judgment on your activity and is fully entitled to express its desire that those resources which are voluntarily given up to general use actually be expended where they are needed. When you rest you belong to yourself; when you work you belong to society.

If you never wish to belong to society, if your work has no social significance, you may be quite sure that you are not working at all, but are spending your whole life flitting like a butterfly from blossom to blossom. Useless labor is not work. If such useless labor is performed fully consciously—that is, if the laboring individual himself recognizes his uselessness and says to himself and others: I am a drone and I want to be a drone, because this pleases me—then of course there is nothing to argue about, because the incurably ill need neither friendly advice nor medical assistance.

But one can say with confidence that the greater part of useless labor in every human society is performed through sheer misunderstanding. In the majority of cases the laboring individual is honestly and sincerely convinced that he is laboring for man-

kind and for society; this enchanting conviction gives him courage and inspires him in his labor. If you shake his conviction he
loses heart; a very onerous moment of disappointment and
despair begins for him. But following this moment there will
come a powerful desire for genuine utility, and a sudden turn
toward some other activity, worthy of a thinking man and a
conscientious citizen. An economy of intellectual resources will
thus be attained, and this economy will be much more significant than it may seem to the reader at first glance. Each individual acts to a greater or lesser extent on everything around him;
the turn toward realism effected in one individual makes itself
felt by many others. . . . Thus I think that our literature could
bring a great deal of utility if it carefully noted and thoroughly
exposed the various manifestations of useless labor which rage in
our society and poison our intellectual life. . . .

Thinking which works for the good of humanity ordinarily
operates along one of two chief avenues: either it brings to bear
on the contemporary life of men results already attained through
the theoretical investigations and scientific observations of leading figures, or it itself attains new results for the future, that is,
conducts investigations, observations, and experiments. Those
sciences which, like history and political economy, subsist only
through the impartial analysis of interpersonal relations, lose much
of their attraction in an age of stagnation. At such a time people
of two sorts devote themselves to these sciences: some write
trite textbooks, while the others are honestly and sincerely convinced that men should sleep forever, but sleep an ennobling
sleep—i.e., see great ideas in their dreams. They charm their
audience with their animated discussions, from which, however,
nothing can ever issue, under any circumstances, except vaporous
raptures.

To this category I assign all honest and intelligent men like
Granovsky.[2] . . .

People will tell me that in Granovsky's field no one could have
accomplished better or more fruitful results. I know. But this
only shows that he should not have selected such a field. To

2. T. N. Granovsky (1813-1855), a professor of history at Moscow University.—TRANS.

this they will reply that something is better than nothing at all. Here again I quite agree, only we must come to agreement on the understanding of the term "something." If I were very hungry I might say pleadingly: "For the love of God give me something to eat!" That is, give me at least a dry crust of bread. But if I am given a piece of rosewood or satin, I am certainly not going to say that this is "something"; rather I shall say that it is "nothing at all." If history were taught in a completely rational manner it would be "something" and would serve society as very nourishing food. But under the artistic mode of teaching, history is turned into a gallery of Rembrandt portraits. It is good, and gay, and it dazzles the eye, and nothing whatever comes of it as a result. Interpret it as you like: the distance from Granovsky to Macaulay is very great, and yet I would most humbly ask any of the great Macaulay's numerous admirers to prove to me clearly and convincingly that all the efforts of this great man have brought England or mankind so much as one grain of real utility. But that the efforts of all scholars and writers like Macaulay have brought exceedingly great harm is not at all difficult to prove. All these gentlemen, consciously or unconsciously, are continually fooling us through elegance.

Young people . . . entering the temple of science find themselves first in a vestibule from which two corridors lead to opposite sides of the building. Go to the left and you will see thousands of pieces of rosewood and satin for you to chew on to satisfy your intellectual hunger. But go to the right and you will be fed, clothed, shod, and bathed, and you will discover, furthermore, how to feed, clothe, shoe, and bathe other people. In the left, or satin-and-rosewood division of the temple of science, there reign the historiography of Macaulay and his countless gifted and ungifted followers, the political economy of the no less countless disciples of Malthus and Ricardo, and moreover the motleyest mob of various forms of "law": Roman, civil, state, criminal, and a multitude of others. And all the satin-and-rosewood similitudes of sciences are carefully brought, with saw and scissors, into strict harmony both with one another and in particular with general contemporary demands. In the right-hand division, on the contrary, is housed the study of nature.

If the question of the two corridors were posed to the young people entering the temple of science as frankly as it is posed here, who would willingly go to the left and chew satin? But unfortunately, very unfortunately for the young people and for all mankind, the left-hand division is crowded with honey-tongued sirens of the Macaulay and Granovsky variety, who occupy themselves solely with charming and seducing inexperienced visitors to the great temple by their melodious songs. The right-hand division has no sirens at all: first, because in general it still has few tenants, and second, because what tenants it has definitely have no time for singing. One is extracting an acid of some sort, another is dissecting a tapeworm, a third is investigating the chemical properties of guano, a fourth is busy with the molar of an *Elephas meridionalis*, a fifth is fitting the severed leg of a frog to a galvanic battery, a sixth is analyzing madmen's urine, and so on and so on, all in the same prosaic way. Tell me, for God's sake—do these occupations lend themselves to melodious serenades, capable of charming and attracting the young visitors who have just entered the temple of science and cannot clearly distinguish the realm of sheer fantasy from the realm of rigorous knowledge? . . .

The reader will probably think that aesthetics is my *cauchemar*, and he will not be mistaken. Aesthetics and realism are irreconcilably hostile to each other, and realism must radically destroy aesthetics, which at the present time is poisoning and making nonsense out of all departments of our scientific activity, from the highest regions of scientific investigation to the most ordinary relations between man and woman. I must try to prove to the reader without delay that aesthetics is the stubbornest element of intellectual stagnation and the surest enemy of rational progress.

The vacuity of all aesthetic judgments consists in the fact that they are pronounced not as the result of reflection but through inspiration, at the prompting of what is called the voice of instinct or feeling. You glance at it, you like it—well, that means it is good, beautiful, fine. You glance at it, you don't like it—that settles it: it is bad, detestable, ugly. But *why* it is liked or not liked is something no aesthetician will ever explain to you. The whole explanation is confined to a reference to the inner voice of immediate feeling. Of course the aesthetician gives you a whole system of subsidiary rules, but to put this whole intricate scaffolding on some sort of foundation he nevertheless refers in the end to immediate feeling.

But surely these feelings must have a definite physiological meaning, or else they simply have no meaning at all. For example, some people cannot eat fish of any kind, and become ill as soon as their digestive tract is presented with the smallest bit of that substance, which they cannot tolerate but which the majority of people regard as tasty and nourishing food. In this case the aversion is perfectly legitimate. It means that in the structure of the stomach or the intestinal tract there is some individual peculiarity which rejects fish. Every sensible physiologist will say, with Lewis, that one must obey the voice of the stomach, because one cannot reason with it, there is no court of appeal against its decisions, and fighting it means only nausea and various other discomforts. Another example: the piercing whistle of a locomotive is absolutely unpleasant, or, to express it in other words, repugnant, detestable, ugly, because this sharp sound pains the auditory nerve. A physiological cause exists, and so again the matter is definitely decided. A third example: a woman, A, feels an unconquerable physical aversion toward a man, B. It is repugnant to her to touch his hand, and kissing him would be real torture. Such phenomena actually exist in nature, and, of course, have some sort of physiological basis, though perhaps contemporary science is not in a position to determine their cause with precision. In this case, too, we must not force nature. Miss A would be acting very imprudently if, despite this physical aversion, she were led to contract a marriage of convenience with Mr. B.

Our organism has its undeniable rights which it asserts, and the violation of which it will not tolerate. But tell me, please, what right of our organism was being claimed, for example, by the French public of Voltaire's day when it systematically hissed off the stage every tragedy which did not have *un amoureux et une amoureuse?* Or what rights of our organism are expressed in the fact that our provincial misses of the thirties and forties liked resplendent uniforms and disappointed heroes almost exclusively? . . . Clearly nature has nothing to do with the matter here; the inner voice of immediate feeling simply parrots what was droned into our ears in earliest childhood. The Frenchman of the eighteenth century constantly saw tragedies of flaming love and constantly heard that such tragedies are considered superb, so he demanded them himself and actually felt a special sympathy toward them. The young lady from her third year to her fifteenth constantly sees her elder kinswomen paying court to Pechorinist [3] officers, and constantly hears that the adult women find such officers charming; it is very natural that this young lady herself, when she puts on her first long dress, will rush to pay court to such officers and will in fact feel a special palpitation of the heart with one glance at an elegant uniform. The passive habit of considering some object good and desirable becomes so strong that it is transformed finally into an actual feeling and an active desire. . . .

Our instincts, our unconscious impulses, our groundless sympathies and antipathies—in a word, all these movements of our inner world of which we can give ourselves no clear or strict account and which we cannot reduce to our needs or to concepts of harm and utility—all these movements, I say, are taken by us from the past, from the soil on which we have been reared, from the ideas current in the society in which we have lived and developed. This legacy constitutes the strength and the foundation of all our aesthetic conceptions. What we like unaccountably, we like only because we have grown accustomed to it. If this unaccountable sympathy is not justified by the judgment of our critical thinking, then evidently it is impeding our intellectual development. If in this clash the sober intellect prevails, we shall move forward to a healthier, which is to say a more socially useful, view of things. If aesthetic feeling prevails we shall take a step backwards, toward the reign of routine, intellectual impotence, harm, and darkness.

3. Pechorin is the central character of M. Lermontov's novel, *A Hero of Our Times.*—TRANS.

Aesthetics, unaccountability, routine, habit—these are all perfectly equivalent concepts. Realism, consciousness, analysis, critical thinking, intellectual progress—these likewise are equivalent concepts, diametrically opposed to the first. The more scope we give to our unaccountable impulses and the stronger our aesthetic feeling becomes, the more passive become our relationships to the conditions of life around us and the more finally and irretrievably is our intellectual autonomy engulfed and enslaved by the senseless influences of our surroundings. . . .

The Frenchmen who worshiped amorous tragedy, Voltaire, La Motte, Belinsky—these men, for all the differences in their views, were all still aestheticians, and this circumstance draws a clear and ineradicable line between such men and the representatives of pure realism. The essential difference does not consist in the fact that the former recognize art while the latter reject it; these are only subsidiary conclusions. One can be an aesthetician without leaving the sphere of purely practical interests, and one can be a realist and lovingly study Shakespeare and Heine as geniuses and great men. The essential difference lies much deeper: the aestheticians always stop at the argument: *because I like it*, and often don't even get to that final argument. The realists, on the contrary, submit even this final argument to analysis.
. . . It is the presence of a supreme ruling idea among the thoroughgoing realists and the absence of such an idea among the aestheticians that constitutes the basic distinction between these two groups. What is this idea? It is the idea of public utility or general human solidarity. Like all men, and even all animals, both the aesthetician and the realist are complete egoists. But the aesthetician's egoism is like the senseless egoism of the child who wants to stuff himself incessantly with the worst sugarplums and honey-cakes. The realist's egoism is the conscious and profoundly prudent egoism of the mature adult who is building up inexhaustible stores of fresh pleasure for his entire future. . . .

A thoroughgoing realism absolutely despises everything that does not bring substantial utility; but we certainly do not take the word "utility" in the narrow sense ascribed to us by our literary antagonists. We certainly do not say to the poet "make boots" or to the historian "bake pies," but we definitely demand that the poet, as a poet, and the historian, as a historian, each according to his specialty, bring *true* utility. We want the poet's creations to depict for us clearly and strikingly those sides of human life which we must know so as to think and act sensibly. We want the historian's investigations to show us the true causes of the flowering and decline of past civilizations. We read books solely to extend the limits of our personal experience. If in this regard a book gives us absolutely nothing—no new fact, no original view, no independent idea—if it in no way stirs and animates our thought, we call such a book empty and rotten, without concerning ourselves with whether it is written in prose or verse; and we are always prepared, with sincere good wishes, to advise the author of such a book to take up making boots or baking pies.

But let us now discuss the question of how the poet, without ceasing to be a poet, can bring society and mankind real and undoubted utility. . . . The poet is first of all a member of civil society, just as each of us is. Meeting him in a drawing room, we are perfectly entitled to require him not to put his feet on the table and twiddle his thumbs; entering into conversation with him, we have full right to require him to argue sensibly and logically. If he does not fulfill these demands, we shall note to ourselves that he is talking nonsense—inspired nonsense, perhaps, but insufferable all the same. To enjoy the love and respect of those who know him the poet must possess the same qualities which cement the love and respect of the people around him for every ordinary mortal. For this a certain dose of intelligence, good nature, integrity, and the like is necessary.

The price at which love and respect are bought in a society rises and falls with the general level of intellectual and moral development. Someone who is considered a fool in England can pass for a very respectable man in Turkey. When society reaches a certain level of development it begins to demand more definite and conscious convictions of its members, and to demand that they adhere to them. Besides ordinary integrity a still higher form makes its appearance—political integrity. Having developed a great sense of political integrity, society begins to make it a duty for each of its members, and all the more for the people who, on the strength of their intellectual gifts, claim the right to act by speech or pen on the development of social convictions. . . .

But sheer integrity and great native talent alone are not enough to make a great poet. . . . The true, "useful" poet must know and understand everything that at a given moment interests the best, the most intelligent, and the most enlightened representatives of his age and nation. Understanding fully the profound meaning of each pulsation of the society's life, the poet, as a passionate and sensitive man, must love with every fiber of his being what seems to him good, true, and beautiful, and must hate with a great and holy hatred that enormous mass of petty and rotten stupidities which prevent the ideas of the good, the true, and the beautiful from clothing themselves in flesh and blood and becoming living actuality. For the true poet this love, indissolubly linked with this hatred, forms and cannot but form the soul of his soul, the only and most sacred meaning of his whole existence and of all his activity. "I write not with ink, like the others," said Börne: "I write with my heart's blood." Thus, and only thus, must every writer write. He who writes otherwise should sew boots and bake pies. . . .

In our time one can be a realist and consequently a useful workman without being a poet; but to be a poet without at the same time being a profound and conscious realist is utterly impossible. He who is not a realist is not a poet but simply a gifted ignoramus, or a clever charlatan, or a minute but conceited insect. From every such importunate creature, realist criticism should carefully guard the minds and pockets of the reading public.

If you should ask me whether we have any outstanding poets in Russia, I should answer without circumlocution that we do not, that we have never had any, that we could never have had any, and that in all likelihood we shall not have any for a very long time to come. We have had either embryo poets or parodies of poets. Among the embryo poets one may name Lermontov, Gogol, Polezhayev, Krylov, and Griboyedov; among the parodies I would include Pushkin and Zhukovsky. . . .

From the beginning of this article I have spoken only of the art of poetry. Of all the other arts—plastic, tonal, and mimetic —I shall express myself very briefly and as clearly as possible.

I feel profoundly indifferent toward them. I definitely do not believe that these arts have contributed to the intellectual or moral betterment of mankind in any way, shape, or form. Human tastes are infinitely diverse: one person likes a glass of vodka before dinner; another prefers a pipe after dinner; a third likes to indulge in the violin or flute of an evening; a fourth goes into raptures and horrors over the screechings of Aldridge as Othello. Well, splendid! Let them enjoy themselves. All this I understand. Likewise I understand that two people who love vodka, or Aldridge, or the violoncello may find it pleasant to chat about the virtues of the object of their love and about the means required to give it still more exalted virtues. From these specialized conversations special societies may be formed. For example: "The Vodka Lovers' Association," "The Society of Lovers of the Chase," "The Theatergoers' Society," "The League of Cream-Puff Lovers," "The Society of Music Lovers," and so on, endlessly. Such societies may have their rules and regulations, their elections, their parliamentary debates, their convictions, their journals. They may grant licenses to genius. As a result there may appear in the world great people of all sorts: the great Beethoven, the great Raphael, the great Canova, Morphy the great chess player, Dussiaux the great chef, Turiat the great billiards player. We can only rejoice at this abundance of human genius and cautiously pick our way past all these "Lovers' Societies," carefully concealing the smile which involuntarily rises to our lips and which can cause much fruitless irritation.

But we certainly have no intention of completely denying the practical utility of painting. Drawing plans is necessary for architecture. Sketches are needed in almost all books on the natural sciences. . . . But neither Rembrandt nor Titian would have taken up drawing pictures for popular works on zoology or botany. And how Mozart and Fanny Elssler, Talma and Rubini could have contrived to apply their great gifts to some rational enterprise, I cannot even imagine. . . .

The lovers of all the arts must not be angry with me for my flippant tone. . . . Freedom and tolerance above all! They enjoy blowing into a flute or portraying their special Hamlet, Prince of Denmark, or decorating a piece of canvas with oil colors, while I enjoy showing in my derisive tone that they are benefiting no one and that there is no reason to place them on pedestals. But no one intends to keep them from their amusements. No one is dragging them to useful work by the scruff of the neck. You're happy—well, enjoy yourselves, dear children! . . .

Human labor is wholly based upon science. The farmer *knows* when to plant his grain, when to reap or mow, in what sort of ground grain can grow, and what to add to the ground to make an abundant harvest. All this he knows very vaguely and only in the most general outlines, but nevertheless this is incipient science, man's first attempts to seize the secrets of living nature. In their time these simple observations on the properties of earth, air, and plants were great and exceedingly important discoveries; it was because of their importance that they became the common property of the laboring masses. They have been merged with life once and for all, and in this respect they have left far behind them all subsequent discoveries, which are more complex and have not yet succeeded in clearing a path for themselves into the working life of the simple poor man. At the present time physical labor and science are in complete rupture over the whole vast face of the globe. Physical labor still subsists on the wretched rudiments of science which were worked out by the human mind in prehistoric times, while science today is accumulating heaps of great truths which remain almost barren, because the masses can neither understand them nor use them. . . .

Such tragic misunderstandings between sciences and life will be repeated until such time as there is an end to the disastrous rupture between brain-work and muscle-work. Until science ceases to be an aristocratic luxury, until it becomes the daily bread of every sound human being, until it makes its way into the head of the craftsman, the factory worker, and the simple farmer, until that time the poverty and immorality of the working masses will constantly increase, despite all the sermons of the moralists, the alms of the philanthropists, the computations of the economists, the theories of the socialists. There is in mankind only one evil—ignorance; for this evil there is only one cure—science; but this medicine must be taken not in homeopathic doses but by the bucket and the barrelful. A weak dose of it only increases the sufferings of the diseased organism. A strong dose will bring radical recovery. But human cowardice is so great that the saving remedy is considered toxic.

Knowledge must be disseminated—this is clear and indubitable. But *how* to disseminate it—that is the question which, though it contains the whole essence of the matter, cannot be considered definitely decided. . . .

To give ordinary people the benefits which education provides, we must create the incentive of which I spoke above. That is, we must see to it that in all of Russian life the demand for intellectual activity is intensified. In other words, we must increase the number of thinking people in those classes of society which are called educated. This is the whole problem. This is the alpha and omega of social progress. If you want to educate the people, raise the level of education in civilized society.

Thus I repeat the question . . . how must knowledge be disseminated? Here is the answer: let every man who is capable of thinking and who desires to serve society act by his own example and by his own immediate influence in the circle in which he permanently resides and on the people with whom he finds himself in daily contact. Study, and draw into the sphere of your intellectual activities your brothers, sisters, relatives, comrades—all the people you know personally and who give you their confidence, their sympathy, and their respect. . . .

In science and in science alone is contained the force, which, independently of historical events, can arouse public opinion and mold thinking leaders of national labor. . . . Society already loves and respects science; but science must still be *popularized*, and popularized with a great deal of skill. It may be said without the slightest exaggeration that the popularization of science is the most important general task of our age. A good popularizer, especially among us in Russia, can bring society much greater benefit than a gifted researcher. A great many investigations and discoveries have already been accumulated by European science.

In the upper regions of the intellectual aristocracy lies a vast mass of ideas; we must now get these ideas moving, change them into bills and coins of small denomination, and put them into general circulation. . . .

Just what sciences must be popularized? In general outline, of course, the reader already knows my manner of thinking; he knows that I am not referring to Sanskrit grammar, Egyptian archeology, the theory of music, or the history of painting. But if the reader supposes that I am going to recommend chiefly technology, practical mechanics, geognosy, or medicine he is mistaken. Science which is already fused with craft, applied science, certainly brings society enormous and incontestable utility, but it is neither necessary nor possible to popularize it. Society needs technologists, geognosts, and mechanics, but it has no use whatever for people who have a general idea of technology, geognosy, or mechanics. In short, the applied sciences must be studied as thoroughly as possible by every man who desires to make them his paying trade. He who studies a science thoroughly addresses himself to its actual sources and not to popular works. Thus popularization is needed only in those regions of knowledge which, not being fused with a special craft, give every man in general, without respect to his particular occupations, a true, rational, and broad outlook on nature, man, and society. Naturally here, as everywhere, the forefront is occupied by those sciences which study all visible phenomena: astronomy, physics, chemistry, physiology, botany, zoology, geography, and geology.

The superiority of the natural sciences over all the other accumulations of knowledge which appropriate the title of science is so evident, and we have so frequently and with such warm conviction spoken of the significance of these sciences, that there is no point in expanding on it now. I shall note only that by "geography" I mean, of course, not the enumeration of states but the overall picture of the globe and the determination of the connections that exist between the earth and its inhabitants.

But the natural sciences, for all their great significance, do not exhaust the whole sphere of objects of which man must have a conception. Man must know man and society. Physiology shows us the different functions of the human organism, comparative anatomy shows us the differences among the human races; but neither of these sciences gives us any conception of how man orders his life and how he constantly subjugates the forces of nature through the force of his own intellect. Both these questions have capital importance for us, but the two departments of knowledge from which we should expect answers to them—history and statistics—have still not attained scientific rigor and definitiveness. History is still nothing more than a vast arsenal from which each literary party selects apt arguments to defeat its opponents. Whether history will some day become a true science is unknown and even doubtful. Scientific history would be possible only if all the materials for compiling detailed statistical tables for all past centuries were preserved. But such a wealth of materials is out of the question. Thus for the study of man in society it remains only to observe contemporary life attentively and to exchange our stock of collected experiments and observations with other investigators. Statistics has already given us many precious facts: it has undermined faith in the usefulness of the penitentiary system; it has proved with figures the connection between poverty and crime. But statistics is only beginning to develop, and we have good reason to expect from it in the very near future practical services a thousand times more important than those it has yet rendered us.

My essay is completed. The reader will see from it that all the aspirations of our realists, all their joys and hopes, the whole meaning and the whole content of their lives is presently exhausted by three words: *love, knowledge*, and *labor*. After all I have said above, these words need no further commentary.

[D M I T R Y   P I S A R E V]

Thinking Proletariat *

Relying on the work they love, which is advantageous to them and useful to others, the new men arrange their lives so that their personal interests in no way contradict the real interests of society. This is by no means difficult. One has only to come to love useful work, and then everything that distracts one from such work will seem an unpleasant disturbance; the more you give yourself up to your favorite useful work the better it will be both for you and for others. If your work maintains you and gives you great enjoyment you will not need to take anything from others, directly or indirectly, either by thieving or swindling or by that kind of exploitation which is not recognized as a criminal offense.

When you work, your interests coincide with the interests of all other working people; you are a worker and all workers are your natural friends, while all exploiters are your natural enemies because at the same time they are the enemies of all mankind, including themselves. If all men worked, they would all be rich and happy; but if all men exploited their neighbors and did no work, the exploiters would devour one another in a week and mankind would disappear from the face of the earth. Therefore, he who loves work also acts for the good of all mankind when he acts for his own good. He who loves work loves himself consciously, and in himself he would love all other human beings if there were indeed no gentlemen who, intentionally or unintentionally, hinder any kind of useful work.

The new men work and they wish for scope and development for their work. In this desire, which constitutes a profound need of their organism, the new men are in agreement with

* Translated by R. Dixon and reprinted, with revisions and corrections for this volume by James P. Scanlan, from Dmitry Pisarev, *Selected Philosophical, Social, and Political Essays*, Moscow, 1958, pp. 635-646. The revisions and corrections were made by reference to the original Russian text in D. I. Pisarev, *Isbrannyye filosofskiye i obshchestvenno-politicheskiye stati*, Moscow, 1949, pp. 651-664.

the millions of working people on earth, all those who consciously or unconsciously pray to God and ask their neighbor not to hinder them from working and enjoying the fruits of their labor. Unity of interests gives birth to sympathy, and the new men have a warm and conscious sympathy for all the real needs of all people. Every human passion is a sign of a force seeking its application; according to the way that force is applied, the passion in question will be called virtue or vice and will bring man benefit or harm, advantage or loss. The forces and passions applied to the exploitation of one's neighbor must be restrained by moral motives, because otherwise they will lead man through vice to the criminal court; but the forces and passions directed to productive work may grow and develop to any desired proportions without any harm.

People who live through exploitation must beware of exclusive selfishness, because such selfishness deprives them of every human aspect and turns them into civilized cannibals who are far more repulsive than savage ones. But the new men, who live by their work and have a physiological revulsion for even the most humane and kindhearted exploitation, may be selfish in the extreme without the slightest danger.

The selfishness of the exploiter runs counter to the interests of all other people. For him to become rich means to deprive somebody else; he is compelled to love himself to the prejudice of all the rest of the world. That is why, if he is good-natured and fears God, he will try to love himself moderately, in such a way that it will not be disadvantageous to himself and *not too painful* for others. But it is very difficult to maintain such moderation, and therefore the exploiter always allows either too much selfishness, so that he begins to devour others, or too little, so that he himself becomes the victim of the selfish appetite of another. As on our wonderful planet exploitation reigns universally in the family, in society, and in international relations, it is the accepted thing for us to raise a hue and cry about selfishness, to call the downright scoundrel a selfish person, and, on the other hand, to accuse people of immorality merely because they do not keep to their own place. The new men are remote from all exploitation, and without the slightest fear of harm for themselves or for others they can plunge into the depths of selfishness and not blemish themselves with the least injustice, solely because they know how to find their place and acquire a passion for their work.

If a man of the old make-up pursues the practice of medicine, his selfishness is expressed in his endeavoring to make as many visits a day as possible and get as many bills of all denominations as possible; he exploits his patients, examining them carelessly, prescribing medicine haphazardly, going to see patients who are not ill at all, and doing everything purely out of love of money. Such a man must, of course, bridle his selfishness and give himself a fairly convincing lecture now and again. The new man pursues medicine only out of passionate enthusiasm; for him every hour is precious because it is devoted to the study he loves; for him money is only a means by which he maintains his life so as to be able to devote it to his work. At the patient's bedside he is a thinker solving a scientific problem. His wish is not to rob his patient but to cure him, because to cure him means to solve a problem. The patient, too, wishes not to be robbed, but to be cured. Thus the interests of the doctor and those of the patient merge, and there is no exploitation; the doctor of the new make-up can follow his selfish inclination in the most unscrupulous manner, and for that he will receive the thanks of his patient, his relatives, and all his fellow citizens. This doctor has no reason to frighten himself with the idea of duty, because for him there is no difference between duty and his free inclination. And why is this? Because he has found the work he loves, because he has found his place. This is an indispensable condition. Without it, it is difficult and perhaps quite impossible to be an honest man at all.

Thus we see that in the lives of the new men there is no discordance between inclination and moral duty, between selfishness and love for mankind. This is a most important characteristic; it is a feature which allows them to love mankind and be honest by the direct urgent inclination of nature which compels each man to ensure his own self-preservation and the satisfaction of the physical demands of his own organism. In their love of mankind there is no forced artificiality; in their honesty there is no overscrupulous pettiness. Their good inclinations are simple and healthy, strong and beautiful like direct productions of a rich nature; and these new men themselves are nothing but the first manifestations of a rich human nature which has cleansed itself of a part of the filth which had accumulated upon it in the course of centuries of suffering. If public opinion does not acknowledge these men to be ordinary but honest represent-atives of their race, if it sees in them something peculiar, some-thing horrifying and sinister, that only means that so-called public opinion has lost all conception of humanity, forgotten its distinctive traits, fears it as something unknown, and accepts as real human beings the strange race of bipeds that Jonathan Swift in *Gulliver's Travels* calls the Yahoos, and whose stupid-ity and wickedness is in such marked contrast to the reason and magnanimity of thinking and talking horses.

Working for themselves, finding their satisfaction and enjoy-ment in the working process, the new men labor for the good of mankind because all productive work is useful for mankind. In the beginning the new men are useful and do good uncon-sciously, but later the very process of being useful and doing good lays the basis of a moral link between the one who is useful and does good and those to whom profit is brought and good done. This link is reinforced by degrees as the worker of the new make-up is more useful and does more good.

It is indeed an old truth that it is human to love those to whom we have done or do good, and this ancient truth finds confirmation at every step. Garibaldi loves Italy more than any other Italian, and probably now the old Garibaldi, having exhausted his life in work and exile and been wounded at Aspromonte by an Italian bullet, loves his Italy more than the ardent youth Garibaldi could have loved it thirty years ago. Then he loved it only as his country; now, in addition, he loves in it all his own feats, his own sufferings, the whole brilliant series of his pure memories. Robert Owen, the "holy old man," as Chernyshevsky's Lopukhov [1] calls him, worked all his life for mankind. Of course, as he grew old his love for mankind was still broader, still warmer, and in any case still more abundant

1. A character in Chernyshevsky's novel, *What Is To Be Done?*—TRANS.

in conscious forgiveness than in the first days of his youth. For men like Owen and Garibaldi there is no such thing as senility. Such men will be new for all times and peoples. But what we note in their lives is common to all men of action and thinkers who devoted their life and their strength to useful work which they loved. In these men love for mankind grows and becomes stronger as they become absorbed in their work and are permeated with the consciousness of its usefulness. They constantly become better and purer; they constantly grow younger instead of becoming flabby and vulgar. Through their life and their rational work they cleanse themselves of the filth that their parents covered them with, that was splattered on them at school and is constantly flung at them by the hellish darkness of the life around them.

Formerly people were beautiful and fresh intellectually only when they were young: ten years went by and all their beauty and freshness disappeared with the glow of their cheeks. Then pettiness and peevishness, reckoning to the last kopek and chickenheartedness crept in; the cock turned into a capon, the brilliant student into a downright Philistine and a "perspicacious" reader. All this was quite natural, because formerly young people did nothing but fly into passions and fits of impetuosity, babble fine phrases, and show pretty sentiments; the amusements of youth had to pass away with youth because they were but amusements. He who did not become firmly attached in his youth to some great and beautiful cause, or at least to some simple but honest and useful work, could consider his youth irrevocably lost, no matter how gay it may have been or how many pleasant memories it had left him. Take with you the feeling of your youth, Gogol said: you will not find it later. And he spoke the truth. But how can you take it with you if you do not invest it entirely in some work to which every fiber of your being will vibrate till the very last minute of your life? He who succeeds in doing that has no reason to be pitied, even if his youth has been spent in hard work away from those who are near and dear to him, without any enjoyment, without the embraces of a woman he loves.

Dear ones, enjoyments, and women we love are all doubtlessly very fine things, but man is dearer to himself than anything else on earth. If at the cost of work and privation, at the cost of spent youth and lost love, he has bought himself the right to have profound and conscious respect for himself, the right to bear with him to the end of the world and maintain with him through all trials an unchanged youthfulness and freshness of mind and feelings, it cannot be said that the price has been too great. He has given up a portion of his life to be able to live the whole of his life like a man; he has deprived himself of two or three enjoyments, but in return he has received the highest delight which embellishes his life and supports him in the moment of his agony; he has received the right to know exactly what he is worth and that he is worth not a little.

That is the selfishness of the new men, and to that selfishness there are no bounds; for that, indeed, they will sacrifice everyone and everything. They love themselves passionately. They respect themselves to the point of worship. But even in relation to themselves they cannot be blind and condescending; they must be on their guard to maintain their love and their respect for themselves at every given moment. Still more precious in their eyes than their love and respect are the direct and sincere relations of their analyzing and controlling *ego* to the *ego* that acts and orders the external conditions of life. If the one *ego* were unable to look the other boldly and resolutely in the eye, if the one *ego* took it into its head to answer the demands of the other with evasions and sophisms, and the other *ego* meanwhile dared to shut its eyes and to be content with the vain excuses of the first, the result of this shameful confusion in the soul of the new man would be such despair and such convulsive horror at his own paltry and defiled person that he would surely spit in his own face and then, having thus befouled himself, would plunge headfirst into the deepest slough.

The new man knows perfectly well how implacable and pitiless he is toward himself. The new man fears himself more than anything else; he is a force, but woe betide him if this force ever turns against itself. If he commits any abomination which produces internal discord within himself he knows that there will be no cure for that discord but suicide or insanity.

It seems to me that such a need for self-respect and such fear of one's own judgment will be more powerful than all the moral barriers that keep men of the old make-up from various abominations, barriers which certain individuals of either sex cross with such freedom to flutter so elegantly one way or the other, barriers for the absence of which the new men have to listen to such boring exhortations from "perspicacious" readers who are masters of the pen or are afflicted with a weakness for edifying eloquence. The new men owe all the advantages of their type to the vivifying influence of the work they love. Thanks to it they may be the most complete egoists: the more profound their selfishness, the greater their love for humanity will become, the more firmly and changelessly their youth and freshness will be preserved, the more their reason and feeling will develop, the more they will treasure their own respect, the stricter their loyalty to themselves will become, and, as a result of all this, the closer they will come to the all-round development of their powers and the boundless fullness of their happiness.

Men who live by exploiting their neighbors or appropriating other men's work are in a state of constant offensive war with the whole world around them. For war one needs a weapon, and it is found in the intellictual capacities. The intellect of the exploiter is applied almost exclusively to outwitting his neighbor or puzzling out the latter's intrigues. To defeat one's neighbor or parry his skillful blows means to reveal the power of one's weapon and one's skill in using it, or, to speak in less warlike terms, it means to display subtle intellect and great experience of life. The intellect is sharpened and steeled for the fight, but we all know by experience that the more adapted the weapon is to fighting, the less suitable it is for peaceful uses. Students, for all their intelligence, have been able to find no other use for their swords than to poke the fire and make punch; but the weapon of war and symbol of honor is a poor instrument even for performing such functions.

The same can be said of the mind which has been educated for internecine strife. Certain of its qualities which are completely useless and even positively harmful to the process of

peaceful thinking are developed. Petty perspicacity, petty sus-
picion, the ability and the inclination to examine with great
attention tiny incidents of everyday life which are not at all
worth studying, the ability and the inclination to fool oneself
and others with sophisms hastily strung together—such are the
qualities which generally distinguish the intelligence of the practical man of our time. His intelligence inevitably becomes shortsighted, because the practical man is always looking down at
his feet so as not to fall into some trap. He is very careful to
guard himself against petty failures, and he often succeeds in
freeing himself from them thanks to his petty circumspection.
But, on the other hand, the practical man loses all control
over the general direction of his life; he treads warily with his
eyes on the ground and then suddenly looks round and does
not know where he has drifted. He is absolutely incapable of
generalizing facts because of the typical features of his intelligence. Neither is he able to account for the general state of
affairs or give any general meaning to his actions. He is carried
along by events, and his greatest wisdom consists in not fighting against the current, which he cannot understand anyhow.

Metternich and Talleyrand may be cited among the greatest
representatives of this type of practical men and exploiters;
nobody will affirm that these gentlemen had no natural intelligence, but anybody will understand that their intelligence,
formed by long training from the cradle, was sharpened and
steeled for absolutely one-sided use, to fool people by sophisms
without ever being affected by the sophisms of the opposing
side. The whole secret of the spectral might of Metternich and
Talleyrand was in their flexibility and characterlessness, their
complete indifference to their own sophisms, and their unceasing
readiness to exchange one sophism for its exact opposite. They
had no power whatsoever over events and did not influence
them in the slightest, just as the weather vane merely shows
changes in the wind and does not produce them. No storm could
shatter Talleyrand because there was nothing in him to shatter;
he had no firm content. If, indeed, Metternich was shattered
by the 1848 revolution, this can only be attributed to the simplicity of the good Germans. They took the signboard of the

principle for the principle itself; they tore down the sign-board, shouted *"Vivat!"* and, of course, were made fools of. The intelligence of Talleyrand, Metternich, and all other exploiters, great and small, is remarkable for its extreme one-sidedness; all it is useful for is to defeat other people in the fight, that is, to lead them by the nose. When gentlemen of this type are guided by the calculations of their own intelligence, we can say beforehand that their calculations will compel them to commit some abomination, because those calculations are shortsighted and the inspirations of narrow and shortsighted selfishness always provide occasion for the most outrageous injustices.

Men of the old make-up know this quite well and that is why they say that our acts must be guided by reason when we clash with other people; but when we are in our own family circle or enter into relations with our friends, we must lay down our fighting weapons and act under the inspiration of our feelings in order not to wound or offend by inadvertence people whom we love really and unselfishly. With men of the old make-up the voice of the feelings and that of reason are in constant discord, and therefore they must always silence one of them when the other speaks, in order to avoid dissonance. Naturally, the result of this is that these people are nearly always harsh and unjust in their business relations and ridiculous and confused in their domestic life.

Healthy people should not split their personalities. Every object which attracts their attention must be considered under its various aspects; the impression that the object produces directly on their feelings is just as important as the official impression which it leaves in our analyzing reason. Any discordance between the demands of our feeling and the judgments of our reason must be eliminated; reason and feeling must be reconciled. However, they must be reconciled not by silencing one or the other, but by carefully and calmly comparing the demands of the feeling with the judgments of reason, seeking the hidden causes of the former and the latter, and, finally, arriving by impartial reflection at a decision which equally satisfies reason and feeling.

With people who live by appropriation there can be no agreement between reason and feeling. Their feeling is manifested in disorderly flares based exclusively on physiological causes, and their reason does not acknowledge the elementary principles of justice because justice—that is, the general good—is in eternal discordance with petty, everyday personal interest. Is it then at all possible to reconcile a feeling which stems from nervous weakness and ceases when one takes cherry drops, with calculations which are based on rubles and kopeks and which cannot see behind those rubles and kopeks either the laws of nature or the sufferings of real men? Of course it is neither possible nor necessary in the least. Really we should destroy both that muddled sensitivity and that muddled stinginess. We should restore the distorted intellect to its original capacity for broad thinking, generalization of individual facts, and understanding the link between causes and effects. We should turn the men of the old make-up into new men. But as such a transformation is absolutely impossible, we must leave them alone. Let them go from office books to cherry drops, from passionate embraces to speculation on the exchange, from well-meaning deception to virtuous emotion over the setting sun.

Having dwelt so long on the intellect and feelings of the old type of people, I may now briefly describe the corresponding features of the intellect and feelings of the new men. In them intellect and feelings are in constant harmony because their intellect has not been transformed into an offensive weapon. It is not used to cheat other people, and therefore they themselves can trust its judgments always and in all things; not being accustomed to deceive their neighbor, their intellect does not deceive its own master. These new men have indeed unbounded trust in their own intellect. This must not be understood to mean that each one of them thinks himself the most intelligent man on earth. By no means. But each of them thinks that every adult human being endowed with normal intellectual capacities can judge his situation and his actions much better and with much greater clarity than they could be judged for him from the point of view of the greatest thinkers of genius. No matter how beautiful and consoling any world outlook is, no matter how many centuries and people considered it an irrefutable truth, no matter how many world geniuses bowed before its power of conviction, the most modest of the new men will accept it only if it suits the demands and make-up of his own intellect.

Each new man has his own inner world in which his own personal intellect rules with unbounded sway. Only that which his personal intellect lets through, only that which by its very nature can acknowledge the mastery of his personal intellect can penetrate into that inner world. If anything will not submit to his personal intellect, the new man will modestly say of it: "I do not understand that," and if anything remains beyond his understanding the new man will not admit it into his inner world, but will show profound respect for it from afar if external circumstances should require.

When an antiquated man has a frank conversation with his own intellect, rather delicate truths come out: "But I know you, my friend," the antiquated man says to his reason, "you are a rare rascal. If I let you have your way you'll invent such a heap of abominations that I shall be horrified, although I am by no means squeamish. Just wait, I'll school you." And then begin the exhortation and intimidation of reason by all sorts of extremely respectable conceptions intended to restrain its too artful desires. It is just as impossible for the new man to play such tricks on his reason as it is for any man to bite his own elbow. First of all, what can you intimidate it with? And secondly, what for? There is neither any means nor any reason for doing so. The new man believes in his reason and in his reason alone; he lets it enter into all circumstances of his life and all the intimate corners of his feelings, because there is no feeling or anything else that his reason can sully or debase by its contact.

When antiquated men fall in love they give their reason an indefinite holiday, and thanks to its absence they commit all kinds of stupidities which often turn into abominations too great to be joked at. After they have forced a girl or a woman to take a decisive step, their judgment comes back from its holiday, and the antiquated man, frightened at the consequences of his innocent joke, beats a calculated retreat and then tries to justify himself by saying that he had taken leave of his senses and was like a madman. Antiquated men do nothing but sin and repent, and one cannot say when they are viler—when they sin or when they repent.

New men neither sin nor repent; they always reflect, and thus they only make mistakes in calculation, which they then correct and avoid on subsequent occasions. In new men goodness and truth, honesty and knowledge, character and reason are identical; the more intelligent a new man is, the more honest he is, because fewer mistakes creep into his calculations. In the new man there is no reason for discord between reason and feeling, because his reason, aimed at useful work which he loves, never advises anything but what is compatible with his personal benefit, which coincides with the true interests of humanity and therefore with the requirements of the strictest justice and the most scrupulous moral feeling.

The basic features of the new type which I have spoken of thus far may be formulated in three main propositions which are very closely interrelated.

I. New men have acquired a passion for work for the benefit of society.

II. The personal benefit of new men coincides with the benefit of society, and their selfishness contains the broadest love of humanity.

III. New men's reason is in perfect harmony with their feeling because neither reason nor feeling is distorted by chronic enmity for other men.

This may be summed up briefly as follows: "new men" is the name given to workers who think, who love their work. So there is no reason to be angry with them.

Book Five

THE POPULISTS

As NIHILISM may be called the leading philosophical attitude in Russia in the 1860's, so Populism came to occupy that position in the seventies. Historically, Populism is the last intellectual trend sufficiently unified to be called a movement in Russian secular thought before the advent of Marxism, which did not begin in earnest until the early 1890's. In many ways, however, the Populists were philosophically more distant from Marxism than the Nihilists were, and even in their social programs the Populist leaders, though dedicated socialists, stand somewhat apart from both the earlier and the later radical trends. PETER LAVROV (1823-1900), the Populists' first and most important philosopher, was attacked by both Nihilists and Marxists—by Pisarev and Chernyshevsky in the sixties, and by Plekhanov (once a Populist himself) in the eighties. NICHOLAS MIKHAILOVSKY (1842-1904), Lavrov's successor as the leader of Populist opinion within the Russian empire, was a major target of the anti-Populist polemics with which Lenin began his literary career in the 1890's.

As a socio-economic doctrine, Russian Populism (*narodnichestvo*) was a form of agrarian socialism based upon a glorification of the Russian people (*narod*)—the common people, thus chiefly the peasantry. In a broad sense Populism has its roots deep in Russian history, and elements of it are clearly discernible in the attitudes of both the Slavophiles and the Westernizers. Alexander Herzen, sometimes styled "the father of Populism," spoke of the "instinctive socialism" of the Russian people and was the first to focus attention on the *obshchina* or peasant village commune as the endemic Russian nucleus of the future socialist order. Nicholas Chernyshevsky advanced the doctrine further in the 1860's. In the hands of the full-fledged *narodniki*, or Populists, of the seventies and after, it became a fully explicit and coherent social philosophy stressing the virtues of the peasantry, the evils of capitalism, and the possibility of avoiding capitalism in Russia by the direct revolutionary establishment of a more or less anarchistic socialist order based on the *obshchina*.

For Populism as a growing movement in the early seventies, however, even more important than its socio-economic program was the moral force which was building around it. Above all, early Populism represents the marshaling and release of a special sort of moral energy, connected with what might be called the *narodnik* mystique, or cult of "the people." Poets and novelists as well as philosophers and economists nourished this mystique. Nicholas Nekrasov (1821-1878), the influential radical publisher and poet of the mid-nineteenth century, generated much Populist sentiment by his portrayals of the hardship and suffering of peasant life. The semi-fictional sketches of the widely read writer Gleb Uspensky (1843-1902) had much the same effect, even though Uspensky took a more critical view of the peasantry and ultimately disavowed Populism. V. V. Bervi-Flerovsky's revealing factual study, *The Condition of the Working Class in Russia* (1869), also contributed powerfully to the growth of Populist feeling. In all of this literature the depiction of popular suffering and degradation was coupled with heartfelt expressions of the peasant's underlying nobility and capacity for regeneration. "The people," viewed as a reservoir of moral strength, became a moral inspiration to the *intelligentsia*.

This inspiration was both heightened and given a firm philosophical foundation in the late sixties by Peter Lavrov, a military professor with radical leanings who had been exiled in 1867, in the repressive aftermath of Karakozov's attempt on the life of Tsar Alexander II. Philosophically, Lavrov was a sophisticated positivist who found fault not only with the spiritualistic metaphysics of the Hegelians but also with the Nihilists' attempts to reduce all the phenomena of human life to matter in motion. In the early sixties he had made himself suspect in radical circles by his criticisms of materialism and by his "subjective" emphasis on the role of ideals in human thought and action. For Lavrov, positivism did not rule out the treatment of moral and historical phenomena on levels of their own, unapproachable by the methods of the natural sciences, and was not incompatible with the vigorous promotion of social ideals. In a series of articles under the general title of *Historical Letters*, written in 1868-1869, Lavrov expanded upon these themes in an attempt to combat what he saw as an excessive emphasis on the natural sciences and on individual self-improvement in radical circles.[1] The *Historical Letters* had an enormous vogue, becoming for the radical youth of the seventies what Chernyshevsky's *What Is To Be Done?* had been for the youth of the sixties—a combined handbook and bible.

Lavrov convinced the young members of the *intelligentsia* not only that it was legitimate to entertain and pursue lofty ideals of the sort scorned by the "thinking realists" or "rational egoists" who followed Chernyshevsky and Pisarev, but also that *they*—as the privileged, educated few—had a special duty to work for social betterment. They owed a debt to the people, Lavrov argued, because it was the toil and suffering of the unprivileged peasant masses which had given them the leisure and the resources needed for their own cultivation. This debt must be repaid, said Lavrov, and repaid through the concerted efforts of dedicated, "critically-thinking individuals," as he called them—no longer stressing the "realism" which to the Nihilists implied materialism, or the "egoism" which could so easily become selfishness. But whether the psychological appeal was to exalted selflessness or to the guilt feelings of the "repentant gentry," as the wellborn among them (Lavrov and Mikhailovsky themselves included) came to be called, Lavrov's message was effective. Nicholas Rusanov, a convert from Nihilism who had previously followed Turgenev's Bazarov in limiting his attention to physiology and anatomy, expressed his sentiments in these words: "To the devil with all these frogs and other objects of science, which have made us forget about the people! Hence-

1. See in particular Pisarev's essay "The Realists," selections from which are printed above (pp. 79-96).

forth our lives must belong wholly to the masses, and only by
dedicating all our strength to the triumph of social justice can
we appear anything but fraudulent bankrupts before our country
and before all mankind." [2]

The same moral emphasis characterized the philosophy of
Nicholas Mikhailovsky, who avoided both arrest and exile and
was the chief voice of Populism inside Russia during the final
quarter of the nineteenth century. Like Lavrov, Mikhailovsky
adopted a positivistic attitude toward religion and metaphysics
and at the same time stressed the "subjective" factor in human
action and history, arguing that only by what he termed "the
subjective method in sociology" could man properly study man.
Objective approaches such as those of Spencer and Comte are
appropriate for the natural sciences, but when the investigator
is concerned with man, Mikhailovsky contends, "the thinking
subject can attain to truth only when he is fully merged with
the thinking object . . . i.e., when he enters into his interests,
lives his life, thinks his thoughts, shares his feelings, experiences
his sufferings, weeps his tears." [3] Thus what Mikhailovsky calls
"teleology" is essential in the study of man. For Mikhailovsky,
as for Lavrov, history becomes an important concern. The
individual who has ideals, and who shares the ideals of others,
is both the proper student of human affairs and the motive force
of history.

Both Lavrov and Mikhailovsky set themselves against any kind
of mechanistic or deterministic theory of history, calling rather
for man's conscious and deliberate pursuit of his ultimate goals.
For Mikhailovsky, these goals are summed up in the concept
of the "integral individual"—the broadly and harmoniously
developed person whom Mikhailovsky sees as the ideal product
of historical progress. The primitive savage, Mikhailovsky contends, developed all his powers comprehensively in varied activity. But modern industrial civilization has narrowed and
perverted man through the division of labor. Mikhailovsky
hoped, by changing the economic base of society to a system
of cooperation in units comparable to the *obshchina*, to reverse

2. N. S. Rusanov, *Biografiya Petra Lavrovicha Lavrova*, n.p., 1899, p. 24.
3. See below, p. 182.

this trend and work toward a society in which there is "the fullest possible and the most diversified division of labor among man's organs, and the least possible division of labor among men." [4] But whatever the ultimate goal, its realization requires deliberate, determined action on the part of the real movers of history, the "critically-thinking individuals" to whom fate has given leisure for their own cultivation and for social action.

The necessary first step, in the opinion of those most influenced by Populist thinking in the early seventies, was to follow Herzen's earlier advice and "go to the people." The *intelligentsia* must carry the Populist message to the wellspring of the new order, educating and propagandizing, preparing for the ultimate social revolution, and also, of course, learning more about the people by the "subjective" method—by sharing in their activities, working alongside them, in short, identifying themselves with the peasant masses. Accordingly, there took place in the spring and summer of 1874 the remarkable movement "to the people!" (*v narod!*), an unorganized, spontaneous crusade in which hundreds and possibly thousands of young zealots left the cities to work and live in the countryside. But to the crusaders' great disappointment, their reception was anything but warm. Misunderstood, resented, and sometimes actively resisted by the peasants, the uninvited "agitators" were either turned over to the authorities by their ungrateful beneficiaries or systematically hunted down by the police. Before long most of them were in prison. The first large-scale activist enterprise by members of the *intelligentsia* since the Decembrist insurrection in 1825 was no more successful than that abortive uprising.

While the movement "to the people" marked the high point of early Populist enthusiasm, its failure by no means spelled the end of Populist thought or activity. It did, however, speed the formation of serious divisions within Populist ranks which had begun to appear as early as 1872, and the subsequent history of Populism as a social movement is a history of factionalism based on differences of both philosophical principle and political contrivance. Lavrov, now living abroad and editing the journal *Vperyod!* (Forward!), was the leader of the party of

4. See below, p. 186.

moderation, which viewed immediate revolution as unwise if not impossible and concentrated on propaganda and education, to prepare men's minds for the coming social transformation. Though Lavrov himself later moved in the direction of revolutionary activism, the "Lavrovists" were known for their gradualism and interest in theory. Determined opposition to this group was mounted by followers of Michael Bakunin, who was still active among Populist-minded Russian expatriates in Switzerland in the early seventies. The Bakuninists, scorning the "theoretical" and hesitant approach of the Lavrovists, advocated immediate revolt; they wished to smash state power and introduce the semi-anarchism of a loose federation of communes.

From the opposition of these two major factions in the early seventies grew a number of other radical groups, shading off into revolutionary terrorism which retained little of the original Populist spirit. Bakuninists predominated in the re-establishment of the underground Land and Liberty (*Zemlya i volya*) organization in 1876, though the society also included Lavrovists such as the future Marxist, George Plekhanov. When Land and Liberty broke up in 1879, Plekhanov was a leader of the moderate Black Repartition faction (*Chyorny peredel*) against the terrorist People's Will party (*Narodnaya volya*). The leading inspiration for terrorism came from the dedicated revolutionary, Peter Tkachyov (1844-1886), one of the first of the Russian radicals to espouse Marxism and the first to take a "Leninist" attitude toward revolution, advocating the seizure and use of state power by an organized, dictatorial elite. Formation of the People's Will party was a victory for this point of view, and a momentous one: led by Andrey Zhelyabov, a former moderate *narodnik*, the People's Will planned and carried out the assassination of Tsar Alexander II in 1881.

In ways more faithful to its original spirit, the Populist idea remained a significant element in Russian political and economic thought after 1881 and indeed into the twentieth century. Prince Peter Kropotkin (1842-1921), the chief philosopher of socialist anarchism after Bakunin, was strongly influenced by Populist thinking in the seventies, and the *narodnik* mystique is also clearly evident in the Christian anarchism of Leo Tolstoy.

The Social-Revolutionary party was the political heir of much Populist sentiment in Russia in the twentieth century. One recent observer finds traces of Populism even under the Soviet regime, as late as 1930.[5]

As a philosophical movement Populism shared many of the fundamental assumptions of the earlier phases of Russian radical thought. That man's earthly, social well-being is his most important concern, that human society is alterable and indeed thoroughly improvable by deliberate human action based upon a rational understanding of society's ills, that improvement consists in the "naturalizing" of social institutions, or putting them into conformity with demands inherent in the nature of man or of Russian man—such assumptions comprise the "social humanism" which is the common intellectual framework of the tradition from Radishchev's day on. The Populist phase of this tradition was distinguished by its specific doctrine of endemic peasant socialism and by its greatly heightened emotional and moral commitment to "the people." The philosophy of the leading Populists was distinguished from that of their predecessors, as well as from that of their Marxist successors, by its unconventional—some have said inconsistent—combination of an anti-metaphysical positivism with a thoroughgoing moral idealism. Above all, Lavrov and Mikhailovsky stress the free, conscious activity of the "critically-thinking individual" who moves history by fighting for moral ideals. Both thinkers are condemned by Soviet philosophers today for their "subjectivism" and rejection of objective laws of social development.

5. S. V. Utechin, *Russian Political Thought*, New York, 1964, p. 139. Utechin's chapter on Populism, pp. 128-147, devotes attention to Populist thought after 1881 as well as before.

PETER LAVROVICH LAVROV
[1823–1900]

WHILE ALEXANDER HERZEN and Nicholas Chernyshevsky were important progenitors of Populism, Peter Lavrov was the thinker whose views were most directly linked with the thoughts and actions of the *narodniki*. The most significant common trait of these men of the 1870's and later, according to one recent commentator, is that to some degree they all followed Lavrov in social philosophy.[1]

Peter Lavrov was born on his family's estate in the province of Pskov in 1823. His father was a cultivated member of the gentry and a retired military man. Peter was educated at home until the age of fourteen, when he was sent to the Artillery School in Saint Petersburg. He received his commission in 1842 at the age of nineteen. Two years later he was named instructor of mathematics at the Artillery School, and subsequently he was called upon to lecture in mathematics and the history of science at other military institutions in the capital. For over twenty years Lavrov pursued a successful career as teacher and scholar in Saint Petersburg, with a brief period on active military duty during the Crimean War. His academic services were highly regarded by the authorities, and he rose to the rank of colonel.

From his youth Lavrov showed a strong interest in philosophy. Through extensive reading and study he acquired a philosophical erudition as broad and solid as that of any Russian thinker of his day. He was well versed in the writings of philosophers from the ancient Greeks to the materialists and positivists of the mid-nineteenth century. In his own views he

1. Utechin, *op. cit.*, p. 128.

was inclined toward positivism, but at the same time he could not avoid the impact of other thinkers whose work he knew and respected—Victor Cousin, Kant and the neo-Kantians, particularly Albert Lange, Hegel and the right- and left-wing Hegelians.

To express his philosophical convictions Lavrov first employed verse, but with the easing of censorship and the increase in journalistic activity after the accession of Alexander II in 1855, he began to write philosophical essays for some of the leading Petersburg journals. One of his major early works, "An Outline of the Theory of Individuality," published in *Annals of the Fatherland* in 1859, provided Chernyshevsky with the occasion for his chief philosophical work, "The Anthropological Principle in Philosophy," [2] in which he criticizes Lavrov for eclecticism. In 1860, Lavrov delivered the first public lectures on philosophy in Saint Petersburg since Nicholas I closed the Department of Philosophy at the University in 1850. Entitled "On the Contemporary Significance of Philosophy," these lectures made a strong impression on the Petersburg public; as we have seen, Pisarev criticized them for their abstract, "scholastic" character and their deviation from materialism in his "Nineteenth-Century Scholasticism." [3]

The philosophical outlook Lavrov developed in these early works formed the foundation for his later *Historical Letters*, and in fact remained essentially unchanged to the end of his life. Lavrov agrees with the Nihilists in placing his trust in "science," but he argues that to identify the scientific approach with materialism is both to assert a view which is "metaphysical" (and therefore illegitimate) and to cripple science. There are three sorts of phenomena with which science must deal, Lavrov contends—material phenomena, "spiritual" phenomena (the phenomena of consciousness), and historical phenomena. The materialist approach of the natural sciences can be adequate only to the first; phenomena of the other two types cannot be reduced to matter in motion. The phenomena of consciousness, in particular, are accessible only to a subjective method—intro-

2. See pp. 29-60 above.
3. See pp. 71-78 above.

spection. And in any properly integrated world-view, the phenomena of consciousness must be regarded as primary, since all
thinking takes its start from them.

The fact that the thinker must start from the data of human
consciousness is what Lavrov chiefly has in mind in calling his
general philosophical outlook *anthropologism*. Developed further, it allows Lavrov to take as given, despite his acceptance of
the reign of objective law among the external phenomena of
material nature, such "facts of self-consciousness" as freedom
of the will and such moral imperatives (ultimately derived from
man's striving for pleasure) as the duty to respect personal dignity. Based more upon Kant than upon the modish thinkers of
the day such as Feuerbach and Comte, Lavrov's anti-metaphysical, phenomenalistic positivism ends in an emphasis on the creative individual who strives to implement ideals of human dignity
and justice; it becomes a moralistic positivism.

While Lavrov did not speak during this period of openly
revolutionary action, his sentiment was clearly moving in the
direction of socialism and agitation for reform. He had read
Fourier while still a student, and he felt particularly indebted
to Proudhon and Herzen. Though he was not regarded as an
ally by the leading socialist radicals, the increasing liberality of
his views made him suspect to the government. Official concern
over his views was probably responsible for his failure to obtain
the chair of philosophy at Saint Petersburg University in 1862,
despite the fact that his bid was supported by the prominent
philosopher, Professor K. D. Kavelin. In 1863, Lavrov was
associated with the Land and Liberty secret society, though he
was not active in its ranks. He was one of the first of the
"radicals" to be arrested following Karakozov's attempt to assas-
sinate the Tsar in 1866, and in 1867 he was exiled to the province of Vologda, north of Moscow.

In Vologda, Lavrov continued his scholarly writing and in
particular continued his campaign against the worship of the
natural sciences by the followers of Chernyshevsky and Pisarev.
This campaign culminated in the *Historical Letters*, first published serially in the journal *Nedelya* (Week) in 1868 and 1869.
The readings which follow are all drawn from this work, which

is Lavrov's most comprehensive statement in the areas of ethical and social philosophy. In it Lavrov applies his moralistic positivism to the phenomena of history, arguing that man must view history teleologically and that modern man must regard "individual development" and "the embodiment of truth and justice in social institutions" as the goals of history. It is by striving to improve social institutions and to extend the conditions of individual development to all men that those who are already cultivated discharge their "debt to the people." The prime movers are the "critically-thinking individuals" who, by diagnosing society's ills and acting to rectify them, continually transform *culture* (the outmoded routines and institutions of the past) into *civilization* (the practices and social forms which are appropriate to vital contemporary needs). Particularly important to Lavrov in this connection is the need for concerted action, and his discussion included below under the heading, "The Need for an Organized Party," is one of the earliest blueprints for party organization in the history of Russian radicalism.

By now a convinced revolutionary, in 1870 Lavrov escaped abroad and began the work of revolutionary theory and practice which was to occupy him for the rest of his life. He went first to Paris, where he took an active part in the Paris Commune. In London he met Karl Marx and Friedrich Engels, becoming one of their closest Russian friends. Settling in Zurich in 1873 he edited the journal *Vperyod!* (Forward!), in which he gave full expression to the Populist socialist doctrines he could not defend in Russia. After 1874 he continued this editorial work in London, but he left the journal in 1876 and returned to Paris when it appeared to him that the "Lavrovists" with whom he was associated were not sufficiently militant in their convictions. From 1883 to 1886 he edited the *Vestnik Narodnoy Voli* (Herald of the People's Will), a theoretical organ of the extremist People's Will party, and he even came to condone terrorism. During this later period of his life Lavrov also continued his scholarly writing, publishing before his death two monumental volumes of an unfinished work, *Essay in the History of Modern Thought* (1894). He died in Paris in 1900.

None of Lavrov's later writings surpassed the *Historical*

Letters either in philosophical significance or in historical influence. And though the categories of Lavrov's social thought became increasingly Marxist,[4] fundamentally he never departed from the moralistic, individualistic orientation of the *Historical Letters*. His appeal remained directed to the free, critically-thinking individual, whose intelligence and determination would usher in the new order.

SELECTED BIBLIOGRAPHY

Works:
Peter Lavrov, *Historical Letters*, trans. with an introduction and notes by James P. Scanlan, Berkeley, 1967.

Secondary Sources:
V. V. Zenkovsky, *A History of Russian Philosophy*, trans. George L. Kline, 2 vols., London and New York, 1953, pp. 348-362.
Franco Venturi, *Roots of Revolution,* trans. Francis Haskell, New York, 1960, pp. 445-468.
S. V. Utechin, *Russian Political Thought*, New York, 1964, pp. 128-147.

4. In his brief autobiography, published in 1885, Lavrov stated that in economics he had regarded himself as "a disciple of Marx" from the time he first became acquainted with Marx's doctrines (P. L. Lavrov, *Izbrannyye sochineniya*, Moscow, 1934, I, 95).

[PETER LAVROV]

Historical Letters *

History versus the Natural Sciences

The natural sciences are the foundation of rational life—this is indisputable. Without a clear understanding of their demands and fundamental laws, man is blind and deaf to his most ordinary needs as well as to his loftiest aims. Strictly speaking, in the modern world a man who is a total stranger to the natural sciences has not the slightest right to be called an educated person.

But once this point of view is accepted the question arises, what is most relevant to man's vital interests? Questions of cellular reproduction, the transformation of species, spectrum analysis, and double stars? Or the laws of the growth of human knowledge, the clash of the principle of social utility with the principle of justice, the conflict between national unification and the unity of all mankind, the bearing of the economic interests of the starving masses on the intellectual interests of the more prosperous minority, and the connection between social evolution and the form of the political system? When the question is put in this way, hardly anyone but a Philistine of learning (they, however, are quite numerous) will refuse to acknowledge that the latter questions are more relevant to man, more important to him, more intimately connected with his everyday life than the former.

In fact, strictly speaking they alone are relevant and important. The former questions are so only insofar as they lead to a better understanding of the latter and facilitate their resolution.

No one questions the usefulness of literacy or denies that it is absolutely indispensable for human development, but literacy hardly has advocates so obtuse as to attribute to it some sort

* Translated for this volume by James P. Scanlan, from P. Lavrov, *Istoricheskiye pisma*, Geneva, 1891. A note at the end of each excerpt indicates the Letter and pages from which it is drawn. The subheadings are supplied by the translator.

of independent, magical force. Scarcely anyone will say that the actual processes of reading and writing are important to man in themselves; they are important only as *aids* to assimilating the ideas man can acquire through reading and communicate through writing. A man who gets nothing from his reading is in no way superior to an illiterate. To call someone "illiterate" is to say that he lacks the basic requisite of education, but literacy in itself is by no means the goal—it is only a means.

The natural sciences play what would seem to be the same role in the overall system of human education. They are simply the *literacy of thought;* developed thought employs this literacy in solving problems that are purely human, and it is these latter problems that constitute the essence of human development. It is not enough to read a book; one must understand it. Similarly, for a cultivated human being it is not enough to understand the fundamental laws of physics and physiology, to be interested in experiments on albumen or in Kepler's laws. For such a person albumen is not simply a chemical compound but a basic constituent of the food of millions of people. Kepler's laws are not simply abstract formulas of planetary motion but acquisitions of the human spirit in its progress toward a general philosophical understanding of the immutability of natural laws and their independence of every sort of divine arbitrariness. . . .

Knowledge of the outer world provides us with absolutely indispensable material, to which we must appeal in solving all the problems which occupy mankind; but the problems for the sake of which we appeal to this material are problems not of the outer but of the inner world, problems of human *consciousness.* Food is important not as the object of nutritional processes but as the product which eliminates the *conscious* pain of hunger. Philosophical ideas are important not as manifestations of the evolution of spirit in its logical abstractness but as the logical forms through which man becomes *conscious* of his own dignity as higher or lower, of the aims of his own existence as broader or narrower; they are important as forms of protest against the present in the name of a desire for a better and more just social order, or as forms of satisfaction with the present.

Many thinkers have noted the intellectual progress man made in coming to see himself as only one among the countless products of the laws of the external world in their unchanging application, whereas formerly he had pictured himself as the center of all existence—in making the transition, in other words, from a subjective to an objective view of himself and of nature. True, this was extremely important progress, without which science would have been impossible and the development of mankind inconceivable; but it was only the first step. A second step inevitably followed: the study of the unchanging laws of the external world *in its objectivity* in order to attain the sort of human condition which would be recognized subjectively as the best and most just. And at this point the great law divined by Hegel, which seems to apply in very many spheres of human consciousness, was borne out: a third step, apparently a return to the first, in fact resolved the contradiction between the first and the second. Man again became the center of the entire world, but this time the center of the world not as it exists in itself, but as it is comprehended by man, conquered by his thought, and turned toward his aims.

Now this is precisely the point of view of history. The natural sciences give man, who is himself a scarcely noticeable part of the world, an account of the world's laws; they inventory the products of mechanical, physical, chemical, physiological, and psychical processes; they find among the products of the latter processes, throughout the entire animal kingdom, a consciousness of pain and pleasure; and they find, in the part of this kingdom closest to mankind, a consciousness of the ability to set up goals and to strive to achieve them. This fact of natural science is the sole foundation of the biographies of the individual creatures within the animal world and the histories of its separate groups. History as a science takes this fact as given and shows the reader how history as the life-process of mankind has resulted from man's aspiration to eliminate what he recognized as pain and to attain what he recognized as pleasure. It shows what modifications took place at the same time in the concepts associated with the words "pleasure" and "pain," and in the classification and hierarchy of pleasures and pains, and what sorts of philosophical ideas and practical social institutions these modifications engendered. It shows by what logical process the aspiration for betterment and justice gave rise to protest and conservatism, to reaction and progress. It shows what connection existed in each age between man's perception of the world—in the form of religious belief, science, a philosophical idea—and the practical theories of betterment and justice embodied in the acts of individuals, in forms of society, and in people's living conditions.

Thus the historian's work is not the negation but the necessary supplementation of the work of the natural scientist. The historian who scorns the natural scientist does not understand history; he wants to build a house without a foundation, he praises education while denying the need for literacy. The natural scientist who scorns the historian simply demonstrates the narrowness and immaturity of his thinking; he is unwilling to see, or is incapable of seeing, that setting up goals and striving to achieve them are facts of human nature just as inescapable and natural as respiration, the circulation of the blood, or metabolism. Goals may be petty or exalted, strivings pitiful or laudable, actions irrational or purposeful; nevertheless, goals, strivings, and actions always have existed and always will exist, and consequently they are no less legitimate objects of study than the colors of the spectrum, chemical elements, or the species and varieties of the plant and animal kingdoms. The natural scientist who restricts himself to the outer world either does not wish to see or cannot see that for men the entire outer world is simply the material of pleasure, pain, desire, and action, and that the most highly specialized scientist studies the outer world not as something external but as something knowable, something which affords *him*, the scientist, pleasure in coming to know it, prompts his activities, enters into his vital processes. The natural scientist who disdains history imagines that foundations are not meant to be built upon, and that man's whole development should be confined to literacy.[1]

1. From the First Letter, pp. 2-6.

The Subjectivity of History

What phenomenological laws have an influence on the distribution and the genesis of events in human history? Laws of mechanics, chemistry, biology, psychology, ethics, and sociology—i.e., laws of *all* the phenomenological sciences; consequently, it is both necessary and in accordance with the demands of science to take them all into account. Which of these laws are especially important for an understanding of history? Here we must take into account the characteristics of the being who is the sole instrument and the sole subject of history—man. It is not special electrical phenomena that distinguish the electric eel from its zoological group, just as particular chemical products do not determine the classification of plants; in both cases, biological phenomena supply the most important indices. Similarly, in all the sciences pertaining to man the criterion of relative importance should be applied in accordance with the characteristic features of man—features which in this case are inevitably fixed by a *subjective* evaluation, since the investigator is himself a man and cannot for a moment detach himself from the processes which he regards as characteristic.

It is possible (even probable) that consciousness is a very minor phenomenon in the overall order of the world. Yet *for man* it has such surpassing importance that he will always first and foremost divide his own actions and the actions of those like him into *conscious* and *unconscious,* and regard these two groups in different lights. Conscious psychic processes, conscious activity in accordance with conviction or opposed to it, conscious participation in social life, conscious struggle in the ranks of this or that political party, with an eye to this or that historical revolution—for man such activities have and always will have a significance completely different from that of mechanical actions performed under the same circumstances. It follows that conscious influences should take first place in the ordering of historical events, to the same extent that they do in human consciousness itself.

From the standpoint of consciousness, what elements have the primary influence on the genesis of events? Human needs and inclinations. How are these needs and inclinations classified as they bear on the individual's consciousness? They can be divided into three groups.

Some needs and inclinations flow *unconsciously* from the physical and psychical structure of man, as something inescapable, and are recognized by him only when they constitute a ready-made element of his activity.

Others come to the individual just as unconsciously from his *social* environment or from ancestors in the form of habits, traditions, customs, established laws, and political arrangements—in general, as *cultural forms*. These cultural needs and inclinations are also apprehended as ready-made, as something *given* for the individual, though not completely inescapable; it is assumed that they had some meaning at the time the cultural forms originated, and scholars search for this meaning and make conjectures about it. But for each individual, living in a particular age under particular cultural forms, they are something external, independent of his consciousness.

Finally, needs and inclinations of the third group are fully *conscious* and seem to each individual to arise in him apart from any external constraint, as free and independent products of his consciousness. This is the province, first of all, of activity based upon the conscious calculation of interest—the individual's egoistic interests and the interests of those dear to him. Second, and still more important for historical progress, it is the province of the need for what is best; of the aspiration to extend human knowledge and to set oneself a higher goal; of the need to change everything given from without in conformity with one's own desire, one's own understanding, and one's own moral ideal; of the aspiration to rebuild the world of thought according to the demands of truth, and the real world according to the demands of justice. Subsequently, scientific investigation persuades man that even these needs and inclinations do not develop in him freely and independently but arise through the intricate influence of his environment and the peculiarities of his personal development. But while he is convinced of this *objectively*, man can never eliminate the subjective illusion which is present in his consciousness and which establishes, for him, an enormous difference between activity for which he *himself* sets the goal and selects the means, critically analyzing the merits of each, and activity which is mechanical, impulsive, or habitual, in which he recognizes himself as an instrument of something given from without.

The three groups indicated have been distinguished from one another on the basis of the phenomenological process which is most important to man in all the sciences treating of him. Consequently, these groups have been established *scientifically*, and their significance for the classification of historical events flows of necessity from their relationship to the conscious process. The most highly conscious needs and inclinations should have predominant importance for the history of man, by the very nature of this history, just as they inevitably have predominant importance for the historian as a human being, by virtue of his personal characteristics. Purposeful conscious activity provides, by its very posing of the question, the central thread around which the other varieties of human activity are grouped, just as the various goals toward which a man strives are arranged in a hierarchy in accordance with his greatest personal interest (for the majority of people) or with his conception of moral value (for the most cultivated people).

The scientific character of the theory results here from the concurrence of two processes which are equally subjective, but of which one takes place in the mind of the historian while the other comes from the observation of historical individuals and groups. The law of the course of historical events becomes, on this view, a determinate object of investigation. The historian must find, for each age, the intellectual and moral aims which the most cultivated individuals of that age recognized as paramount, as the truth and the moral ideal. He must discover the conditions which gave rise to this outlook, the critical and uncritical thought processes which developed it, and the ways in which it was subsequently modified. He must arrange in their historical and logical sequence the different outlooks which thus arose. He must dispose around them, as causes and effects, as helps and hindrances, as instances and exceptions, all the other events of human history. Then from a kaleidoscope of hetero-

geneous events the historian passes of necessity to a law of the
historical sequence.

In such an investigation all the chief objects and tools of
research belong to the subjective world. Subjective are the
various goals which individuals and groups of individuals pursued in the given age. Subjective is the outlook in accordance
with which these goals were appraised by their contemporaries.
And subjective is the criterion which the historian applies to
the different outlooks of the age so as to select from them
what he considers central and paramount, and to the whole
series of outlooks so as to determine the course of progress in
human history, to identify progressive and retrogressive periods
and their causes and effects, and to show his contemporaries
what is possible and desirable at the present moment. But the
sources of the subjectivity in these cases are different, and the
means for eliminating the errors which might result from the
use of this method are also different.

The subjectivity of particular goals and of their moral evaluation in a given age is a fact, quite unavoidable and scientific,
which should be observed and investigated in all its aspects. To
avoid error here the historian must simply study the individuals'
cultural surroundings and stage of development in the particular
age with the utmost thoroughness and care. He is gathering
facts as in any other science, and his personal views have or
should have an extremely small role in establishing these facts.
If he ascribes to Sesostris or Tamerlane the intricate diplomatic
calculations of Louis XIV or Bismarck, he simply does not know
his period. If he reads Hegel's dialectic into the thought of
Heraclitus, again he has not sufficiently mastered the difference
between two periods. If he gives the predominant significance
in history to cultural phenomena, state expansion, or the conflict of nations, he has not become clear as to the characteristic
features of human nature as man himself conceives it. In all
these cases, the best means of eliminating errors is to make
scientific information accurate, broad, and comprehensive.

But objective appraisal of the different world-views of a given
age or of the theory of historical progress which the historian
formulates is quite a different matter. Here the most precise

erudition cannot eliminate error if the author sets up a false ideal. Here is reflected the historian's personal, individual development, and only through concern for his own development can he find the way to make his conception more correct. Consciously or unconsciously, a man applies the level of moral development which he himself has attained to the entire history of mankind. One person seeks in the life of mankind only that which furthers the formation or destruction of powerful states. Another follows primarily the conflict of nations, their rise and fall. A third tries to convince himself and others that the victors always had more right on their side than the vanquished. A fourth is interested in facts to the extent that they have implemented this or that idea which he accepts as an absolute good for mankind. They all judge history subjectively, according to their view of moral ideals. Indeed they cannot judge it otherwise.[2]

History as the Course of Progress

Thus, willy-nilly, a man is bound to evaluate the historical process subjectively: that is, having acquired, in accordance with his level of moral development, one or another moral ideal, he is bound to put all the facts of history into perspective according to whether they have promoted or opposed this ideal, and to give primary historical importance to those facts in which this promotion or opposition is most vividly exhibited.

But here two further significant circumstances present themselves. First, from this standpoint all phenomena become identified as beneficial or harmful, as morally good or evil. Second, in the historical perspective set by our moral ideal we stand at the end of the historical process; the entire past is related to our ideal as a series of preparatory steps which lead inevitably to a definite end. Consequently, we see history as a struggle between a beneficent principle and a harmful principle, where the former—in unchanging form or through gradual development—has finally reached the point at which it is for us the supreme human good.

Not that the beneficent principle was in fact bound to triumph

2. From the Second Letter, pp. 23-28.

without fail, or that each successive period necessarily drew
nearer to our moral ideal. No, many observers are perfectly
aware of the fact that epochs of retrogression are quite common
in history; others are only too willing to complain of the predominance of evil in this "vale of tears" and of the corruption
of modern generations; still others frankly maintain that a better
future for mankind is impossible. Nevertheless, when these
people begin to survey historical events they inevitably arrange
the entire past in perspective according to what they consider
best. The only events which stand out are those which have
furthered the development of their ideal, or have most hin-
dered its realization.

If the thinker believes that his moral ideal is actually realized
now or will be realized in the future, he will arrange the whole
of history around the events which paved the way for this
realization. If he transfers his ideal to a mythical region beyond
the grave, then history is simply a preparation for the creed
that entails beatitude in the future world. If he renounces all
possibility of realizing his ideal, it remains the highest inner
conviction which history has produced in the mind of man,
and again all past events, important and unimportant, are displayed before him as the preparation for this moral conviction,
which is unrealized now and unrealizable in the actual future,
but has been realized in the sphere of human consciousness as
the pinnacle of human development.

This approach of historical facts to a real or ideal best of
which we are conscious, this evolution of our moral ideal in
the past life of mankind, is for everyone the *only* meaning of
history, the only *law* of the historical ordering of events, the
law of *progress*—whether we consider the progress to be in
fact continuous or subject to fluctuation, whether we believe in
its actual realization or only its realization in consciousness.

Thus we inevitably see *progress* in history. If we support a
principle which is triumphing in our time, we regard our age
as the crown of all those which preceded it. If our sympathies
belong to a principle which is clearly on the wane, we believe
that our age is critical, transitional, or pathological, and that
after it will come an age in which our ideal will triumph either

in the real world, or in a mythical future world, or in the consciousness of the highest representatives of mankind. Those who have believed that the end of the world was imminent—and the world seemed to them full of evil—believed that beatitude for the righteous was sure to follow. Those who have accepted the idea of a primitive state of perfection have advanced from the very next step to a theory of progress. Even the proponents of the cyclical theory of history (which, however, we shall not develop here) have unwittingly submitted to this general law of human thinking. By the inevitable necessity of this thinking, *for man* the historical process is always more or less clearly and consistently a struggle for progress, a real or ideal development of progressive aspirations and progressive understanding, and only those phenomena were historical, in the strict sense of this word, which affected this progress.

I know that a great many people will find my conception of the word "progress" distasteful. All those who wish to endow history with the same objective impartiality which characterizes the processes of nature will be indignant because I make progress depend upon the personal views of the investigator. All those who believe in the absolute infallibility of their own moral outlook would like to convince themselves that the elements of the historical process which are most closely connected with the principles of their outlook are more important not only *for them* but *in themselves.*

But really it is time for thinking people to learn one very simple thing: that distinctions between the important and the unimportant, the beneficial and the harmful, the good and the bad are distinctions which exist only *for man;* they are quite alien to nature and to things in themselves. While man of necessity applies to everything his human (anthropological) way of looking at things, by an equally inescapable necessity things in their totality follow processes which have nothing to do with the human point of view.

For man general laws rather than individual facts are important because he understands things only by generalizing them; but science with its general laws of phenomena is characteristic only of *man,* while outside man there is nothing but simulta-

neous and successive concatenations of facts, so minute and frac-
tional that man can scarcely even apprehend them in all their
particularity. *For man* some of the thoughts, feelings, and deeds
of a person (or a group of persons) are marked out from the
unbroken thread of life's commonplaces and allotted to biographies and histories as being paramount, having ideal significance, historical importance—but this selection is made only
by *man* himself. Unconscious natural processes develop the
idea of universal gravitation and the idea of popular solidarity,
just as they develop the hairs on a beetle's leg or the shop-
keeper's desire to extract an extra penny from his customer.
Garibaldi, Varlin, and others like them are, for nature, exactly
the same sort of nineteenth-century specimens of the human
race as any senator of Napoleon III, any small-town German
burgher, or any of the self-satisfied nonentities who strut along
the *Nevsky Prospekt.* On scientific grounds, the impartial investigator has no right to transfer his moral judgment concerning
the significance of a general law, a genius, or a hero from the
realm of *human* understanding and desire to the realm of unconscious and passionless nature.[3]

The Nature and Extent of Human Progress

Everything I have said in the foregoing Letter demands, of
course, that I give the reader a definite statement of what
exactly I take the goal of human progress to be. This I shall
do. . . .

*The physical, intellectual, and moral development of the
individual; the incorporation of truth and justice in social institutions*—here is a brief formula embracing, I believe, everything which may be considered progress. And I may add that
I view nothing in this formula as my personal property: it
is present, more or less clearly and fully expressed, in the minds
of all thinkers of recent centuries, and in our time it is becoming
a truism, repeated even by those whose actions are inconsistent
with it and who desire something quite different.

I regard the concepts contained in this formula as fully
definite and as not open to different interpretations for anyone

3. From the Second Letter, pp. 29-32.

who takes them seriously. If I am mistaken, then in any event it is the task of ethics rather than of the theory of progress to define these concepts, to prove the propositions contained in the formula, and to develop the formula in detail. Just as truths of chemistry need not be proved in a treatise on physiology, so it is unnecessary to develop truths of ethics when the question is one of their application to the historical process. I believe that the proposed formula, for all its brevity, is open to extensive development, and that by developing it we can obtain a complete theory of both individual and social morality. Here I am taking this formula as a basis for what follows, and I shall proceed directly to the investigation of some of the conditions necessary for the realization of progress in the sense indicated.

The *physical* development of the individual is possible only when he has acquired a certain minimum of hygienic and material comforts, short of which pain, illness, and constant anxiety are far more likely than any sort of development, and the latter becomes the property of exceptional individuals only, while all the others are doomed to degeneration in a continual struggle for existence with no hope of improving their lot.

The *intellectual* development of the individual has a firm foundation only when the individual has cultivated in himself the need for a critical view of everything which presents itself to him, the conviction that the laws which govern phenomena are unalterable, and the realization that in its consequences justice is identical with the pursuit of personal interest.

The *moral* development of the individual is likely to take place only when the social environment permits and encourages the development of independent convictions in individuals, when individuals have the opportunity to defend their different convictions, and by the same token are constrained to respect the freedom of conviction of others, and when the individual recognizes that his dignity resides in his convictions, and that respect of another's dignity is respect of his own dignity.

The incorporation of truth and justice in social institutions presupposes, first of all, the opportunity for scientists and thinkers to advance propositions which they regard as expressions of truth and justice. It presupposes, further, a certain minimum of general education in society which will permit the majority to understand these propositions and to evaluate the arguments adduced in favor of them. It presupposes, finally, social institutions which would permit of change as soon as it appeared that they had ceased to serve as embodiments of truth and justice.

Only when the physical development of the individual is possible, his intellectual development firmly grounded, and his moral development likely, only when society is so organized as to contain sufficient freedom of speech, a sufficient minimum of secondary education, and sufficient openness to change in social institutions—only then may the progress of society as a *whole* be considered more or less assured. Only then may we say that all the conditions of progress are present, so that only external catastrophes can stop it. Until all these conditions have been fulfilled, progress can only be accidental and partial, providing no guarantee for the most immediate future; until then we may always expect an age of stagnation or reaction after an age of apparent advance. Under the most disadvantageous conditions for society as a whole, favorable circumstances may put some individual in a position to develop far beyond the level of his environment. These favorable circumstances may even exist for a group of individuals. But they remain nonetheless an ephemeral phenomenon, while society as a whole is left to stagnation or reaction. The law of large numbers will never be slow to demonstrate, with relentless rigor, what little historical significance there is in the development of a small group of individuals under exceptional circumstances. A majority of society must be placed in a position where its development is possible, likely, and firmly grounded before we may say that society is progressing.

While I counted on the reader's unquestioning acceptance of the brief formula of progress set forth above, I am not nearly so confident that he will accept the conditions of progress I have mentioned. But this is the common fate of formulas. A great many people will consent to them so long as they are not elucidated; as soon as elucidation begins, the people who have accepted them begin to realize that, while they have been adhering to one and the same formula, they have not entirely understood one another. To me these conditions seem necessary, and I leave it to anyone who disagrees with me, but retains the formula, to supply other conditions.

But having supplied *these* conditions, I shall venture to ask the reader whether we have any right today to speak of the progress of *humanity*. Can we say that the *elementary* conditions of progress have already been fulfilled for a majority of the 1,400 millions who today constitute humanity? That even *some* of these conditions have been fulfilled? And for what portion of these 1,400 millions? And can we reflect without a certain horror on the *cost*, to the wretched millions of the generations which have perished, of realizing progress for the handful of individuals whom the historian may regard as representatives of civilization?

I should consider it an insult to the reader if I doubted for a moment how he will answer the question of whether the elementary conditions of progress have been fulfilled. Only one answer is possible here: the conditions of progress have not *all* been fulfilled for *a single person*, and *none* of them has been fulfilled for the *majority*. Only isolated individuals or small groups have sometimes, here and there, found themselves in sufficiently favorable circumstances to win some sort of progress for themselves and to pass on the tradition of fighting for betterment to other small groups, to whom fate also has given a somewhat more advantageous position. Everywhere and always, individuals who have cultivated progress of some sort have had to combat innumerable obstacles and waste the greater part of their strength and their lives in this struggle, simply to uphold their right to physical and intellectual cultivation. Only under particularly favorable circumstances have they succeeded. Only in exceptional situations have individuals not had to struggle for existence, so that time and energy could go to the fight for an increase in pleasures. Still more exceptional was the situation of those who could profit to such an extent by a fight which other individuals carried on for them, that they were able to strive for the moral pleasure of consciously cultivating humane principles and embodying them in social institutions. And in all these cases the struggle demanded so large a portion of their strength and their life that extremely little of either was left for actually realizing the goal of the struggle.

Thus it is small wonder if mankind, even in its most privileged part, has yet achieved so little. Indeed it is surprising that under such unfavorable conditions a certain portion of mankind has nevertheless achieved something which can properly be called, not the realization of, but perhaps the preparation for true progress. But then how small is this portion which has succeeded? And what has it cost the rest? [4]

The Cost of Progress and the Obligation To Repay It

Mankind has paid dearly so that a few thinkers sitting in their studies could discuss its progress. It has paid dearly for a few little colleges where it has trained its teachers, who to this day, however, have brought it little benefit. If one were to count the educated minority of our time and the number of people who have perished in the past in the struggle for its existence, and estimate the labor of the long line of generations who have toiled solely to sustain their lives and allow others to develop, and if one were to calculate how many human lives have been lost and what a wealth of labor has been spent for each individual now living a *somewhat* human life— if one were to do all this, no doubt some of our contemporaries would be horrified at the thought of the capital in blood and labor which has been lavished on their cultivation. What serves to soothe their sensitive consciences is that such a calculation is impossible.

Perhaps what ought to be horrifying, however, is not that the progress of the minority has been costly, but that it has been *so* costly and that for this price *so* little has been achieved. If the minority had troubled itself sooner and more diligently with disseminating the development achieved in the sphere of culture and thought, the quantity of wasted lives and labor would not be so great; the debt incurred by each of us would

4. From the Third Letter, pp. 37, 41-43, 45-48.

be smaller and would not increase so enormously with each generation.

We have no power over the laws of natural necessity, and for this reason a reasonable person should accept them, limit himself to calm investigation of them, and as far as possible make use of them for his own ends. We have no power even over history; the past simply gives us facts, which at times may help us to improve the future. We are responsible for the sins of our fathers only to the extent that we continue these sins and profit by them, without attempting to rectify their consequences. We have power to some degree only over the future, since our thoughts and our actions are the material out of which the whole content of future truth and justice is created. Each generation is answerable to posterity only for what it *could have* done but did not do.

Thus in light of the verdict of posterity we, too, shall have to answer certain questions: How much of the evil contained in the process to which we give the high-sounding title of "historical progress" is unavoidable and natural? To what extent did our ancestors—who provided us, the civilized minority, with the chance to enjoy the advantages of this progress— needlessly increase and prolong the sufferings and toil of the majority which has never enjoyed the advantages of progress? In what instances may the responsibility for this evil fall also upon us, in the eyes of future generations?

The law of struggle for existence is so universal in the animal world that we have not the slightest ground for blaming primitive men when this law was applied among them, too, so long as a sense of mutual solidarity and the need for truth and justice had not awakened among men. Since a sense of solidarity could hardly have awakened so long as men, mutually exterminating one another, had not reached the point of substituting exploitation for murder, we must regard the whole long period of strife among individuals, bands, clans, tribes, and nations as simply a zoological fact.

As for the growth of knowledge and the development of a conception of right and duty, one can scarcely imagine it as at first anything but a process occurring in the few who were placed in particularly favorable circumstances—that is, in individuals who had leisure, the best food, and the best education at the expense of other individuals who furnished the former with these advantages through an increase in their labor, if not at the price of their own lives or of considerable suffering. Before one can be taught, one must have teachers. The majority can develop only through the action upon it of a more cultivated minority. Thus, either mankind had to remain undeveloped, or the majority at first had to carry the more fortunate minority on its shoulders, work for it, suffer and die for it. This, too, would seem to be a law of nature.

Given this law, it remains for us either to say that we want no part of a development bought at such a price, or to regard this, too, as an anthropological fact. But since I have already included comprehensive development in the very formula of progress at the beginning of the previous Letter, to repudiate development in general would be to fall into a contradiction. Let us, then, accept the fact that for his development it was necessary for man to provide himself, at a very, very high price, with the teachers' college and the more cultivated minority, so that the science and the diversified practical experience, the thinking and the techniques which accumulate at these centers would gradually spread to a greater and greater number of people.

The necessary, natural evil in progress is confined to the foregoing, and beyond the bounds of these laws begins the responsibility of human generations, more particularly of the civilized minority. All the blood which has been shed in history beyond the immediate struggle for existence, in the period of the more or less clear recognition of man's right to life, is blood criminally shed and lying within the responsibility of the generation which shed it. Every civilized minority which was unwilling to be *civilizing*, in the broadest sense of this word, bears the responsibility for all the sufferings of its contemporaries and of posterity which it *could have* eliminated, had it not confined itself to the role of representative and custodian of civilization but assumed also the role of its motive force.

If from this standpoint we assess the panorama of history down to our own day, we shall no doubt have to acknowledge that every generation in history has shed rivers of blood even without having the justification of the struggle for existence, and that in almost all times and places the minority, while priding itself on its civilization, has done extremely little to disseminate it. A few individuals have troubled themselves with broadening the sphere of learning among men; a still smaller number with strengthening thought and searching for more just forms of society; as for members of the civilized minority who have endeavored to convert such forms into fact, they are encountered in very small number.

Many brilliant civilizations have paid with their own destruction for this inability to link the interest of a greater number of individuals with their existence. In all civilizations without exception, the majority of those who have enjoyed the comforts of culture have never given a thought to all those who did not and could not enjoy them, much less to the price at which the acquired comforts of life and thought had been purchased.

There has always been quite a number of people, however, who at each stage of civilization have considered that stage the limit of social development and have indignantly rebelled against any critical attitude toward it, against any attempt to spread the blessings of civilization to a greater number of persons, to diminish the toil and the suffering of the majority who do not enjoy it, and to introduce more truth into thought and more justice into social institutions. These apostles of stagnation are terrified at the thought that all history is an inexorable steeplechase in pursuit of the better, where everyone who has lagged behind promptly drops out of the circle of historical figures, disappears into the mob of anonymous, dumfounded spectators, and perishes in animal insignificance. Those incapable of such a race persuade the others to stop also, to rest, to enjoy peace and quiet—as if this were possible for a man who wishes to remain a man. The apostles of stagnation have very rarely succeeded in erecting a complete barrier to social progress, but they have often succeeded in retarding it and in increasing the sufferings of the majority.

In view of this, we must admit that the benefits of modern
civilization have been purchased not only with *unavoidable* evil
but moreover with an enormous quantity of absolutely *needless*
evil, the responsibility for which rests with the preceding generations of the civilized minority—partly because of its lack
of concern and partly because of its direct opposition to every
civilizing endeavor. This evil in the past we can no longer correct. The suffering generations of the majority have perished,
their labor unrelieved. The present civilized minority is profiting by their toil and sufferings. More than that: it is profiting
by the sufferings and toil of a vast number of its contemporaries,
and can contribute to an increase in the toil and sufferings of
their grandchildren.

Since for this last circumstance we have borne and shall bear
the moral responsibility before posterity, historical investigation
of the cost of the progress which has been made leads to the
next practical question: what resources does the present generation have for lessening its responsibility? If living representatives of the different levels of development were to ask themselves: what must we do so as not to answer to posterity for the
fresh sufferings of mankind? and if they all *clearly understood
their tasks*, the answers would, of course, be diverse.

A member of the majority who are fighting daily for physical
existence, as their ancestors did in the earliest periods of the life
of mankind, would say to himself: Fight, to the best of your
knowledge and ability! Defend the right to life for yourself
and for those you love! This was the law of your fathers, and
your plight is no better than theirs. This is the only law for you,
too.

A more unfortunate member of this same majority, in whom
civilization has aroused a sense of his own human dignity but
has gone no further, would say to himself: Fight, to the best
of your knowledge and ability. Defend your own dignity and
the dignity of others. Die for it, if necessary!

A member of the civilized minority who desires only to
augment and insure his own pleasure, but is inclined to seek
it more in the sphere of material comforts than in the sphere
of thought, would say to himself: You can find pleasure only

in a society where solidarity more or less reigns. Oppose, then, in yourself and in others, whatever is incompatible with this solidarity. You, too, suffer from the discord of contemporary society, when you realize that this discord is a social disease. Reduce, then, your own sufferings by striving to improve the lot of the majority: what you sacrifice in present benefits with this aim will return to you in the knowledge that you have alleviated in some small measure the disease of society—a disease which brings suffering to you, too. So consult your own *true* interest: reduce the sufferings around you and in yourself. This is what benefits you most.

A member of a small group within the minority, who finds pleasure in his own development, in the search for truth, and in the realization of justice, would say to himself: Each of the material comforts which I enjoy, each thought which I have had the leisure to acquire or to develop, has been bought with the blood, sufferings, or toil of millions. I cannot correct the past, and however high the cost of my cultivation I cannot repudiate it: it constitutes the very ideal which arouses me to action. Only a weak and uncultivated person collapses under his responsibilities and flees from evil to the Thebaid or to the grave. Evil must be corrected as much as possible, and this can be done only in life. Evil must be corrected *vitally*. I shall relieve myself of responsibility for the bloody cost of my own development if I utilize this same development to diminish evil in the present and in the future. If I am a cultivated person I am obliged to do this, but for me this obligation is very light, since it coincides exactly with what constitutes pleasure for me: by seeking and disseminating greater truth, by coming to understand what social order is most just and striving to realize it, I am increasing my own pleasure and at the same time doing everything I can for the suffering majority in the present and in the future. And so my task is limited to one simple rule: live according to the ideal which you yourself have set up as the ideal of a *cultivated* man.

This would all be so easy and simple if every individual understood his task, but the trouble is precisely that very few understand it. The foregoing rules are followed only by a portion of those in the first category and by a few in the other categories. The remaining portion of those who are struggling for their physical existence do not defend themselves with sufficient energy—not because they lack the knowledge or ability to do so, but through lack of determination, through apathy. The majority of persons in the second category sacrifice their dignity for their daily bread and are abased in their own eyes —without, for all that, having the chance to escape from their predicament. The majority of persons in the third category fail to understand their own true interest; they follow routine and do not know how to counteract, even in small degree, the social malady which brings suffering to each individual and consequently also to themselves: that is, while they seek to avoid suffering, they do not know how to lessen in themselves the sufferings which flow from social discord. As for the majority of persons in the last category, either they set up idols in place of truth and justice, or they limit themselves to truth and justice in thought but not in life, or they do not want to see what an insignificant minority enjoys the advantages of the progress of civilization.

And the cost of this progress keeps mounting.[5]

The Duty of the Critically-Thinking Individual

My last two Letters lead ultimately to one and the same conclusion. A society is threatened with stagnation if it stifles critically-thinking individuals; a society's civilization, whatever its merits, is threatened with destruction if it becomes the exclusive property of a small minority. Consequently, however limited the progress of mankind, what progress there is depends exclusively upon the critically-thinking individuals. Without them, it is absolutely impossible; without their firm desire to disseminate it, it is extremely precarious. Since these individuals ordinarily assume that they are entitled to be considered cultivated, and since it is precisely for *their* cultivation that the terrible price discussed in the last Letter has been paid, it is upon them that the moral duty to repay the cost of this progress is incumbent. This repayment, as we have seen, consists in the greatest possible

5. From the Fourth Letter, pp. 72-78.

extension of material comforts and of intellectual and moral development to the majority, and in the introduction of scientific understanding and of justice into social institutions.

Let us, then, consider for a moment these individuals who are the sole instruments of human progress. Whatever its characteristics may be, it depends upon them. It will not spring from the earth like a weed. It will not propagate itself from germs wafted in the air, like infusoria in a decomposing liquid. It will not suddenly appear among men as a result of the mystical ideas which were discussed so much forty years ago and which many still discuss even now. Its seed is in fact an idea, but not an idea mystically present in mankind: it is conceived and developed in the brain of an individual, passes from there into the brains of other individuals, grows qualitatively with the increase in the intellectual and moral stature of these individuals and quantitatively with the increase in their number, and becomes a social force when these individuals recognize their unity of thought and resolve upon united action; it triumphs when the individuals imbued with it have introduced it into social institutions.

If a person who talks about his love of progress is not willing to reflect critically on the conditions for its realization, then in reality he has never desired progress and has never even been capable of desiring it sincerely. If a person who recognizes the conditions of progress waits passively for it to realize itself without any effort on his part, then he is the worst enemy of progress, the most detestable obstacle in its path. All those who complain about the corruption of the times, about the worthlessness of men, about stagnation and reaction, should be asked: and *you* yourselves, you with eyes among the blind, you who are healthy among the sick, what have *you* done to promote progress?

I am not referring to those who fight all their lives for a crust of bread. I mentioned them in the last Letter, and no accusation falls upon them. If progress has passed them by without allowing them to develop at all, then they are nothing but its victims. If intellectual development has brushed them, if an awareness of what is best has kindled in them a hatred of falsehood and of evil, while circumstances have crushed every manifestation of

this awareness and have confined their lives to preoccupation
with their daily bread; if at the same time they have nevertheless preserved their human dignity, then by their example and
by their existence they remain the most vigorous promoters of
progress. In historical importance, the greatest figures in history
are insignificant in comparison with these invisible heroes of
humanity who have not performed a single striking deed. If the
latter did not exist, the former could never have carried out a
single one of their undertakings. The visible heroes fight for
what is best, and often even perish in the struggle; but at the
same time, despite unfavorable circumstances, the invisible heroes
sustain in society the tradition of human dignity and the consciousness of what is best. And when one of the great figures in
a hundred succeeds in putting his ideas into practice he suddenly
finds around him a group of stalwart men, hardened by toil and
steadfast in their convictions, who cheerfully offer him their
hands. It is from these invisible heroes that the ground for reform is created at every great historic moment. They preserve
within themselves the whole potential of the future. In a society
without them all historical progress would cease at once. Morally, the subsequent life of such a society would differ in no
respect from the life of other social animals.

But these vigorous figures contain only the *potentiality* of
progress. Its actualization never is or can be their task, for a very
simple reason: each of them who set about bringing progress into
being would soon die of hunger or sacrifice his human dignity,
in either case vanishing from the progressive ranks. The actualization of progress belongs to those who have freed themselves
from their most oppressive concerns for their daily bread. But
of these latter, *anyone* who thinks critically can bring progress
into being among men.

Yes, anyone. Please do not say that you lack the talent and the
learning. Neither special talent nor great learning is needed here.
If your talent and learning sufficed to give you a critical attitude
toward what exists around you and to make you aware of the
need for progress, then they will suffice to put this criticism and
this knowledge into practice. But do not miss a single opportunity which life actually presents. Suppose that your activity is

trifling: all substances consist of immeasurably small particles; the most enormous forces are composed of infinitely small impulses. Neither you nor anyone else can estimate the quantity of good your action will produce: it depends upon a thousand different circumstances, upon a multitude of coincidences impossible to foresee. The best intentions have often had appalling consequences, just as actions which at first glance seem unimportant have had countless ramifications.

But we can expect, with some degree of assurance, that by imparting the same direction to a whole series of actions we shall obtain only a few contrary results, while at least some of the actions will coincide with conditions favorable to appreciable results in the direction intended. We, perhaps, shall never witness these results, but certainly they *will exist*, if we have done everything in our power. The farmer, having cultivated the soil and sown his seeds, knows that many of the seeds will die and that he can never completely protect the cornfield against cattle damage, crop failure, and nocturnal marauders; but even after a crop failure he returns to the field with another handful of seeds, expecting a future harvest. If everyone who thinks critically will constantly and actively strive for what is best, then however insignificant the sphere of his activity, however circumscribed the arena of his life, he will be an influential motive force of progress and will repay his share of the terrible cost of his development.[6]

The Transformation of Culture by Thought

Hence it becomes necessary to determine which elements, in the complex system of society, constitute the *ground* to be acted upon and which constitute *instruments* of action. Where is the more or less tinseled but in itself dead form, and where is the living strength?

Needs give rise to the processes of the organic world, the growth of vegetation, the reproduction of animals. They constitute one of the most important topics of physiology, human psychology, and sociology, and they also constitute the inescapable starting point for the explanation of every historical phe-

6. From the Fifth Letter, pp. 79-83.

nomenon. Wherever there is an act of the will, there is a need at the basis of the act; thus all the elements of historical phenomena can be reduced to the various needs of individuals.

Physiological and habitual needs unite all the classes of the animal world and do not in any way distinguish man from the other vertebrates or from the invertebrates. In fact the latter sub-kingdom presents the most striking examples of their manifestation—namely, the societies of ants, bees, and other creatures closely related to them.

These needs constitute the most solid, if it may be so expressed, and the most naturalistic element in the life of societies. They provide the unalterable economic and statistical laws and the reciprocal determination between the physical conditions of a country and its civilization which underlie human history. They give rise to the first technology and hence to the first science. It is under their influence that human beings, like other animals, are first drawn together. Social life, issuing from this source, is already a *cultured* life; and man, inconceivable without needs, is by the same token inconceivable without some sort of culture. Just as do certain of his fellows from the world of insects and vertebrates, man belongs to the class of cultured animals.

With the first individualized inclinations a second group of needs makes its appearance in the organic world—needs which are more complex, more diverse, and less common. They are observed in anything like determinate form only in the higher classes of vertebrates (among birds and mammals), and even here they are developed fully only in certain families, genera, and species. They are expressed in *choice* which seems to be voluntary, in various feelings of attachment and aversion which cannot be reduced to a need shared by all, in the variability of inclinations, which range under quite similar circumstances from complete indifference to an uncontrollable passion which makes the individual forget self-preservation, drowns out all other needs, generates sometimes completely reckless and sometimes cunningly calculated action, and manifests itself in man as heroism or as crime.

This second group of *affective* needs plays a large role in the private biographies of individuals, but a very negligible one in the overall history of mankind. The brevity of the life of individuals prevents them, even when they occupy very influential positions, from leaving any very appreciable traces of their affective states in the life of society—especially since affective states by their very nature vary from individual to individual, and, for the most part, in the diversity of the affective states of co-existing individuals these influences cancel out one another.

Physiological and habitual needs would reduce every culture to the perpetually repeated forms of the beehive or the ant heap. Affective needs would give rise to personal dramas, but could not create history. History takes place only under the influence of the work of *thought*. It is engendered by yet a new type of needs, observed only in man, and there only in the small groups of individuals for whom the sufferings of generations have produced exceptional cultivation. These are the progressive, historical needs, the needs of *development*.

The first technology and the first calculation of utility are already products of *thought*, and the culture of societies becomes diversified as their thought develops. Under the influence of its operation, needs multiply and inclinations change; calculation gives rise to a whole line of expedient actions which push immediate inclinations aside. The inclinations themselves, in the form of desires and passions, become the springs of activity calculated to provide the best satisfaction of the desire. Finally there comes a moment when the critical work of thought is directed not to the *satisfaction* of an immediate inclination but to the inclination itself. Then thought weights inclinations and arranges them according to the *worth* they prove to have when examined critically. On the other hand, thought itself becomes a favored objective and arouses a desire; the satisfaction of this desire directed to the product of thought becomes a new, purely human, higher need. The actual cultivation of thought—thought as an absorbing goal, as the sought-for *truth*, as a desirable *moral good* —becomes a need for a cultivated individual.

Under the unceasing work of critical thought, on behalf of *development* in general as the end, all needs and inclinations are arranged in various perspectives, as better and worse inclinations, as higher and lower needs. There arises a need for truth and justice, independent of utility. The beginnings of science and of art are created. There arises a need to set ideals of life for oneself and to realize them through a moral life. Man becomes capable of resisting his inclinations and needs and of giving himself up wholeheartedly to an idea, a notion, a life goal—sometimes to an illusion—sacrificing everything to them, and often without it even occurring to him to submit them to critical examination. As soon as thought's work on the cultural terrain has leavened social life with the demands of science, art, and morality, then culture has been transformed into civilization and human history has begun.

The results of the intellectual labors of one generation are not confined to the sphere of thought for succeeding generations. They become habits of life, social traditions. For people who have received them in this form their origin is a matter of indifference; the most profound thought, repeated habitually or in accordance with tradition, is no higher phenomenon for mankind than the customary actions of the beaver and the bee are for beavers and bees. The invention of the first ax and the first baked clay pot was an enormous labor of elementary technical thought, but today man uses axes and baked clay no more consciously than a bird builds its nest. . . .

Generally speaking, the ancestors' contribution to civilization, in the form of customs and traditions, is nothing but a zoological, cultural element in the life of the descendants. This second-order customary culture must be operated upon critically by the thought of the new generation so that society will not sink into stagnation—so that among the customs and traditions which it has inherited it will discern those which present an opportunity for the further work of thought on the path of truth, beauty, and justice, will discard the rest as obsolete, and will create a new civilization—a new system of culture, revitalized by the work of thought.

And in each generation the same process is repeated. From nature and from history man receives a complex of needs and inclinations which are in large measure determined by cultural customs and traditions. He satisfies these needs and inclinations through the ordinary usages of life and through inherited social institutions, craftsmanship, and routine technology. All this constitutes his culture, or the zoological element in the life of mankind.

But among the inherited customs of every civilization is the custom of critical inquiry—and it is this which gives rise to the humane element in history—to the *need for development*, and, in the light of this need, to the *work of thought*. Scientific criticism introduces more truth into world-views; moral criticism extends the application of science and justice in life; aesthetic criticism promotes a fuller grasp of truth and justice, gives life more harmony and culture more humane refinement. To the extent that culture-principles prevail in a society and the work of thought is stifled, to that extent the society, however brilliant its culture, is approaching the social order of ants and wasps; it is nothing more than a difference in degree, a difference in the form of the needs and inclinations. To the extent that the work of thought—the critical attitude toward one's culture—is vigorous in a society, to that extent the society is more humane and further distinguishes itself from the world of the lower animals, even if the strife engendered by the work of thought—by the critical examination of what exists—has melancholy scenes as its specific consequence, has recourse to the weapons of social or intellectual revolution, and disturbs the public order and tranquility.

Very often it is only through temporary agitation and disorder, only through revolution, that one can buy a better guarantee of order and tranquility for the majority in the future. . . .

A society's culture is the environment which history has provided for the work of thought, and this environment determines what is *possible* for that work in a given age, just as inevitably as the immutable laws of nature set its limits in all ages. Thought is the only factor which *humanizes* social culture. The history of thought, conditioned by culture, in connection with the history of culture as it changes under the influence of thought—this is the entire history of civilization. The only events which can enter into the rational history of mankind are those which elucidate the history of culture and thought in their interaction.

Needs and inclinations are given by nature or engendered by

culture, and they give rise to social institutions. To introduce truth and justice into these social institutions is the task of thought. What *nature* has contributed to social institutions, thought cannot alter and must simply take into account. Thought cannot relieve man of the need for food and air, cannot abolish sexual attraction, cannot arrange things so that children will not exist along with adults, cannot change the process of its own dissemination in such a way that the individual will cease to be its necessary organ. But everything which *culture* has introduced into social institutions is subject to the critical examination of thought. In the work of thought, culture must be taken into account as the historically-given environment, but not as an unalterable law. If we compare the cultures of different ages we can easily observe the extent to which the most basic elements of culture are liable to alteration. Nevertheless, for those who lived during the age of the ascendancy of a given culture this culture formed the environment within which each individual had to act, with no chance of making this environment different. Natural needs and inclinations, under the influence of the critical activity of thought, must forge for themselves social institutions which contain the greatest quantity of truth and justice that the given status of the culture will permit.

Thus, before us is the specific task of progress: *culture* must be reworked by *thought*. Before us, too, is the specific and the only real agent of progress: the *individual* who defines his abilities and the work which he can do.[7]

The Need for an Organized Party

"The voice of one man is the voice of no one," says an ancient proverb, and the individual who confronts society with a critique of social institutions and a desire to infuse them with justice is, of course, as a powerless unit, insignificant. Yet such individuals, by becoming a force which sets society in motion, have created history. How have they accomplished this?

First of all, it must be acknowledged that if the person in question is really a critically-thinking individual, he is never alone. In what does his critique of social institutions consist? In the fact that he has come to understand the inadequacies of

7. From the Sixth Letter, pp. 97-105.

these institutions, their lack of justice for the present day, more clearly and more profoundly than others. But if this is so, then a great number of individuals will be suffering and groaning, writhing and perishing under the burden of these institutions. They, as individuals whose thinking is not sufficiently critical, do not understand *why* they are so miserable. But if they were told, they could understand; and those who do will understand just as well as he who first expressed the thought—perhaps even better, because they may have suffered the truth of this thought much more fully and comprehensively than has its original proclaimer. . . . They are everywhere, and the truer and more just the ideas, the more of them there are. This is a force which is invisible, intangible, not yet manifested in action. But it is already a force.

For this force to be manifested in action, an example is needed. For the individual to feel that he is not alone, he must know that someone else not only understands how wretched he is, and why, but furthermore is taking action against the evil. Not words alone but deeds are needed. Vigorous, fanatical men are needed, who will risk everything and are prepared to sacrifice everything. Martyrs are needed, whose legend will far outgrow their true worth and their actual service. Energy they never had will be attributed to them; the best ideas and the best sentiments of their followers will be put into their mouths. For the multitude they will become unattainable, impossible ideals. But on the other hand their legend will inspire thousands with the energy needed for the fight. The words they never uttered will be repeated—at first only half-understood, then understood better and better. The ideas which never animated the original ideal historical figure will be embodied in the work of succeeding generations as if inspired by him.

The number of those who perish is not important here: legend will always multiply it to the limits of possibility. And history shows that the conservators of social institutions, with commendable selflessness, have themselves always supplied slaughtered champions for the multitude to worship, in sufficient numbers for those who oppose some social institution to be able to compile a long martyrology.

In this phase of the struggle the critically-thinking individuals already have before them an actual force, but it is a disordered one. . . . The force has shown itself, but it is spent in vain. Nevertheless, it is now a force which has become conscious of itself.

So that the force will not be spent in vain, it must be organized. The critically-thinking, determined individuals must be determined not only to fight but to win; to this end it is necessary to understand not only the goal toward which one is striving but also the means by which it can be attained. If the struggle has been in earnest, those who are combating outmoded social institutions will include not only individuals who are fighting in the name of their own suffering, which they have come to understand only through the words and thoughts of others, but also individuals who have thought through the state of affairs critically. They must seek each other out; they must unite, and bring order and harmony to the disorderly elements of the historical force which has arisen. Then the force will be organized; its action can be focused on a given point, concentrated for a given purpose. Its task is then purely technical: to do the most work with the least expenditure of strength. The time for unconscious suffering and dreams has passed; the time for heroes and fanatical martyrs, for the squandering of strength and for futile sacrifices, has also passed. The time has come for cool, conscious workmen, calculated strokes, rigorous thinking, and unswerving, patient action.

This is the most difficult phase. . . . Let us see, then, in what the chief difficulties of this phase consist, because only by overcoming these difficulties do individuals become a real organic force in society in the fight for truth and justice.

Because critically-thinking individuals, who must join together to organize the party, are more capable and vigorous than other men, they possess a more marked individuality. They have worked out their *own* mode of thinking, and thus to adopt another's point of view and submit to it is more difficult for them than it is for others. They have cultivated independence of action, and thus to force themselves to act in a way which they think is not entirely best is more difficult for them than for someone else. They have been able to defend their independence in the midst of social routine more successfully than others, and thus it is easiest for them to act in isolation. Yet it is precisely these people, who think and act independently and are accustomed to moral solitude, who now must come together, unite, think together, act together, and organize something strong and single, but strong as a collective force, and single as an abstract unity. Their own individuality, which they have protected from the smothering influence of routine—the individuality to which they have become so accustomed and which they value so highly —must vanish in the common direction of thought and the common plan of action. They create an organism, but they reduce themselves to organs within it. And they do so voluntarily. . . .

Each individual must separate the essential from the customary in his opinions. Each must enter the association determined to sacrifice the customary, though it be very dear, for the sake of the essential. Each must consider himself an organ of the overall organism. He is not a lifeless instrument, not an insensate mechanism, but he is nevertheless *only* an organ. He has his own nature and his own functions, but he is subordinate to the unity of the whole. This is a condition, and a necessary condition, of the life of an organism. It is a condition of harmonious action, a condition of victory.

But if discord is disastrous, if concessions with respect to what is *customary* are necessary, and if individuals must submit to the common cause—concessions on what is *essential* would be just as disastrous, and it is just as necessary that the party members remain *thinking* individuals without being transformed into machines to serve another's ideas. He who has yielded on what is *essential* to his convictions has no serious convictions at all. He serves not a cause which he has understood, reflected upon, and desired to promote, but a meaningless word, an empty sound. To be sure, victory is impossible without a firm alliance, without unity of action; and of course victory is desired by all who fight. But victory *in itself* cannot be the goal of the thinking person. Victory must have some inherent meaning. It is not *who* has won but *what* has won that is important. It is the triumphant idea that is important. And if through compromises the idea has lost all content, then the party has lost its meaning: it has no cause, and the dispute is simply one of personal predominance. . . .

Thus the party is organized. Its nucleus is a small number of highly developed, deliberate, vigorous people, for whom critical thinking is inseparable from action. Around them are members of the intelligentsia who are less highly developed. But the party's real foundation is its inevitable allies, the social groups suffering from the evil which the party has been organized to combat.

The distinction which has been established between the essential and the inessential in personal beliefs determines both the freedom of action within the party and what the party will tolerate from without. However widely its members may differ on points considered inessential, they are nonetheless useful and inevitable party allies for the future.

All members of the party—actual and potential—are under its protection. Every thinking person who has entered into the party organism becomes a natural defense attorney not only of those who already belong to it but of those who may enter it tomorrow. . . .

Beyond the bounds of the inessential, the freedom of action of the party's members and its tolerance of those outside it ceases. If any member oversteps these bounds, he is no longer a member of the party, but its enemy. If anyone outside the party disagrees with it on essential issues, he, too, is its enemy. Against these enemies the party directs and must direct the whole force of its organization, fighting as one man, with all its resources, concentrating its blows.

Just as each member of the party is a natural defense attorney of his actual and potential allies, so too he is a natural prosecutor of all his avowed enemies. . . .

Thus grows the social force, proceeding from the solitary, weak individual to include, first, the sympathy of other individuals, then their unorganized cooperation, until finally a party is organized which imparts unity and direction to the fight. At this point, of course, the party encounters other parties, and the question of victory becomes a question of numbers and tactics.[8]

8. From the Eighth Letter, pp. 118-125, 128-130.

Idealization

But at a particular moment in history, how are we to know where progress lies? Which party is its representative? Great words are inscribed upon all the banners. All the parties preach principles which, under certain conditions, have been or will be motive forces of progress. This principle is good, but so is that. How, then, are we to choose? . . .

No word has had an exclusive right to progress; progress has never been squeezed into a single institutional frame. Behind the word, look for its content. Study the conditions of the day and of the given social institution. Make yourself a person of learning and conviction. This is indispensable. Only one's own understanding, one's own conviction, one's own determination make an individual an individual, and apart from the individual there are no great principles, there are no progressive institutions, there is no progress whatever. What is important is not the banner, and not the word inscribed upon it, but the thought of him who bears it.

In order to discern this thought more readily, one must come to understand the process by means of which people sometimes conceal the foulest things under great words.

Part of the world and a slave of nature, man has never liked to acknowledge his slavery. Submitting constantly to irrational impulses and fortuitous circumstances, he has never liked to call his motives frankly irrational or his action a product of accidental influences. In the inmost depths of his soul there is an urge to conceal from himself his dependence upon the immutable laws of unconscious matter and to embellish somehow in his own eyes the inconstancy and inconsistency of his actions. This he has done through idealization.

It works as follows: I have performed an act, good or evil, on the spur of the moment—without even giving a thought to whether it is good or evil. After the act has been performed, there is an appraisal. If in my opinion the act is good, I am gratified. But if I were to admit to myself that I have performed a good act without even considering its value, I should not gain much credit in my own eyes. Perhaps I *had* considered it, but do not remember. But now I remember: actually, I *had* quickly grasped that it was good, and the rapidity of my reflection increases my merit still further; I am both a good man and one who grasps things quickly.

Let us assume, however, that I am endowed with a sufficiently good memory so as not to make a mistake on that score. Very well. I have performed a good act without reflecting upon it, without calculating, but through an inner, natural inclination. This means that my nature is so permeated with goodness that I can perform good acts without even having to recognize, intellectually, how valuable they are. I am a good man not through intellectual cultivation but by nature. I am, then, one of those men who are exclusively good.

Or else still another method is followed, which is effective given religious modes of thought. I did not perform the good act of my own volition: it was inspired in me from on high, by a deity who directs the will and the actions of men without the mediation of their conscious reflection. God chose me as His instrument to carry out the divine purpose of effecting this good act. The seeming humility of this last method conceals still greater self-glorification than the methods previously examined.

In each of these cases, from a completely unthinking act which, through its consequences, has accidentally turned out to be good, idealization has drawn the conclusion that I am a very good man and remarkably quick of comprehension, or that I am exclusively good by my very nature, or that I am a person chosen by God for good acts.

When the act is evil the methods of idealization are somewhat different, but they fall into the same categories. First, the last method works here too, without alteration: I did not perform the act of my own volition but was the instrument of God's wrath and judgment. God selected me for an act which only *seems* evil to feeble human reason; the Supreme Reason judges differently, and if it has decided that the person chosen is to perform this act, then in reality the act is not evil. The rationalist will speak not of God but of a higher law which guides events and draws good consequences from evil actions; of a higher harmony of all that exists, where the acts of individuals are the particular notes which grate upon the ear if we hear them separately, but which are necessary for the overall harmony. It turns out that the evil deed, as a necessary element in the universal harmony, is by no means evil and had to be performed; while I, from being the perpetrator of an evil deed, have become a valuable participant in the universal concert.

But the method which people are most fond of using here is the method of a supposed higher consideration. Taken in itself the act is, let us say, evil. But memory quickly produces a long list of *great principles* and tries them on my act, and if any of them even remotely fits, imagination suggests that I had in mind precisely that principle in performing my act. I have quarreled with a friend and killed him in a duel: I was defending the great principle of honor. I have seduced a woman and thrown her and the child into the street with no means of subsistence: I was following the great principle of freedom of attachments. I have concluded a contract with peasants which is disadvantageous to them, and have through lawsuits reduced them to penury: I was acting in the name of the great principle of legality. I have informed against a conspirator: I was upholding the great principle of the State. In a time of trial for literature, out of personal spite I trample in the mud the last remaining ideological organs of my own party: I am a champion of the great principle of independent opinion and the purity of literary manners. There is scarcely any such foul act which it would be absolutely impossible to bring under one of the great principles. It seems that from a higher point of view my act not only is not evil, it is good. Once again an unthinking act, despite the fact that its consequences have shown it to be harmful, has made me out to be a defender of great principles, a valuable participant in the universal harmony, the chosen instrument of a higher will.

The domain of idealization is very vast. In all aspects of its development it is based upon the urge to impart, in man's imagination, a conscious character to unconscious and semi-conscious actions, and to elevate conscious actions from a more elementary level to a higher one. At the same time, however, we must discriminate between, first, the cases of idealization which are *inevitable* since they are determined by the very nature of human thinking; second, the vast province of that *false* idealization against which the work of critical inquiry must be directed in the name of truth and justice; and finally, the few cases of *true* idealization, where this same critical inquiry must defend the real and rightful needs of men against those who would deny them.

The only idealization which is absolutely inevitable for man is the notion of *free will*, in virtue of which he cannot in any way rid himself of the subjective conviction that he voluntarily sets goals for himself and chooses means of achieving them. However convincingly objective *knowledge* demonstrates to man that all his "voluntary" actions and thoughts are nothing but necessary consequences of an antecedent series of events—external and internal, physical and psychic—the subjective *consciousness* that these actions and thoughts are voluntary remains a constant, inescapable illusion, even in the very process of demonstrating the universal determinism which rules both in the external world and in the spirit of man.

What is inevitable must of necessity be accepted. In the realm of human activity this involuntary idealization of one's motives becomes a fruitful basis of vast provinces of human intellectual labor, both scientific and philosophical. Quite independently of the extent to which the ends man sets himself and the means he chooses to achieve them are *in fact* real or illusory, these ends and means arrange themselves in his mind into a definite hierarchy of *better* and *worse*.

But scientific criticism sets to work establishing the *correct* hierarchy among them. An indisputable truth is set against a probable hypothesis, a faulty argument, an invention of fantasy, a contradictory concept. The ineffective means is distinguished from the effective, the harmful from the beneficial. The moral motive is distinguished from the whole mass of irrational, fortuitous, passionate, and selfish motives. To the province of those motives, thoughts, and actions in which man himself cannot discover the traces of a conscious will, he opposes the province of his other motives, thoughts, and actions, concerning which he cannot rid himself of the idea that he willed them, that he is responsible for them, and that other people similarly consider him to have this responsibility—however subject all of this is, equally with the former province, to the universal determinism.

By a process as inevitable for the human mind as the objective laws which rule in nature, the fundamental inner idealization of the voluntary establishment of goals and the voluntary selection of means sets before every individual a hierarchy of morally better and morally worse goals, leaving him only the ability to determine critically whether it is necessary in this critical examination to refashion the hierarchy and to regard something *else* as better and worse. The decision of the will and the choice of one or another action as a result of this decision prove always to be inevitable, but ethical criticism can credit this choice with a higher or lower significance and can charge the individual with responsibility for this choice in his own eyes and in the eyes of others who share the same convictions. This makes it possible to compare the province of theoretical *knowledge* with the province of moral *consciousness,* and in the latter province to take one's departure from the primary subjective *fact* of free will *for oneself,* independently of the theoretical significance of this fact. It provides a solid foundation for practical philosophy, and has permitted me in these Letters to speak to the reader of the moral duty of the individual, of the moral need for individuals to fight against moribund social institutions, of moral ideals, and of the historical progress which flows from them.

If the principle of personal responsibility for everything a man regards as a manifestation of his will must be recognized as an inevitable idealization, and for that reason cannot be eliminated, it is the only idealization entitled to this privilege. Everything avoidable should be admitted only on the basis of critical examination. . . .

Social institutions are the product of natural needs and inclinations. To the extent that these needs and inclinations are natural, to that extent, but no further, the institutions produced by them are legitimate. In history, however, an institution which is a product of one need has often proved suitable, for lack of something better, for satisfying other needs as well. As a result such an institution has been turned into an organ having the most diverse functions, and in this form—by being subjected to true and false idealization—it could be proclaimed as a party banner, as a highly important instrument of progress.

In such a case the task of critical thought is twofold. First, it must determine what real ambitions of the parties are concealed behind the words inscribed upon their banners. Second, it must discover the natural, and consequently the legitimate, need which called into existence the institution which is proclaimed on a party's banner as its fundamental principle. Through the former procedure, critical thought destroys the false idealization of those who advance an institution—which may in essence even be worthy of respect—in defense of ambitions that have nothing in common with it. Through the latter, critical thought combats both those who have made a fetish of a high-sounding word without understanding its meaning, and those other false idealizers who *deny* the legitimacy of a need that is entirely natural, and in so doing give rise either to a perversion of human nature or, more commonly, to hypocrisy.

The latter task has a positive as well as a negative side. By revealing a natural need or a natural inclination at the basis of a given social institution, critical thought thereby recognizes the legitimacy of these bases and demands the construction of social institutions on a foundation of *sincerity* of feeling, i.e., on a foundation of sincere regard for the needs and inclinations inherent in the nature of man. This realization in social institutions of moral ideals which are rooted in the very nature of man is a legitimate and truly human idealization of man's natural needs, in opposition to their *false* idealization in the guise of historically generated cultural institutions that in no way correspond to them.

This truly human idealization is fully scientific, because the element of subjective opinion is present in it only to the extent that it is completely inevitable in any investigation of psychic phenomena. A need is a real psychic fact, the particular features of which must simply be studied as fully as possible. Once a need has been established as natural it must be satisfied within the limits of its healthy operation, and social institutions must be sought which will best satisfy it. I may be mistaken in my definition of the natural need which underlies a particular social institution. I may be mistaken as to the consequences which in my view necessarily flow from a sincere regard for this need. A more expert investigator may uncover new sides to the latter and consequently construct a more correct theory of the corresponding social institutions. But the possibility of errors and their successive elimination in no way destroys the scientific character of the overall method. The tracing of social institutions to the needs which generate them, a sincere regard (i.e., a straightforward regard, one free from irrelevant considerations) for these needs on the part of the investigator, the demand to adapt social institutions to them—these can operate apart from all personal arbitrariness, apart from all dogmatic blindness, apart from all work of creative fantasy. This operation can be carried out strictly methodically, with all sources of personal error being eliminated. Consequently it is scientific, and its result—a theory of social institutions as they *ought to be* on the basis of clearly understood human needs—is a product of true and scientific idealization in accordance with need.

Thus every need admits of a legitimate and truly human idealization appropriate to it, just as we may reject only what has been introduced into it by culture; this is the limit of thought's relationship to it. By denying a law of nature we shall not abolish it, but shall only call forth a more pathological manifestation of the law, while hypocrisy prevails in the social institution. False idealization cannot make the slightest change in a law of nature. It only introduces falsehood into social institutions, which always makes it possible for the more cunning and less moral person to oppress the less cunning and more moral.

But it is precisely this falsehood and injustice, introduced into social institutions by petty egoistic interests under the screen of false idealization, that generates constant irritation and makes the existing social institutions precarious. The only way to make them more durable is to introduce real vitality into them, i.e., to replace their false idealization by true. It is in this that the work of thought on cultural institutions, which constitutes the advance of civilization, chiefly consists.

As the reader can see, in this process there is, properly speaking, nothing negative, destructive, or revolutionary. Thought strives constantly to make social institutions more durable by discovering their true bases in genuine human needs; through studying these needs, it fortifies social institutions with science and justice. What thought's critical inquiry rejects is exactly the

element that is making social institutions unstable. What it destroys is precisely what is threatening to destroy civilization. It
strives to prevent revolution, not to provoke it.[9]

Idealization and the State

Though it cannot be said of a single great social principle that
it has not been abused by idealization, in recent times scarcely
any principle has been subjected to this operation so extensively
as the principle of the *state*. . . .

All this compels us today to deal much more critically with a
principle which only recently was deified, compels us to expose
its false idealization and replace it with true: that is, by penetrating to the natural basis of the state in its simplest form, to
show in what way this principle is open to progress—to show
how it can satisfy the conditions of individual development and
of the embodiment of truth and justice in social institutions.

As long as people live together pursuing economic, moral, and
intellectual aims which each may freely modify or even renounce without fear of constraint, they constitute a *social* association to which everything juridical and political is alien. As
soon as they enter into a contract which is binding upon the
contracting parties their society enters a new phase of its existence. It is bound together only *juridically* if the compulsory
power which supervises the execution of the contract is vested
in persons who are not parties to the contract. It becomes
political when the authority which obliges the members of the
society to execute the contract is set up within the society itself.
A political society becomes a *state* when it causes the contract
which is binding upon the members who have entered into it to
be binding also upon persons who have never been asked to give
their consent to it or who consent only because they fear personal harm in the event of opposing it. Examples of the first three
forms are a scientific society, a legal trade association, and a
secret political organization.

It is clear from the foregoing that the state is as old as the
forcible subjection of individuals to conditions which are not

9. From the Ninth Letter, p. 145, and the Tenth Letter, pp. 146-151,
155-158.

of their own choosing. Since there has always been an immense number of persons in society who, through lack of intellectual cultivation, knowledge, or energy, have needed other persons who are more intelligent, knowledgeable, and energetic to choose a mode of life for them, so the state system had its root in the first pre-clan groups and clans, in the first nomadic tribes, and is still by no means limited to the so-called *political* organs of society. Wherever a man, without deliberation, submits to conditions of life which are not of his own choosing, he is submitting to the principle of the state. . . .

The principle of state obligation is, of course, a perfectly natural product dating from remote antiquity, and in fact the further we go back in antiquity the more extensive is its application. Initially it appears as the physical domination of some persons by others, subsequently it turns into an economic dependence, and finally—now by way of idealization—it becomes a moral force.

But in the earliest stages of the development of the state the principle of contract also appears, distinguishing the state from the simple subjection of one person to another. The head of the family, adult and strong, rules over the young children and the weaker women not on the basis of the state principle of compulsion but on the basis of personal pre-eminence. Similarly, the prophet commands the faithful as a result of his personal influence. The state principle makes its appearance in the family when there are adult members who *could* disobey the head but who instead *help* him govern the others; in the religious sect, when the prophet is surrounded not only by followers but by *aides* as well. And in general the state arises whenever a group of persons, in the name of their own interests, well or poorly understood, voluntarily *uphold* the obligatory character of certain decisions issuing from a person, an institution, or an elected council—an obligatory character which extends to other persons who have *not* entered this union voluntarily. Thus to the principle of *compulsion* is here joined the principle of *contract*— with this peculiarity, that the contract is concluded by a smaller number of people, while the compulsion extends to a larger number.

Of course, this extension of the principle of contract changes it materially. The whole moral and legal meaning of contract resides, as we have seen, in the obligation of the *honest* man to fulfill a condition which he has deliberately *accepted*. But here the contract is actually concluded by *some* persons, while the fiction of a contract is extended to *others* as well. The conclusion of a contract by one person in the name of others who have not the slightest comprehension of the contract which is being concluded, but who nevertheless are obliged to fulfill it, violates the most elementary demands of justice and thus contradicts the idea of progress.

What would a jurist think of a contract which is binding upon hundreds, thousands, even millions of people, but of which it is known with certainty that it had been drawn up, ratified, and made obligatory by a few persons who were in no way authorized to sign such a contract? How far can we regard as just a contract which is concluded by one generation and is binding upon all succeeding generations until they finally decide to break it by force or to drown it in blood? There is, of course, no justice in such contracts, and they presuppose one thing only: the existence of a powerful organization, or of a considerable majority of persons, for whom the contract is advantageous and who, thanks to their organization or their numbers, forcibly compel all those who are dissatisfied with the state contract to submit to it. Leave the state or fulfill the state contract—such is the dilemma confronting every subject.

If the number of those who are dissatisfied is small, they alone feel the force of this dilemma. They must either endure the painful yoke of laws which are odious to them or content themselves with sacrificing the most elementary comforts of life, with imprisonment, banishment, or execution, for failing to carry out these laws or for combating them. They can, in the end, emigrate. As long as the malcontents are scattered individuals, they will always be suppressed. The more prolonged the suppression and the more perverted the legal order under which it takes place, the more completely does such an environment demoralize its inhabitants by atrophying their clarity of thought, their strength of character, their capacity to have convictions and to fight for them, and finally their sense of social solidarity.

But as the malcontents join together in a growing social force and organize, it is no longer possible to ignore them, and the state system itself is threatened. The threats are of two sorts. If the malcontents are spread over the entire territory of the state or are concentrated in its chief centers, the state is threatened with alteration of its fundamental laws through reform or revolution. If, on the other hand, they are concentrated in one part of the state, it is threatened with disintegration. In both cases the cohesion of the state is precarious, and this because its laws represent a fictitious contract rather than a genuine one: a considerable number of persons are obliged to submit to the state contract who have never been consulted about it, have never consented to it, and submit to it only through weakness, want of energy, or inability to recognize their own rights and powers.

As the participation of individuals in the state contract increases, the contract becomes more stable: first, because its discomforts are more readily recognized, more properly discussed, and can more easily be eliminated through reform rather than revolution; second, because a greater number of individuals regard the law of the state as a contract binding upon them, while its opponents feel increasingly powerless and more readily submit to it. It is clear that the ideal state system is a society all members of which view the law as a mutual contract, consciously accepted by all, which permits of alteration by the general consent of the contracting parties, and which is compulsory only for those who have consented to it, precisely because they *have* consented to it and are subject to a penalty for violating it.

But the reader will see at once that the ideal thus derived from the very essence of the state principle works to negate this same principle. The state is distinguished from other social institutions by the fact that its contract is adopted by a *smaller* number of persons and is maintained by them as binding upon a *greater* number. The two sources of state cohesion—the natural principle of compulsion and the deliberative principle of contract—come into conflict because the latter, in the name of justice, strives to diminish the compulsion. Hence the inescapable conclusion that political progress has had to consist in the reduction of the role of the state principle in social life. And thus it is in reality. . . .

Does it seem a direct contradiction to make reduction of the role of the state principle in society a requirement for political progress? Does it seem that by weakening this principle, in the name of demands for progress in general, the party of progress is depriving itself of the best weapon for combating its opponents?

The idea that the role of the state principle decreases with the progress of society is by no means new. It was already expressed, incidentally, by the elder Fichte in a work which appeared in 1813, and it has been expressed repeatedly since that time. The anarchists made elimination of the state fundamental to their doctrine, denying the need for it even in a time of stubborn struggle against powerful opponents of progress—but with this it is now difficult to agree.

Reduction of the state element depends, of course, upon abatement of the need to defend the weak, to protect freedom of thought, and so on, with *state* force. As long as there are men who monopolize capital under the protection of the laws, and as long as the majority does not possess even the elementary means of development, state power is an indispensable weapon which a party fighting for progress or for reaction strives to appropriate. Given these conditions, critically-thinking individuals should regard it simply as a weapon in this fight, and can bend every effort to gain possession of this indispensable weapon and direct it toward the cultivation of progress and the suppression of reactionary parties.

But in using this weapon, those who fight for progress must remember that it has its peculiarities which oblige the agent of progress to treat it with extreme caution. In a battle it is perfectly natural to concern oneself with strengthening the weapon with which one is fighting; but strengthening the authority of the state can, by the very nature of this authority, be detrimental to social progress the moment it goes a little beyond what is absolutely necessary in the case at hand. It always coincides with an increase in the obligatory, compulsory element in social life, always stifles the moral development of the individual and the freedom of critical thought. This also is what constitutes the chief obstacle to progressive activity through state means. It has been responsible for the failure or the harmful influence of the eminent reformers who have decreed progress in a society unprepared for it.

It is difficult to define in each particular case the limit to the use of state power in the struggle for progress, but it seems most correct to assume that this power can be used to advantage only negatively—that is, only to overcome the obstacles to the free development of society posed by existing cultural forms. But this is an extremely debatable question.

As long as the state is a powerful factor in the struggle for progress and for reaction, the critically-thinking individual is justified in using it as a weapon to protect the weak; to extend truth and justice; to provide individuals with the means of developing physically, intellectually, and morally; to provide the majority with the minimum of comforts required to enter upon the path of progress; to provide the thinker with the means of expressing his ideas, and society with the opportunity of appraising them; to give social institutions the flexibility which will prevent them from ossifying and open them to changes which promote a broader understanding of truth and justice. This is true not only for the state such as it is in a particular age, but also for all the social institutions encountered by the individual in his cultural environment, as was said above in the Eighth Letter.

But, in working *with the aid* of the state for the scientific satisfaction of human needs in other social institutions, the agent of progress must remember that in itself the institution of the state does not correspond to any separate real need. Consequently, it can never be an *end* of progressive activity but is in all cases only a *means* for it, and thus must be modified in conformity with other *ruling* ends.

When vital functions are extremely unsound, very vigorous treatment may be needed. When the patient's condition is improving, the medication should be milder. A physician knows that his patient is not well until regular hygiene is sufficient and therapeutic measures can be completely eliminated.

Can human societies really aim at perpetual political therapy rather than a healthy life in accordance with the precepts of sociological hygiene? [10]

10. From the Thirteenth Letter, pp. 198, 201-205, 223-225.

NICHOLAS KONSTANTINOVICH MIKHAILOVSKY

[1842–1904]

THE SECOND MAJOR PHILOSOPHER of Populism was Nicholas Mikhailovsky, for a quarter of a century the Populists' theoretical guide within the Russian empire.

Mikhailovsky was born in the province of Kaluga, southwest of Moscow, in 1842. His father was a landowner whose financial position was so unfavorable by the end of the 1840's that he was forced to sell his land and serfs. The family moved to the town of Kostroma on the upper Volga, where Nicholas attended the local *gymnasium*. Orphaned by the age of thirteen, Nicholas was sent to Saint Petersburg in 1856 to pursue his interest in the natural sciences at the Saint Petersburg Mining Institute. In the capital he was rapidly swept up in the radical student enthusiasm of the post-Crimean period, and although he had a good record at the Institute and had completed the program, he was expelled without a degree in 1861 for leading student disturbances. In 1860, he had already begun to write for *Dawn*, the journal which had given Pisarev his start two years before, and he soon became known as a champion of radical causes, particularly women's rights.

Mikhailovsky shared the views of John Stuart Mill on the emancipation of women, and Mill's utilitarian moral philosophy in general was one of the chief intellectual influences on the young writer. He also drew inspiration from the Russian radical thinkers who preceded him, from Herzen and Belinsky to Lavrov; Lavrov's first philosophical essays began to appear soon after the young Mikhailovsky arrived in Saint Petersburg. Like

Lavrov, Mikhailovsky was strongly drawn to Proudhon, whose preaching of personal dignity and social justice contributed powerfully to the intensely moralistic cast of the thinking of the leading Populists. Their devotion to justice and the inseparable connection they saw between justice and truth are nowhere better expressed than in Mikhailovsky's often-quoted remarks (first written in 1889) on the meaning of the Russian word *pravda*, presented as the first selection below.

Mikhailovsky contributed to a number of journals during the sixties, but his literary career did not begin in earnest until 1869, when he became an editor of *Otechestvennyye Zapiski* (Annals of the Fatherland). All of Mikhailovsky's major theoretical writings were first published in this journal, which succeeded Chernyshevsky's *Contemporary* and Pisarev's *Russian Word* as the most influential and respected organ of Russian radicalism. First to appear was the long essay, "What Is Progress?" (1869), Mikhailovsky's fullest statement of his general philosophical outlook; excerpts from this essay form the second selection below.

In "What Is Progress?" Mikhailovsky formulates a moralistic positivism comparable to Lavrov's "anthropologism." Acknowledging that positivism has performed great services from the point of view of theoretical knowledge, where it shows man "the limits beyond which he faces eternal and invincible darkness," Mikhailovsky argues that in the practical sphere positivism is seriously inadequate, because it attempts to abstract from the "subjective" factor the feelings and desires which form an essential element in human action. Mikhailovsky subtitled his essay, "An Examination of the Ideas of Herbert Spencer," and he was particularly concerned to show that Spencer's attempt to approach human progress in a purely "objective" manner cannot succeed: progress can be understood only through a "subjective method" which explicitly introduces teleological considerations. Responding to Spencer's definition of progress as an increase in social complexity or heterogeneity, Mikhailovsky argues that Spencer has overlooked "human joys and sorrows," or the fate of the real individual: as society becomes more heterogeneous through the division of labor, the individual is mutilated by narrow specialization. Emphasizing the human evils of the division of labor, Mikhailovsky contends that not society but the individual should become more heterogeneous, while remaining integrated: the goal of progress must be to produce the "integral individual" whose diverse capacities are harmoniously developed.

Mikhailovsky's view of human progress brought him into conflict not only with Spencer but with Darwin as well—or at least with the Social Darwinists. Here, as in other areas, Mikhailovsky was indebted to the ideas of his friend and literary associate, the young Russian biologist Nicholas D. Nozhin (1843-1866). Nozhin, rejecting the application of Darwinian theory to the study of society, argued that cooperation, rather than struggle or competition, typically prevails among members of the same biological species. Mikhailovsky explored this subject in a number of important essays, among them "Darwin's Theory and Social Science" (1870), from which the third selection below is drawn. Representing competition as a natural product of the stultifying division of labor, Mikhailovsky foresees its replacement by cooperation. And accompanying such changes in social organization are changes in philosophical outlook, according to Mikhailovsky; speculative metaphysics, for example, is a product of a divided society and will disappear under true cooperation. Mikhailovsky went further than any Russian thinker before his time in developing a "sociology of knowledge."

A third evolutionary thinker with whom Mikhailovsky takes issue is, of course, Auguste Comte, who comes under criticism in both of the longer selections below. Mikhailovsky follows Comte in dividing the history of mankind into three stages, but in place of Comte's "theological," "metaphysical," and "positive" stages Mikhailovsky presents divisions which, characteristically, are defined by the type of *teleology* each involves. The first or lowest stage Mikhailovsky calls *objectively-anthropocentric:* in it man views himself as the center of reality, the focus of nature's concerns. At the second or *eccentric* (excentric) stage, man still attributes purposes to nature but finds them present equally in all of nature's parts rather than focused uniquely in him. Only in the highest or *subjectively-anthropo-*

centric stage does man realize that purposes do not reside in nature at all but issue solely from him—that they are human products, grounded in nothing outside man. At this stage all forms of supernaturalism are abandoned and man reigns supreme over nature. Mikhailovsky's further elaboration of the theory of cultural evolution includes a distinction between *level* and *type* of civilization: while, for example, industrialized Western nations occupy a level of civilization higher than that of agrarian Russia, the latter, with the commune, represents a superior *type* of civilization capable of greater ultimate advance.[1]

In 1873, Mikhailovsky was invited by Lavrov to join him in Paris in editing the revolutionary journal, *Forward!* But Mikhailovsky declined to emigrate, preferring to remain a legal if less outspoken advocate of Populist socialism in the homeland. He played a major role in disseminating Populist ideas in the seventies, despite the fact that he was sometimes critical of the Populists' tendency to idealize the commune. Although he subsequently moved more in the direction of revolutionary activism, and in the late seventies was associated with the underground People's Will party, Mikhailovsky managed, through circumspection and through mastery of the "Aesopian" language for evading censorship, to escape any official action against him aside from a short imprisonment in 1866 and occasional periods of banishment from Saint Petersburg.

In 1884, *Annals of the Fatherland* was forced by the government to cease publication, and Mikhailovsky went into semi-retirement. By 1892, however, he was back in the literary forefront—this time as an editor of the journal, *Russkoye Bogatstvo* (Wealth of Russia). Revered as the grand old man of Populist socialism, he carried on what he had earlier named "the struggle for individuality"—now chiefly against the Marxist socialism of Plekhanov and others—until his death in Saint Petersburg in 1904.

1. See the discussion in Thomas G. Masaryk, *The Spirit of Russia*, trans. E. and C. Paul, New York, 1955, II, 147-148.

SELECTED BIBLIOGRAPHY

Works:

Aside from the following selections, none of Mikhailovsky's writings has been translated into English. "What Is Progress?" has been translated in full into French as *Qu'est-ce que le progrès?* (Paris, 1897).

Secondary Sources:

James H. Billington, *Mikhailovsky and Russian Populism*, Oxford, 1958.

Thomas G. Masaryk, *The Spirit of Russia*, trans. E. and C. Paul, New York, 1955, II, 136-190.

V. V. Zenkovsky, *A History of Russian Philosophy*, trans. George L. Kline, 2 vols., London and New York, 1953, pp. 362-374.

Francis Randall, "Mikhailovski's 'What Is Progress'," in J. Curtiss, ed., *Essays in Russian and Soviet History*, New York, 1963.

[NICHOLAS MIKHAILOVSKY]

Pravda *

Every time I think of the word *pravda* I cannot help admiring
its striking inner beauty. Apparently there is no word like it in
any European language. Only in Russian, it seems, are truth and
justice designated by the same word and fused, as it were, into
one great whole.

Pravda in this vast sense of the word has always been , the
goal of my endeavors. I have always been not merely dissatisfied but outraged when *pravda* as truth is separated from
pravda as justice, when the *pravda* of the theoretical heavens
is cut off from the *pravda* of the practical earth. And con-
versely, the noblest worldly practice, the most exalted moral and
social ideals have always seemed to me pitifully impotent when
divorced from truth and science. I have always believed and I
believe now that it is possible to find a point of view from
which *pravda* as truth and *pravda* as justice can go hand in
hand, each enriching the other. In any case, to elaborate such
a point of view is the highest task with which the mind of man
can be confronted, and to fulfill it no effort is too great. To look
reality and its reflection—*pravda* as truth, objective *pravda*—
fearlessly in the eye while at the same time preserving *pravda*
as justice, subjective *pravda*—such has been the task of my
whole life.

It is not an easy task. Too often the serpents of this world
are not lacking in dove-like purity, and the doves in serpent-
like wisdom. Too often the men who set out to rescue some
moral or social ideal are turned aside by an unpleasant truth,
while others, on the contrary, men of objective knowledge, too
often strive to raise a naked fact to the level of an immutable
principle.

All the problems which have occupied me at various times—
problems of free will and necessity, the limits of our knowledge,

* Translated for this volume by James P. Scanlan, from the Preface to
Sochineniya N. K. Mikhailovskovo, St. Petersburg, 1896, I, v-vi.

the organic theory of society, the application of Darwin's theory to social questions, the problem of public interests and public opinions, problems of the philosophy of history, ethics, aesthetics, economics, politics, literature—have occupied me exclusively from the standpoint of this great dual *pravda*. I have engaged in countless polemical bouts, have responded to the most diverse issues of the day, once again to promote the establishment of this same *pravda*, which, like the sun, must be reflected both in the boundless ocean of abstract thought and in the smallest drops of blood, sweat, and tears shed in a given moment.

[NICHOLAS MIKHAILOVSKY]

What Is Progress? *

Spencer repeatedly cites Guizot's *History of Civilization*, drawing arguments from it to support his analogies and conclusions. But he seems to have overlooked a suggestion the book contains that is not devoid of interest—the suggestion, namely, that there are two types of progress—the progress of society and the personal development of man—and that these two types of progress do not always perfectly coincide and sometimes form unequal parts of the sum total of civilization. The word "progress" is used here in the generally accepted sense of improvement in the direction of welfare—the sense Spencer repudiates as interfering with research.

Whatever Guizot's inferences and conclusions, his thesis of the dual character of progress has its share of truth. And however assiduously Spencer tries to avoid the teleological sense of the word "progress," his survey of the possible types of evolution must contain either an estimate of *both* personal evolution and the evolution of society, or else an indication that these two types of progress coincide. Now he has shown very well and in quite adequate detail that society—the ideal person—evolves like an organism: it proceeds from the homogeneous to the heterogeneous, from the simple to the complex, through gradual disintegration and differentiation. Very good. But what is happening all this time to the real person—the member of society? Does he himself experience the same process of evolution, on the model of organic progress? Spencer answers this question in passing, affirmatively. We shall try to answer it in more detail, negatively.

Primitive society is on the whole an almost completely homogeneous mass. All its members are occupied with the same tasks, possess the same knowledge, have the same customs and

* Translated for this volume by James P. Scanlan, from *Chto takoye progress?*, Secs. 3-5, 10, as printed in *Sochineniya N. K. Mikhailovskovo*, St. Petersburg, 1896, I, 31-32, 34-36, 41-42, 54-56, 64, 70-72, 75-76, 148-150.

habits. But each of them taken separately is quite heterogeneous: he is a fisherman, a hunter, and a herdsman; he knows how to make boats and weapons, how to build himself a hut, and so on. In a word, each member of primitive, homogeneous society combines in himself all the powers and capacities which can develop, given the cultural level and the local physical conditions of the time.

But then the society first begins to divide into rulers and ruled. Certain individuals come from without or are singled out from the most homogeneous mass, and in the course of time they adopt a mode of life distinct from that of the remainder of the society; they leave the muscular labor to others, while they themselves gradually become specialists in activity of the nervous system. The society has taken a step from homogeneity toward heterogeneity, but the individuals who make it up have moved, on the contrary, from heterogeneity to homogeneity. With some, the muscular system has begun to develop at the expense of the nervous system, and with others, vice versa. Previously, each member of the society knew how to build a hut and how to catch animals, but now half of them have lost the habits connected with these occupations, while on the other hand they have learned how to rule, to heal, to tell fortunes, and so on. . . . Subsequent differentiations within the ruling class have the same dual character: they breed heterogeneity within the social order and, on the contrary, homogeneity and narrowness in the separate individuals.

We get the same result when we compare primitive society with the present condition of the lower classes. Take the labor of the savage on the one hand and of the contemporary factory worker on the other. The savage decides to build himself a hut. He himself chooses the right trees, fells them himself, hauls them into place himself, makes the framework and does the finishing himself. Suppose that the hut he has built is a very poor one—that is not the point. All the time he was working he was living a full life. While he was sweating and straining in the forest his labor was not merely physical: the choice of trees, of the route for transporting them, of the place to build—all this demands a certain intellectual effort. Furthermore, all the time he is working the savage is thinking of his future life in the hut he is struggling to build, thinking of the comforts that will grace his life and the life of his family; every corner and every chink suggests things to him. Similarly, he brings his pitiful conception of beauty into play in planning the hut and puts to work all of his meager knowledge of physics and mathematics. In short, in his work the savage is living with his whole being.

Quite the contrary picture is presented by the labor of the factory worker today in those areas in which the division of labor has proceeded furthest. For example, the manufacture of pocket watches, according to Babbage, consists of 102 separate operations, in accordance with the number of separate parts in the watch mechanism; each of a hundred men engaged in this work spends his entire life bent over the same wheels or screws or cogs, and only the master watchmaker who puts the separate parts of the mechanism together knows how to do anything besides his own specialty. Naturally such monotonous occupation excludes any kind of intellectual activity, or at least reduces it to the bare minimum. As Schiller says: by eternally occupying himself with some fragment of the whole, man himself becomes a fragment.

In the armaments works at Tula, the division of labor has been carried to such a point that the gunsmith not only spends all his life fashioning triggers or firing pins or boring the holes in barrels, but bequeaths his specialty to his children. Unvarying, monotonous activity can only result in simpler rather than more complex organization, and in the organism must lead to a more or less extensive homogeneity, which its posterity could acquire simply through the hereditary transmission of the organism's characteristics, were it not that in this case the natural factor of inheritance is further intensified by the social factor. It is understandable, then, that in the course of a few generations of Tula gunsmiths we encounter an ever-increasing transition from heterogeneity to homogeneity. Their ancestors made entire guns, and thus had to take into consideration facts which are completely unnecessary and useless to the descendants, who are only boring barrels or making firing pins. Thus the ancestors were more heterogeneous than the descendants, and at the same time the rise of these specialist descendants has promoted the heterogeneity of society, i.e., its evolution.

In constructing his outline of social evolution, Spencer refers to the works of economists in which there are detailed descriptions of the transition of industrial organization from homogeneity to heterogeneity through the division of labor. But Spencer seems to forget here that, if not the corporation economists, then their adversaries have examined in no less detail the double import of the division of labor, namely its property (retaining Spencer's terminology) of increasing the heterogeneity of society while at the same time diminishing the heterogeneity of the worker. . . .

If every development of the whole can take place only at the expense of the development of the parts, if in every particular act of evolution there exist two elements: one active, progressive, passing from homogeneity to heterogeneity, and the other passive, a victim of evolution, as it were, passing from heterogeneity to homogeneity—then how is the evolution of society reflected in the fate of its members? The answer is clear: if society makes a transition from homogeneity to heterogeneity, then the process of integration in the citizens which corresponds to this transition must proceed from heterogeneity to homogeneity. In short, individual progress and social evolution (on the model of organic evolution) are mutually exclusive, just as the evolution of organs and the evolution of the whole organism are mutually exclusive. . . .

What do the advocates of the so-called "woman question" (which in reality is just as much a man's question) want? They are demanding the extension of women's intellectual horizons and a certain role for women in social affairs, i.e., they are demanding individual heterogeneity, which must make society less heterogeneous, for to a certain degree it lessens the difference between men and women. What do their opponents want? To maintain the *status quo*, i.e., to keep women homogeneous and society heterogeneous. In what do the reforms of the present reign consist? In making society less heterogeneous and the individual more heterogeneous. What are the abolitionists striving to attain? The reduction of the differences between the white and colored populations, i.e., social homogeneity, and at the same time the extension of the rights of the colored people and a rise in their moral and intellectual level, i.e., individual heterogeneity. In a word, every social question takes both of these forms at once, because the differentiation of society, as a whole, is always and everywhere accompanied by the integration of the citizens, as parts. . . .

To plumb Spencer's error to the bottom, let us examine the analogy he sets up between an organism and society. . . .

Though Spencer counsels us not to forget what is, according to his own opinion, the most important point of difference between society and an organism, he nevertheless forgets it himself. This is shown most clearly in the cleverest part of his analogy—the parallel between Parliament and the brain. If the individual's brain receives not the actual sensations immediately impressed upon the nerve-endings, but rather representations of these sensations, nevertheless the organism, possessing a corporate consciousness, experiences pain and pleasure as a whole. Consequently, to express it in the metaphorical language of Spencer's analogy, the interests of the brain are solidary with the interests of the whole organism, and in it there are no Tories and Whigs, no radicals and Chartists. But the English workers in no way benefit from the fact that their interests and sufferings are not immediately felt by the House of Commons but are "represented" in it. In an organism it is the whole that experiences pain and pleasure, not the parts; in society it is the parts that experience pain and pleasure, not the whole. And no cleverness or erudition can abolish this fundamental difference, connected with the fundamental difference between the physiological and the social division of labor, which in its turn is connected with the equally fundamental difference between organic and social evolution.

This is in fact the third time Spencer has ignored human joys and sorrows, though all three times the wings of his thought have beat against them and he has bypassed them by the most diverse routes. Ordering art to depict past life only, he omits the concerns of the present through simple oversight, since the principle of contrast does not exclude from the tasks of art the communication of contemporary phenomena. Pursuing the parallel between organic and social progress, he consciously turns away from the happiness of mankind, since he frankly declares his disapproval of this point of view. Setting up an analogy between natural and social organisms, he ignores the pain and pleasure of men through a double oversight: he forgets not only the pain and pleasure but also his own reminder of them.

If in all these cases Spencer had actually reached the truth, we would say nothing and could say nothing against his objective method. In this event success would justify the means, whatever we had thought of them apart from their results. But we see that this is not so; . . . in all three of these cases he has fallen into gross errors. And since there can be no question of Spencer's intellectual prowess, the question arises: Is it legitimate to eliminate the teleological element from sociological investigations? Can the objective method give good results in sociology? Perhaps the sociologist has no logical right, so to speak, to eliminate man from his work—man as he is, with all his sorrows and desires. Perhaps the terrible image of suffering humanity, in league with the logic of things, revenges itself upon anyone who forgets it, upon anyone who is not imbued with a sense of its sufferings. Perhaps the objective point of view, obligatory for the natural scientist, is completely unsuitable for sociology, the object of which—man—is identical with the subject. Perhaps, as a consequence of this identity, the thinking subject can attain to truth only when he is fully merged with the thinking object and is not separated from him even for an instant—i.e., when he enters into his interests, lives his life, thinks his thoughts, shares his feelings, experiences his sufferings, weeps his tears. . . .

In the first half of the present century a new philosophical school arose in the West which sought to avoid . . . the interference of the subjective element. We speak of positivism. . . .

Every ethico-political doctrine has its motto, by which, as an end, its practical motives are summed up. But on the banner of positivism there is no such motto. Its principles are purely scientific, not philosophical. Positivism prides itself on the fact that in it philosophy and science blend into one whole—and it so prides itself with perfect justice. By this I do not mean to credit the principles of positivism with philosophical significance, but only to say that positivism does not embrace all aspects of life.

The principle of the conformity of phenomena to laws is as pure and irreproachable as a virgin. But like a virgin it may remain sterile, for it contains no fertilizing principle; as with a virgin, there is no guaranteeing into whose hands it will fall and what it will give mankind. Comte himself felt this. "One must be very careful," he says, "that the scientific conviction that social phenomena are subject to immutable natural laws does not degenerate into a systematic tendency toward fatalism and optimism, which are equally immoral (*dégradants*) and dangerous; thus only those whose moral level is sufficiently high can profitably study sociology" (*Cours de phil. pos.*, Vol. IV, p. 190). . . .

But why, from the point of view of positivism, are fatalism and optimism immoral and dangerous? "Without praising or condemning political facts," Comte says, . . . "positive sociology, like all other sciences, sees in them nothing but simple objects of observation and views each phenomenon from a dual point of view—from the point of view of both its harmony with co-existing facts and its connection with antecedent and subsequent states of human evolution" (*Cours*, IV, 293 . . .). How can we connect this purely objective attitude toward political facts . . . with deprecatory remarks about fatalism and optimism? Fatalism and optimism are simply political facts, not subject to condemnation from the standpoint of positivism; they necessarily harmonize with co-existing facts and are connected with antecedent and subsequent facts. If it is said that the expressions "immoral" and "dangerous" themselves define the connection of fatalism and optimism with subsequent facts, this can only mean that the program of approaching political facts objectively is unrealizable; that in the realm of the phenomena of social life observation is inevitably linked with moral evaluation to such a degree that one can refrain from "praising or condemning political facts" only by failing to understand their significance. But moral evaluation is the result of a subjective process of thought, whereas positivism particularly prides itself on using an objective method in sociology.

Further, if the objective method is fully adequate to sociological investigations, then why is a high moral level needed? Apparently the conviction that phenomena conform to law is, by itself, not enough. Very good. But how is one's presence on a higher moral level expressed in sociological investigations? Evidently from this height a man can see something which is not accessible to the objective investigation which alone is recognized as legitimate by positivism. Thus it turns out that there is something lacking in Comte's system, and something very important.

I am pleased to be able to refer here, in support of my own cursory observations, to an outstanding article by Mr. P. L. [Peter Lavrov], "Problems of Positivism and Their Solution" (*Contemporary Review*, May): "The objective element in ethics, politics, and sociology," says this esteemed author, "is limited to the actions of individuals, to social institutions, and to historical events. These are subject to objective description and classification. But to *understand* them, it is necessary to consider the *ends* for which the actions of individuals are only means, the *ends* which are embodied in the social institutions, the *ends* which generate the historical event. But what is an end? It is something desirable, agreeable, obligatory. All these categories are purely subjective and at the same time are accessible to all individuals. Consequently, when these phenomena are involved in an investigation they compel us to employ a subjective method and at the same time permit us to do so fully scientifically" (137). In another place Mr. P. L. quite rightly observes that by eliminating the subjective method in politics and ethics, positivism even prevents itself from justifying its own existence.

Teleology, in the sense of a doctrine of the ends which the individual sets himself, has no place in positivism, as a consequence of the absence of the subjective method and consequently of moral evaluation. Thus when Comte or one of his disciples . . . approves or disapproves of some social phenomenon, then however apt the evaluation, it is alien to the system, is not connected with it organically. Where there is no teleology there can be no moral rules, no praise or blame such as Comte himself pronounces, as we have seen. . . .

Similarly, when Comte says: "This new social philosophy (i.e., the positive), by its nature, is capable of realizing today all the legitimate desires which revolutionary politics can produce" and so on (*Cours*, IV, 148)—when Comte says this, the expression "legitimate desires" is left quite undefined. We know what desires are legitimate from the standpoint of the present political theories of the reactionaries, the conservatives, and the revolutionaries, from the standpoint of the individualists, the socialists, the clericalists, the eclectics, and so on. . . . From the standpoint of the objective method which is the characteristic feature of positive sociology, the expression "legitimate" desire can mean only "attainable" desire. But every ethico-political doctrine that has ever existed has regarded its desires as attainable. Let us suppose that positivism, linked so closely with science, can determine better than other philosophical systems and political theories which desires are attainable and which are not. But to do so it is first necessary to have a desire, and while of course every *positivist* has them, *positivism* poses no ideals, because an ideal is the result of a subjective attitude.

Mankind has harbored many unattainable and in that sense illegitimate desires, and many minds and lives have been destroyed by them. Perhaps the greatest service of positivism is to show man the limits beyond which he faces eternal and invincible darkness. To try to transcend these limits is to have unattainable and illegitimate desires. So teaches positivism. We shall go further. These illegitimate desires are a crime against that humanity to the service of which all man's powers should be dedicated. We are speaking here of purely theoretical questions, of the essence and the beginning of things, of ultimate principles, and so on.

But in the realm of practice the matter is complicated both by the complexity of the questions themselves and by the absolutely unavoidable interference . . . of the subjective element, i.e., personal feelings and desires. On a given practical question at any given moment several diametrically opposed desires may be attainable, and in this case what solution a positivist will adopt will depend upon his personal character. But this, of course, will always be the case, and not with positivists alone. The difference is that the follower of any other doctrine receives from it a more or less powerful immediate impulse in one direction or another. But the positivist receives no impulse from his doctrine. He can remain a positivist and move to the right or to the left, can, like Dumas, Nélaton, and other scientific luminaries of present-day France, prove to be the most humble servant of the Second Empire, or follow some completely different program. . . .

The exclusive use of the objective method in sociology—if that were possible—would be tantamount to measuring weight with a yardstick. From this it does not follow, however, that the objective method must be completely eliminated from this field of investigation, but only that the supreme control must be vested in the subjective method.

But then the question arises: if the objective method cannot satisfy all the demands of social science, cannot give it a supreme principle, which of the several subjective principles that can be suggested should be chosen as the best? This is the question we have been answering in this entire article. The fullest possible and most diversified division of labor among man's organs, and the least possible division of labor among men—such is the principle we propose, such is the goal we point to as the best.

It seems to us that this principle is free from every one of the defects inherent in all the principles of politics, ethics, and economics hitherto accepted. They are all either intended for one particular field, as a consequence of which no reconciliation can be effected between the different departments of social science; or else they are reached by a metaphysical route, are lacking in empiricism, and illegitimately ignore the science of nature, as a consequence of which no reconciliation can be effected between science and life. On the other hand, our principle embraces all realms of human activity, all aspects of life. We do not draw it from the depths of our personal spirit.

and we do not recommend it as acquired via a supernatural route. It is firmly rooted in objective science, because it flows from exact investigation of the laws of organic evolution. It is true that Spencer, Draper, and many others, men of substance and authority, have taken their departure from these same laws and have arrived at diametrically opposed conclusions. But this circumstance in no way shakes our principle, since guided solely by it we have shown the complete groundlessness of Spencer's views and have even found it possible to suggest their historical causes.

Setting aside everything that is unfinished and incompletely expressed here, the reader is left with a clear and simple question: can the division of labor among individuals and the division of labor among the organs of a single individual be reduced to a common denominator, as Spencer and others suppose, or are they two phenomena which are mutually exclusive and which exist in eternal and inevitable antagonism, as we affirm? This question can be decided by the facts of objective science, and moreover by facts which are already established and are not open to doubt. If these facts actually support Spencer's answer to the question of the division of labor—which we consider the fundamental question of social science—all our considerations must fall by the wayside. If not, if truth is on our side, it remains only to apply the principle we have proposed, as a sociological axiom, to the solution of particular questions.

To the question we have posed—what is progress?—we answer: Progress is the gradual approach to the integral individual, to the fullest possible and the most diversified division of labor among man's organs and the least possible division of labor among men. Everything that impedes this advance is immoral, unjust, pernicious, and unreasonable. Everything that diminishes the heterogeneity of society and thereby increases the heterogeneity of its members is moral, just, reasonable, and beneficial.

[NICHOLAS MIKHAILOVSKY]

The Three Stages of History *

The disturbed mental state of the man who has withdrawn into himself and sees himself as the special object of protection or persecution by the surrounding world sometimes assumes manifestly pathological forms, accompanied by illusions and hallucinations. Now many anthropologists have repeatedly observed that a very fruitful parallel can be drawn between certain pathological phenomena in modern civilization and phenomena in the life of primitive man. While we cannot fully accept this parallel in the general form in which it is usually expressed, the psychological facts referred to can, it seems, help to explain the early stages of human history. Primitive man, naked, dirty, and alone, having barely become man, having not yet come to know anything but his personal desires and needs, must naturally spend all his life in a disturbed, egocentric frame of mind. And without a doubt the source of that strange phenomenon in the life of savages which is known, thanks to many observers, as "pantophobia" (fear of everything) lies in the insufficient development of a system of cooperation among men and in the paucity of sympathetic feelings and impressions experienced by them.

Imagine this savage, two-legged beast, in whom, however, human thoughts already swarm. Imagine him in the luxuriant tropics, full of sounds both terrible and delightful, full of dangers and at the same time bountiful to the point of superfluity. Or imagine him in the cold and gloom of the north, where a freezing wind howls and snowy plains stretch out endlessly. And amid all this grandeur, amid these terrors and luxuries, amid this reign of cold and hunger, man lives and moves. He hears the thunderclap, the roar of the surf, the wailing of the wind, the murmur of the treetops in the dense forest

* Translated for this volume by James P. Scanlan, from N. K. Mikhailovsky, "Teoriya Darvina i obshchestvennaya nauka," *Sochineniya N. K. Mikhailovskovo*, St. Petersburg, 1896, I, 196-197, 199-201, 205-208, 210-215.

which he enters timorously, glancing from side to side and pricking up his ears at every rustle. What are these noises? He has a ready answer. He knows the inflections his own voice takes when he is pleased or displeased, when he is hungry or filled: he seizes upon this wretched analogy and erects a whole world-view upon it. Man creates gods for himself, in his own image and likeness.

But if the thunderclap signifies someone's wrath, to whom is it addressed and whom does it threaten? Whom indeed! Does this two-legged beast really know anyone besides himself? Can he really take into consideration the fact that right there, not two steps from him, another of these same two-legged creatures has taken the same thunderclap to be addressed to *him*, while over there still a third two-legged beast has recoiled in terror from a bush in which he heard the sinister sound of a rattle-snake, and the fact that in the head of this third two-legged beast there already dimly glimmers the same egocentric resolution of the question of the significance of this sound? Isn't this two-legged beast just like [a modern man] who has withdrawn completely into himself, and knows, sees, and understands nothing but his own individuality?

Over many centuries the individualistic existence of primitive man is gradually broken up through cooperation with his fellows. He comes to recognize the solidarity of his interests with the interests of his family, his clan, his tribe, and so on. He learns to know another's life vicariously, and his teleology broadens. Its character, however, for a long time yet remains unchanged, i.e., for a long time yet man sees himself as the object of the special protective or hostile attention of the surrounding world. If this objectively-anthropocentric teleology undergoes any alteration, it is not qualitative but purely quantitative. Depending upon the course of historical events, there is now a broadening and now a narrowing in the focus of nature, in the object of the special attention of all forces, natural and non-natural—i.e., there is a reduction or an increase in the number of cooperating individuals who see themselves as under the protection of the same forces. . . . In accordance with these fluctuations in the growth and the historical forms of coopera-

tion among men, the direction and the intensity of the objectively-anthropocentric teleology change as well. It attains the
highest stage of its development when no one ethnological, political, or professional caste but rather all mankind, humanity
in general, is taken as the center of nature. Such is the exalted
teaching of Buddha. Higher than this the objectively-anthropocentric teleology cannot go. And after this final quantitative
alteration in the primitive teleology, a qualitative alteration takes
place. The last straw at which a drowning anthropocentrism
clutches disappears from sight, and it turns out that

> . . . *unfühlend*
> *Ist die Natur:*
> *Es leichtet die Sonne*
> *Über Bös und Gute . . .*[1]
>   —Goethe

Learning, observation of the phenomena around him con-
vinces man that nature is in no way especially concerned with
his fate. But the same human thinking that has arrived at this
negative conclusion is affected by the existing forms of social
cooperation. Surrounded on all sides by an eccentric social
system—i.e., by a system in which cooperation takes place
through the division of labor—this thinking erects a new teleology, the eccentric teleology.

We have already spoken of the fate of human thought under
the influence of the division of labor. We have seen that, along
with the final practical division of labor into intellectual and
physical, man is bisected with respect to theory as well; that
science and philosophy strive to run off in different directions,
i.e., a practical split occurs even among those who specialize
in intellectual activity. Just as the representatives of intellectual
labor and physical labor enter into a terrible if not always
bloody struggle for existence with one another, so the representatives of science and philosophy join combat with one
another. The former bury themselves in trifles, making no
attempt to unite them into one whole, and with a disdainful

---

1. "Nature is unfeeling: It makes the sun shine on both the good and the
bad."—TRANS.

smile they oppose the paltry results they attain by empirical means to the arbitrary transcendental generalizations of metaphysical philosophy. The metaphysicians, on the other hand, view these pitiful drudges, these "slaves of the senses and experience," with no less disdain, and endeavor to explain and embrace the whole universe by pure thought (pure in the sense that it is free of any admixture of sense impressions).

Eccentrism, the breaking up of man into independent and mutually hostile fragments, stupefies some and paralyzes others. The stupefied cannot raise their eyes to the heavens, the paralyzed do not examine the earth. The characteristic feature of the eccentric period in the evolution of thought consists, as we have seen, in the attempts of bifurcated, sundered men to renounce their empirical substance. Some think it possible to get along without any theory; others, on the contrary, think they can construct a theory by disregarding experience and observation.

In fact, however, both prove to be equally impossible, for however much history has done to fragment man he is still a single whole, and thought is connected with sense impressions by an indissoluble bond. The data of experience necessarily group themselves in a certain order—i.e., they are generalized, theorized about—while theories necessarily flow from the data of experience and observation. The fact is, as Haeckel says, that "the pure empirics are content with an incomplete and unclear philosophy of which they themselves are unconscious, while the pure philosophers are content with an equally unsatisfactory empyrean.". . . Hence one cannot rely on the assurance of the specialist-empirics that they adhere to no philosophy; though this philosophy in all likelihood is very meager and poor, it unquestionably exists. Similarly one cannot believe the metaphysicians who maintain that they have procured the data of their philosophy through pure thought independent of sense perception; though their generalizations rest upon very poorly investigated facts of experience and observation, there can be no doubt that they really flow from these facts.

The metaphysicians who embrace the universe by pure thought proudly reject the ancient superstition that had placed the human personality—either the individual, real personality or the juridical, ideal personality—at the center of nature. This superstition lies at their feet, vanquished by the successes of science and social cooperation. But the metaphysicians, in scornfully trampling one historical form of teleology underfoot, are establishing a new one. "No," says the eccentric, "man is not the focus and goal of nature. That is the wretched, crude, egoistic teleology. In studying nature we must forget that we are human beings, must forget our aspirations, desires, and needs, and then we shall see that the true, legitimate teleology consists in finding purposefulness in nature in general, in the belief that nature realizes itself through a certain pre-established plan which has no one set center but antecedently determines the location, direction, and force of the action of each tiny atom. Let us cast off the preconceived notion that nature cares more for us than for any of its other parts; it is realizing its goals not for man but at every step it takes, in every infusorian, in every crystal."

Thus speaks the eccentric-metaphysician, recommending his conclusion as having been reached through contemplation by pure thought. It is not difficult, however, to uncover the quite real, observational supports on which this eccentric teleology is constructed. Likewise, it is not difficult to show that, despite the fundamental difference between this teleology and the teleology of primitive people, the two have many more features in common than they may appear to have at first glance. It is not difficult, finally, even to become convinced of the fact that the eccentric teleology actually involves no renunciation of human needs, aspirations, desires, preconceived opinions, that self-delusion here is rooted simply in the lack of control by consciousness. . . .

Mysticism, i.e., the erection of a subjective idea to the level of an objective existence, and anthropomorphism, i.e., copying God's person from the person of man and the circumstances surrounding him—this is the ground shared by the objectively-anthropocentric and the eccentric system of thought. Without doubt the fact that they have these features in common was significant in leading Haeckel, and many others as well, to confuse these world-views under the general name of "dualistic" or "teleological" as opposed to "monistic" or "mechanistic." Only eccentrism is strictly dualistic, and if both the objectively-anthropocentric and the eccentric world-views are with equal right called teleological, nevertheless between them there is, from the human—i.e., the only scientific and just—point of view a very material distinction. . . .

Ever since thinking ceased to be a means and became an independent end—a *Selbstzweck*, as the Germans say—accessible only to one part of society, the bond between this part and the rest of society has been broken, or at least the consciousness of this bond has been lost. The thinking part of society significantly broadens its psychical substance in a particular direction. Experience and observation gradually convince these people who gain security through the labor of others that the beliefs of their ancestors and of the representatives of physical labor who live side by side with them are nothing but fairy tales produced by frightened fantasy. On the other hand, the same result is attained by the modification, brought about by the division of labor, in the direction and intensity of sympathetic feeling among men. If history could proceed in such a way as not to admit of anything resembling organic evolution in society—i.e., the emergence of heterogeneous parts having special functions—then the growth of learning would lead mankind from objective anthropocentrism directly to subjective anthropocentrism. Man would straightway, without any eccentric detours, have been convinced that the formula, everything is created for man's use, is perfectly just, but in a subjective rather than an objective sense: that nothing has been created for man, that he has to obtain everything by his own sweat and blood, but that by virtue of his interests he himself, through the power of his consciousness, stands at the center of nature and bends it to his will.

But the growth of learning under a system in which cooperation takes place through the division of labor does not carry a view of the world this far. Thinking, as a specialized function of the social organism, provides only the negative result: nothing has been created for man. But eccentric thought, in its purity and its isolation from physical labor and the impressions of the senses, seeks its supports within itself: consequently, observing in itself certain aspirations and purposes, it imposes these upon nature as well. Now if purposes and aspirations exist in nature, they must issue from some man-like person—a deity. This is not, however, the primitive anthropocentric's deity, who gave the rattlesnake his unique tail so that he would forewarn man of the danger by the noise he makes, and created the snake itself to punish and frighten man.

The man of eccentrism has already been so fragmented, has to such an extent ceased to be an indivisible *man* and approached the condition of some isolated *organ,* that the purposes of Providence can no longer reside for him in *man;* he sees them as spread over all space and time, being distributed in conformity with the special physiological function which man in his capacity as a special organ of the social organism has cultivated at the expense of the rest. Such is the essential difference between the objectively-anthropocentric and the eccentric teleologies.

Evidently Auguste Comte did not sufficiently consider the meaning and significance of what he calls the metaphysical phase of evolution (which, as we have already indicated, relates to eccentrism as part to whole) when he says: "Evidently the theological system of belief rests upon the idea of a universe directed in the interests of man. The absurdity of this idea must inevitably become clear even to the most ordinary minds as soon as it is shown that the earth is not the center of the celestial movements but only a minor planet revolving about the sun just like its neighbors Venus and Mars, the inhabitants of which have just as much ground to ascribe pre-eminent significance to themselves. Semi-philosophers, wishing to retain the doctrine of purposefulness and providential laws, but rejecting current views of the significance of the purposes of nature and the activity of Providence, have fallen, it seems to me, into a very important and material inconsistency. For having excluded every clear and tangible consideration of the interests of man, one can no longer see any sort of intelligible goal in providential activity. Thus recognition of the earth's movement necessarily destroyed the foundation of the whole theological edifice" (*Cours de philosophie positive*, II, 117).

By "semi-philosophers" here Comte evidently means the English and French deists of the last century. But greater familiarity with the German philosophy of his day would have shown him that, whether or not the eccentric world-view is consistent, its root (and consequently the root of metaphysics) consists precisely in locating the goals of nature outside of man; that precisely here lies the boundary between dogmatic theology and metaphysics. And the idea of the earth's movement undermined only the primitive, objectively-anthropocentric teleology. All metaphysics is based on the conviction that by observing the state of our spirit we can acquire an exact conception of the phenomena of the external world. Our actions are purposeful, and this fact is extended by metaphysicians to nature as well: they see purposefulness in it. The other branch of theoretical eccentrism—specialization and empiricism—leads, on its side, to the same result. . . .

The teleological views of Voltaire are interesting in this connection. Voltaire was never imbued, of course, with the fantastic, infantile fancies which hang like a dense fog over the first stages of the evolution of mankind. At least he never wrote a single line in which one could find an echo of an objectively-anthropocentric attitude. On the contrary, nearly his whole long career was a fierce and passionate struggle against this world-view and all its consequences. In his works one finds many characteristically direct, powerful, and venomous attacks on objective anthropocentrism. Thus in his poem on man Voltaire has mice praise God for the wonderful arrangement of their burrows; then ducks, turkeys, and rams appear on the scene, declaring in turn their conviction that the focus of nature resides precisely in ducks, turkeys, and rams. The jackass bluntly maintains that proud man himself has been created for the express purpose of taking care of him, the jackass, since man cleans his stall, carries in fodder, brings him a she-ass, and so on.

But if Voltaire so correctly understood the absurdity of the objectively-anthropocentric teleology, it was only occasionally and, evidently, with great effort that he was able to free himself from the fetters of the eccentric teleology. *Causae finales* had a tenacious hold on this extraordinary mind. . . . He could not tear himself away from his anthropomorphic idea of God the workman, God the thinker, God the artist. However strong was Voltaire's reaction against the primitive world-view, he was at one with it with respect to the creation of God in his own image and likeness. A thinking artist, he imagined the deity, too, to be a thinking artist. And more than once he expressed the thought that nature is not nature but art; that the universe is a great artistic production. . . .

A confirmed optimist who denied the very existence of evil in the world, Voltaire began to sing a completely different tune in 1755, the year of the notorious Lisbon earthquake. That terrible event set many men thinking and caused a profound upheaval in many minds: the destruction of a magnificent city and the loss of sixty thousand lives in a few short moments had grave and painful reverberations in the hearts and minds of men. . . . Voltaire was completely transformed. From this man—who until that time had maintained that "to know that the earth, men, and animals are such as they ought to be according to the order of Providence, is the mark of the man of wisdom" . . .—were now suddenly wrung sounds full of grief, irony, and doubt. . . . Three weeks after the earthquake he wrote to Tronchin: "How cruel nature is! It is going to be difficult to say why the laws of motion should produce such dreadful devastation in this best of all possible worlds. What a mournful play of chance is the game of human life! This should teach man not to persecute man. While one is plotting to devour another, the earth swallows them both." Then came the deeply felt and profoundly satirical *Candide;* Voltaire mercilessly ridiculed his recent teachers—Bolingbroke, Shaftesbury, and Pope—who maintained that all things are ordered in the best possible way. Thus did the Lisbon earthquake convulse the eighteenth century's "king of thought."

It would be interesting to compare these results with the apt observations Buckle makes concerning the influence of earthquakes in strengthening superstition and delaying the development of science. This comparison would show how one and the same phenomenon under different conditions can have diametrically opposed effects on people. Buckle believes that the conception of earthquakes and of terrifying natural phenomena in general as divine retribution is the product of superstition, which in turn is itself fed by these same phenomena. This is, of course, to a certain extent true, and no doubt the gradual acceptance over many generations of the law of the causal connection of phenomena significantly clears the ground for the replacement of objectively-anthropocentric conceptions by more correct ones. But it is also not difficult to see here the influence of sympathetic experience and social cooperation.

Voltaire even earlier had ridiculed man's faith in the centrality of his position; even before the Lisbon earthquake he had understood very well that the forces of nature do not operate to punish and reward man. Clearly, his sudden agitation was caused by the thought of the death of thousands of innocent people. He lived through the last terrible minutes in the lives of these unfortunate victims of blind, deaf nature, and even his eccentric teleology began to crack. But the world had not yet lived through the great revolution which would finally assure Europe that the system of the division of labor would be replaced by a system of simple cooperation; sympathetic experience had not yet attained sufficiently broad realms of application. And Voltaire stopped halfway. It is pitiful to see this bold and powerful intellect grow confused and hesitant when speaking of the significance of evil in the world: . . . "It seems to me poor consolation when Pope says that God sees as equal the death of a heroic human being and the death of a sparrow, the destruction of thousands of planets or of a single atom; or when Shaftesbury asks why God should alter his eternal laws to accommodate a wretched creature like man. . . . This doctrine is comfortless, distressing. The question of the origin of evil remains an insoluble riddle, from which there is no other salvation than faith in Providence."

Or: . . . "the whole world says: How can God be the source of such sufferings? But if our reason is only part of the universal reason, only an emanation from the supreme being, how can we presume to fathom all the intentions and ultimate purposes of this supreme being? That three is half six, that a diagonal divides a rectangle into two equal triangles—this we can know as truly as God knows it. But we remain only a part and can comprehend only a part of the world. The supreme being is powerful, we are weak; we are as necessarily limited as the supreme being is necessarily infinite. Knowing that a single ray means nothing as against the sun, I humbly submit to the higher light which must instruct me in the gloom of this world.". . .

What senile impotence these lines breathe, how feeble is the irony that creeps through here in places! The "king of thought" regrets the fact that he cannot believe that "eternal laws are altered to accommodate a wretched creature like man." This king of thought, irrevocably banished from paradise, apparently does not even suspect that, besides the objectively-anthropocentric and the eccentric resolution of the question occupying him, still another is possible—the subjectively-anthropocentric resolution. He does not realize that man can say:

> *Un jour tout sera bien, voilà notre espérance,*
> *Tout est bien aujourd'hui, voilà l'illusion—* [2]

and therewith can pin his hopes not on a "higher light," as Voltaire does, but on himself, on his own hands and his own head. Man can say: yes, nature is merciless toward me, it knows no distinction, with respect to rights, between me and a sparrow. But I myself shall also be merciless to it, and by my own blood and toil subdue it, compel it to serve me, wipe out evil and create good. I am not the goal of nature, and nature has no other goals. But I have goals, and I shall attain them.

---

2. "Some day all will be well—that is our hope; all is well now—that is the illusion."—TRANS.

Book Six

CRITICS OF RELIGION
AND CULTURE

THE RUSSIAN THINKERS who have been labeled "Westernizers," "Nihilists," and "Populists" in previous sections of this work were chiefly literary and social critics who, taken together, form a more or less coherent movement in nineteenth-century Russian philosophy—a secular, politically radical movement, inspired by the West, which in the light of later developments may be called the dominant stream of Russian thought during this period. But while they and their followers moved toward socialism and revolution, other dissenting voices were raised in Russia—the voices of individual giants, as often creators of literature as literary critics, who belonged to no defined movement. On some points these thinkers were in accord with the dominant tradition, but more often they were opposed to it. Indeed they were often opposed to one another, and certainly their dissent proceeded from no shared philosophical foundation. Yet in the more indigenous, independent, and spiritual character of their protest against many features of the Russian secular and religious culture of their day they constitute a distinguishable group in the history of Russian philosophy—a group capacious enough to include two of the greatest names in world literature—FYODOR DOSTOEVSKY (1821-1881) and LEO TOLSTOY (1828-1910)—as well as men of eccentric genius such as CONSTANTINE LEONTYEV (1831-1891) and VASILY ROZANOV (1856-1919).

It was the members of this loosely defined group who dominated sophisticated conservative thought in Russia during the last quarter of the nineteenth century. And since by that time the radicals were largely excluded from the legal Russian press, these thinkers shared with the more systematic theologians and philosophers of the time (who will be considered in the following section) the dominance of the cultivated legal press in Russia during this period. At the same time there were, of course, official and quasi-official "government conservatives"— such men as Constantine Pobedonostsev (1827-1907), Alexander III's tutor and subsequent chief minister who was the most outspoken defender of the status quo during these years, and Michael Katkov (1818-1887), once a professor of philosophy and a moderate Westernizer, who after the Polish rebellion in 1863 became an ardent nationalist, supporter of the Tsar, and opponent of reform. The critics of religion and culture shared some of the attitudes of these latter-day champions of "Orthodoxy, Autocracy, and Nationalism," but they expressed these attitudes with greater independence of thought and more far-reaching implications. In an important sense many of them were *more* reactionary than men like Pobedonostsev and Katkov: their opposition to Western "progress," if implemented, would entail sweeping social changes of a sort different from those the radicals advocated but fully as disruptive of existing Russian institutions.

Perhaps the best single intellectual characterization of these critics is that they represented the waning heritage of Slavophilism. Originally a more unified body of beliefs than Westernism, Slavophilism had a briefer and more diffuse career. As an identifiable movement it hardly outlasted the 1850's. Yet in different ways it significantly affected the thinking of these later critics. A case in point is that of Nicholas Yakovlevich Danilevsky (1822-1885), the Russian historian and philosopher whose work has been called the principle source of Oswald Spengler's theories of history.[1] Early attracted to Fourier and, like Dostoevsky, a member of the Petrashevsky Circle in the forties, Danilevsky was interested in the natural sciences and took an advanced degree in botany. But basing himself on science, he developed a theory of history having distinct Slavophile over-

1. D. S. Mirsky, *A History of Russian Literature*, ed. Francis J. Whitfield, New York, 1958, p. 339.

tones. In his most important work, *Russia and Europe* (1869), Danilevsky argues that world history exhibits no single, universal civilization but rather a number of fundamentally distinct cultures produced by distinct national types. The Slavs represent one such national type, and led by the Russians they have produced distinctive cultural patterns such as the institutions of Russian Orthodoxy. Danilevsky does not attempt to establish the superiority of Slavdom over the West; but he follows the Slavophiles in maintaining that Western institutions, as alien to Slavic culture, must be rejected by the Slavs, and he contends that while Western culture is declining, Slavic culture is on the upswing. Danilevsky became an enthusiastic supporter of Pan-Slavism, and his ideas found a broad circle of admirers, Dostoevsky among them.

A particularly ardent admirer of Danilevsky was the philosopher and critic Nicholas Nikolayevich Strakhov (1828-1896), whose collaboration with Dostoevsky, close friendship with Tolstoy, and influence on Leontyev and Rozanov give him a central position among the thinkers under consideration here. Strakhov comes the closest of all to orthodox Slavophilism. With the Dostoevsky brothers—Fyodor and Michael—and the critic Apollon Alexandrovich Grigoryev (1822-1864), Strakhov gave the journal *Vremya* (Time) a distinctive character as the organ of second-generation Slavophile thought for a brief period in the sixties, and subsequently developed at length the theme of Russia versus the West in his writings during the seventies and eighties.

The theory of "organic criticism" which gave the *Time* collaborators their banner had originally been worked out by Grigoryev in the fifties, while he was an editor of *Moskvityanin* (The Muscovite), a Slavophile journal published by the conservative historian Michael Pogodin. Grigoryev, admittedly influenced by Schelling, advanced the view that literature, and indeed art in general, should be an organic outgrowth of a nation's cultural "soil" (*pochva* in Russian—whence the name *pochvenniki* for those who adhered to this trend). For Grigoryev this meant that Russian art should spring from the distinctively and traditionally Russian—i.e., non-Western—aspects of the national "soil," to which the true artist would have an "intuitive" relation. Pushkin and Ostrovsky were such artists, according to Grigoryev.

The Dostoevsky brothers and Strakhov adopted essentially the same view of criticism, and in their collaboration with Grigoryev on *Time* they gave it its fullest expression, calling for a rejection of Western "rationalism" in favor of what Zenkovsky has called "a restoration of 'organic wholeness' in man's intuition of the world." [2] Strakhov, in particular, was led by these conceptions to a wholesale critique and rejection of the rationalism and secularism of Western culture, very reminiscent of the attacks of the original Slavophiles. Like them, and like his fellow *pochvenniki*, Strakhov reaffirms the significance of religious faith —though his own views of the proper content of this faith are closer to Tolstoy's than to the traditional Russian Orthodoxy emphasized by Grigoryev. In his chief philosophical work, *The World as a Whole* (1872), Strakhov argues that the world is a hierarchically organized, spiritual, organic whole having man as its center and focus. Like Danilevsky, he strongly emphasizes differences of cultural type, defending the distinctive elements of traditional Russian culture. Strakhov's many critical essays incorporating these views were collected into three volumes under the general title, *The Struggle with the West in Russian Literature* (1882-1896).

In his later years Strakhov developed an increasing admiration for the thought of his friend and correspondent, Leo Tolstoy. Both were impressed by their reading of Schopenhauer. Both emphasized the necessity of a religious foundation for true culture and sought this foundation in a non-ecclesiastical interpretation of Christianity. Tolstoy agreed not only with Strakhov but with the original Slavophiles on a number of other points as well: like them, he opposed the Western cult of science and technology, and advocated greater simplicity and "immediacy" in man's relation to his native cultural "soil." Tolstoy at times even accepted a conception of Russia's unique historical destiny, affirming that Russia might lead the world to salvation

2. V. V. Zenkovsky, *A History of Russian Philosophy*, trans. George L. Kline, 2 vols., London and New York, 1953, p. 406.

because the Russian people "are less civilized than others—i.e., less intellectually corrupted and still possessed of a dim conception of the essence of the Christian teaching." [3] Still, it is only in a highly extended sense that Tolstoy can be called a descendant of Slavophilism. In his concern for the common humanity of men, which draws his attention away from national and cultural differences, and in the clear and simple rationalism of his approach to religion, Tolstoy is at odds with some of the Slavophiles' basic motifs.

Indeed while Tolstoy, as a critic of Western culture and religion, shares a number of views with the Slavophiles and the *pochvenniki*, in other respects his outlook harks back to the doctrines of the Nihilists. In his anti-aristocratic and anti-ecclesiastical bias, in his opposition to useless and "unnatural" luxuries and institutions and to the idle rich, and in general in the sweeping extent and severity of his negations, Tolstoy was on common ground with Chernyshevsky and Pisarev. In aesthetics, to which he devoted one of his most noteworthy books, *What Is Art?*, Tolstoy arrived at the same deprecation of "traditional" aesthetic values as the Nihilists had; he came to prefer *Uncle Tom's Cabin* to his own *War and Peace*, and simple peasant songs to Beethoven symphonies. What is more, he arrived at this point on much the same basis as the Nihilists had: he subordinated aesthetic values to moral values, arguing that the sole justification of art is its social service to humanity—in Tolstoy's case, its service in "infecting" men, as simply and directly as possible, with moral feelings—particularly feelings of "the fatherhood of God and the brotherhood of man." Similarly Tolstoy, like Pisarev, took a moral and utilitarian view of science, disparaging "pure" science in favor of science which is directed to concrete human problems. Tolstoy did not, of course, share the atheism or the inclinations toward revolutionary socialism of the Nihilists, but the above comments are sufficient to indicate some of the parallels existing between the radical, secular movement considered in previous sections and a critique like Tolstoy's which proceeds from a different basis.[4]

3. See p. 222 below.
4. See pp. 213-234.

With Leontyev and Rozanov the anti-radical criticism of the last quarter of the nineteenth century reaches extremes of passion, pessimism, and eccentricity reminiscent of Nietzsche— with whom, in fact, both thinkers have been compared. Leontyev, whose aesthetic immoralism is the precise opposite of Tolstoy's subordination of the aesthetic to the moral, returns again to a position closer to Slavophilism. Like Tolstoy, he adopts a religious basis in criticizing modern culture, but it is one vastly different from Tolstoy's. He criticizes both Tolstoy and Dostoevsky for their weak and overly optimistic views of Christianity, himself emphasizing fear of God rather than love of God as the primary religious motive. He became famous as a reactionary thinker who completely disavowed all egalitarian and democratic principles and rivaled Nietzsche in his vehement condemnation of the common man. Strongly influenced by Danilevsky, Leontyev stressed the differences between Western and Russian culture, hoping to save Russia from the godlessness and the democratic institutions that had overcome the West by simply stopping all Western "progress" in Russia. At the same time, he had little hope that it could really be stopped. He did not shrink from the pessimism implied by these views, but on the contrary regarded pessimism as a necessary concomitant of a genuine religious outlook.

Rozanov was an enthusiastic admirer of Strakhov and Dostoevsky, and his essays have been called continuations of the style of social and political writing adopted by Dostoevsky in the sixties.[5] Like his older friend Leontyev, Rozanov had his intellectual beginnings in conservatism and Slavophilism. He soon, however, abandoned the theme of Russia and the West, and his critique of Western Christianity became an anguished, lifelong struggle against Christianity itself. With Leontyev and Tolstoy he rejected both the secular social world of the revolutionaries and the dominant religious conceptions of his day. But while Leontyev and Tolstoy developed their own forms of Christianity on which to base their thinking, Rozanov castigated the religion of the New Testament as a "religion of death" and elaborated a highly imaginative metaphysics of sex and family

5. Zenkovsky, *op. cit.*, p. 414.

life which he considered closer to the spirit of the Old Testament.

Thus the myriad personal and doctrinal links among the thinkers discussed above cannot obscure the fact that there are fundamental philosophical differences among them. If we were to venture further afield, to include such thinkers as the poets Fyodor Tyutchev and Afanasi Fet, who also contributed to the anti-radical intellectual currents in the latter half of the nineteenth century, this basic philosophical diversity would only be increased. Yet all these thinkers diagnosed Russia's cultural ills in ways which set them apart from the dominant radical current of the times, and all offered means of dealing with these ills other than science and revolution. Even the voices of these giants, however, were not enough to stem the tide.

LEO NIKOLAYEVICH TOLSTOY
[1828–1910]

THE LITERARY ACHIEVEMENTS which have caused Leo Tolstoy to be considered one of the world's greatest masters of fiction have understandably eclipsed the achievements of Leo Tolstoy the philosopher. Like many of the Russian thinkers included in this volume, Tolstoy was not a professional philosopher; in fact he had no formal training in philosophy. Nonetheless he was ardently concerned with certain philosophical issues, and the years of intellectual concentration and moral fervor he devoted to them, coupled with the unorthodox character of the answers at which he arrived, give his philosophical views an interest quite independent of his literary reputation. He expounded these views not only in novels and short stories but in a great many works of nonfiction as well; during his later years Tolstoy wrote voluminously on philosophical and theological themes.

Count Leo Tolstoy was born in 1828 at the family estate of Yasnaya Polyana, some hundred miles south of Moscow. He was educated by private tutors and raised by other members of the family after the death of his mother in 1830 and his father in 1837. In 1844, he entered Kazan University, but in 1847 he returned without a degree to Yasnaya Polyana, bored and eager to manage the estate which now belonged to him. This occupation, too, failed to satisfy Tolstoy's vigorous nature and in 1851 he joined the Army, seeing active service in the Caucasus and later in the siege of Sevastopol during the Crimean War. It was during his Army service that Tolstoy began to write fiction which met with immediate critical and popular acclaim. After leaving the Army in 1856 and traveling in Western

Europe, he settled once more at Yasnaya Polyana, which remained his chief residence for the rest of his long life. There he began his educational and philanthropic work with the peasants and, after his marriage in 1862, worked on his two great masterpieces, *War and Peace* (1863-1869) and *Anna Karenina* (1873-1877).

Literary fame and an active domestic life did not bring Tolstoy contentment, however. From 1875 on he was beset by severe fits of depression, intensified by the death of two of his young children. He experienced a melancholy compounded of an obsession with death and a growing despair at the failure of all his attempts to find a reason for living. Movingly described in *My Confession* (written in 1879), Tolstoy's anguished search was terminated in 1878 by a final moral crisis and his "conversion" to Christianity—first to the orthodoxy of his youth and subsequently to his own, ethical interpretation of Christianity which emphasized universal love and brotherhood. Henceforth all of Tolstoy's thought and activity revolved around his intense religious outlook, which soon led him to pacifism and anarchism.

The years immediately following his conversion—1879-1883 —were largely devoted to a study of theology and the Christian Scriptures. The unconventional and anti-ecclesiastical views he continued to expound led to his excommunication from the Russian Orthodox Church in 1901, though by this time his writings and charitable activities had brought him such widespread public adulation that he was effectively sheltered from the ordinary sanctions of his two great adversaries, Church and State. After 1883, Tolstoy resumed the writing of fiction, and some of his best-known works date from the post-conversion period, including *The Kreutzer Sonata* (1890) and *Resurrection* (1899). But nonfictional vehicles for his ideas became at least as important to him: *My Confession* was followed by *What I Believe* (1884), *On Life* (1888), *The Kingdom of God Is Within You* (1893), and finally, at the age of eighty, the "last testament" from which the following selections are taken, *The Law of Violence and the Law of Love* (1908). Tolstoy died at Astapovo in 1910, following a sudden decision to flee from what had become an onerous family situation at Yasnaya Polyana.

The intellectual content of Tolstoy's post-conversion outlook was in many ways a response to earlier influences and a crystallization of former attitudes. Without doubt the greatest single philosophical influence on Tolstoy was that of Rousseau, whose primitivist opposition to modern technical civilization and whose idealization of "naturalness" and the untutored peasant greatly affected Tolstoy as early as his fifteenth year (he wore a Rousseau medallion around his neck at the time) and remained prominent in his mature outlook. The only other philosopher for whom Tolstoy expressed such high regard was Schopenhauer, whom he studied intensively in 1869; there is evidence of Schopenhauer's pessimism in Tolstoy's later views.[1] Again, Tolstoy early expressed opposition to State authority, and is said to have made a vow in 1857 never again to serve any government.[2] Finally, specific anticipations of Tolstoy's later views can be found in *War and Peace*, which, with its sprawling, worldly vitality, is often considered the antithesis of the later religious outlook. Not only does the philosophy of history which Tolstoy advances in the novel stress the role of the great masses of common people, it also rejects the very assumption that Tolstoy calls a "gross" and "horrible" superstition in *The Law of Violence and the Law of Love*—the assumption that human intelligence can significantly predict and control man's social future.

This anti-intellectualist theme in Tolstoy's philosophy of history does not extend, however, to the substance of his mature religious outlook, which may be viewed as an attempt to remove everything mystical, mysterious, or "unreasonable" from the moral kernel of Christ's teaching. According to Tolstoy, Christ was not uniquely divine (*all* men are God's sons) and no mythical "miracles," absurd doctrines such as the Resurrection and the Trinity, or ecclesiastical rituals or authorities can be allowed to obscure the simple moral truths advanced by Christ, which are both perfectly understandable to all men and the only rational means by which all men can attain the well-being they desire. In *What I Believe*, Tolstoy sums up this moral teaching in five basic commandments: (1) refrain from anger and live

1. V. V. Zenkovsky, *op. cit.*, pp. 391-392.
2. Theodore Redpath, *Tolstoy*, London, 1960, p. 90.

in peace with all men; (2) do not lust; (3) do not bind your-self by oaths; (4) resist not evil; and (5) love everyone without distinction of nationality. The first, fourth, and fifth of these, taken together, essentially comprise what Tolstoy calls "the law of love," which is the distinctive content of Christianity. The fourth commandment is particularly important, since in Tolstoy's view it absolutely prohibits the use of force or violence, even to combat evil.

From here it is an easy step to anarchism as a social theory, and Tolstoy takes it with relentless consistency, refusing to sanction or participate in *any* use of force by man over man, whether in war or through any State institution, however "legal." There is, then, no justification for any social instrument of coercion—army, police, law court—or for the institutions which these instruments sustain—private property, differential social privileges, warfare, taxation. True Christianity and the State, as a form of organized violence, are simply incompatible. The present essay, *The Law of Violence and the Law of Love*, is noteworthy for its attempt to refute, one by one, the obvious "common-sense" objections to Tolstoyan anarchism. In the end Tolstoy always insists on the irrationality of any social system based on force: to maintain that peace and the good can be attained through violence (which is both belligerent and evil) is to fall into a contradiction.

Nor is Tolstoy's view without a rational metaphysical basis, also suggested in the present essay: love must guide human life because it is of the essence of human life; love is "the principle of everything." More exactly, my true reality (as opposed to my "animal personality"—a distinction developed in Tolstoy's important essay, *On Life*) is the universal divine reality, which manifests itself in me as love. Consequently it is only when I am the vehicle of universal love that I live my own true life, "a life divine and free."

Much has been made of the contrast between Tolstoy's expressed views on the one hand and his own character and conduct on the other—not only his youthful profligacy but his mature enjoyment of the aristocratic comforts of Yasnaya Polyana and the intense pride and even haughtiness he sometimes exhibited. But these lapses in no way weakened the moral impact of his views. Ironically, the Bolshevik revolution effectively prevented Tolstoy, who in many ways epitomizes the "maximalism" and ethical focus of so much of Russian philosophy, from maintaining any considerable philosophical following in Russia. But his influence on thinkers abroad has been great. He is, of course, one of the inspirers of "non-violent" social protest, as adapted first by his admirer and most eminent disciple, Mahatma Gandhi, and subsequently by many others, including contemporary anti-segregationists in the United States. In recent years his writings, both fictional and nonfictional, have come to have increasing interest for existential philosophers. Martin Heidegger's discussion of death in *Being and Time* has been called "an unacknowledged commentary" on Tolstoy's story, "The Death of Ivan Ilyich." [3]

SELECTED BIBLIOGRAPHY

Many different editions of Tolstoy's works are available in English translation. A useful collection of his chief religious writings is *Lift Up Your Eyes: The Religious Writings of Leo Tolstoy*, intro. Stanley R. Hopper, New York, 1960. Of the vast secondary literature on Tolstoy, an excellent brief study of his life and thought is Theodore Redpath, *Tolstoy*, London, 1960, which contains a useful guide to the literature.

3. Walter Kaufmann, "Existentialism and Death," *Chicago Review*, Summer, 1959, p. 81. See the discussion in *Lift Up Your Eyes: The Religious Writings of Leo Tolstoy*, intro. Stanley R. Hopper, New York, 1960, p. 10.

The Law of Violence and the Law of Love *

I am writing this only because I, who stand on the brink of the grave, cannot keep silent when I know the one thing that can free the people of the Christian world from their frightful corporal sufferings and, more important, from the spiritual corruption into which they are sinking deeper and deeper.

It must be clear to all thinking men today that contemporary life—not only Russian life but the life of all the nations of the Christian world—with its continual increase in the need of the poor and the luxury of the rich; with its war of all against all, of revolutionaries against governments, of governments against revolutionaries, of oppressed nations against their oppressors, of state against state, of West against East; with its continual increase in armaments that devours the energies of the people; with its exquisiteness and its depravity—that such a life cannot go on, that the life of the Christian nations, if it is not changed, will inevitably become increasingly calamitous.

This is clear to many, but unfortunately men often fail to see the cause of this calamitous plight, and still more often fail to see the means of deliverance from it. The most diverse circumstances are identified as its cause, and the most diverse means of deliverance are proposed. Yet there is only one cause, and only one means of deliverance.

The cause of the calamitous plight of the Christian nations

---

* Translated for this volume by James P. Scanlan, from "Zakon nasiliya i zakon lyubvi," as printed in Leo Tolstoy, *Polnoye sobraniye sochineni,* Vol. 37, Moscow, 1956, pp. 149-213. Tolstoy wrote this long essay in the form of short untitled chapters, each with a number of epigraphs. The epigraphs have been omitted in the present volume, but the chapter divisions are indicated by spacing between paragraphs. The present selections are drawn from the Preface and Chapters 3-4, 7-9, 13-17, and 19 (pp. 149-150, 156-158, 160-161, 166-171, 173-176, 192-193, 196-203, 205-208, 212-213), with some omissions, as indicated, within the passages selected.

is that they have no shared supreme conception of the meaning of life, no common faith or rule of conduct flowing from a common faith.

The means of deliverance from this calamitous situation—a means not fantastic or contrived but entirely natural—consists in the adoption by the men of the Christian world of that supreme conception of life and that rule of conduct flowing from it which were revealed to them nineteen centuries ago and which meet the demands of the present age of mankind: i.e., *the Christian doctrine in its true meaning.*

The majority of men in the Christian world are aware of the ever-increasing calamity of their situation, and to deliver themselves from it they employ the only means which, in accordance with their world outlook, they consider effective. This means is the use of violence by some men against others. Some men, considering the existing order advantageous to them, strive to maintain it by violent state action; others, by equally violent revolutionary action, strive to destroy the existing order and to set up another, better order in its place.

Many revolutions have been effected and many revolutions have been suppressed in the Christian world. External forms have changed, but the essential features of the state system—the power of a few over many; corruption, falsehood, and fear of the oppressed on the part of the ruling classes; oppression, enslavement, stupefaction, and irritation on the part of the masses—these features, if they have changed in form, in their essence not only have not diminished but have markedly increased and are still increasing. What is happening in Russia today shows particularly clearly not only the utter futility but the manifest harmfulness of employing violence as a means of uniting men.

In every newspaper recently, while there are fewer and fewer accounts of banks robbed, policemen and officers killed, and assassination attempts discovered, there are more and more accounts of executions and death sentences.

For two years now they have been shooting and hanging people without cease; thousands have been executed. Other thousands have been torn to pieces by revolutionary bombs. But since lately more and more people are being killed by the authorities and fewer and fewer by the revolutionaries, the ruling classes exult; it seems to them that they have won, and that now they will be able to continue their ordinary life, supporting fraud by violence and violence by fraud.

The error of all political doctrines without exception, from the most conservative to the most progressive, the error which has brought men to their present calamitous predicament, is essentially this: the men of this world have thought it possible, and still think it possible, to unite people by violence in such a way that they will all, without resistance, submit to the same order of life and to the same rule of conduct following from it.

Men can, of course, under the sway of passion, forcibly impose their wills on people who do not agree with them. One can by force push or drag a man where he does not wish to go. (Both animals and men always act in this way under the influence of passion.) This is comprehensible, but quite incomprehensible is the reasoning according to which violence is called a means of persuading people to perform the actions we desire them to perform.

All violence consists in this: some men, under threat of pain or death, make other men do what the latter do not want to do. Thus those who are subjected to violence do what they do not want to do only as long as they are weaker than those employing the violence, and cannot evade that with which they are threatened for failing to do what is demanded of them. The moment they are the stronger party, naturally they will not only cease doing what they do not want to do, but, angered by the struggle against those who overpowered them and by everything they were forced to bear, they will first free themselves from their oppressors and then, in their turn, make those who disagree with them do what they consider good and necessary for themselves.

And thus one would think it clear that the struggle between the users of violence and the victims of violence can in no way unite men, but on the contrary only divides them more the longer it continues. One would think this so clear that it would not be worth mentioning, were it not that the lie that violence can benefit and unify men has been so widespread since ancient times and has been tacitly accepted as the most indubitable truth, not only by those to whom violence is advantageous but even by the majority of the very men who have most suffered from it and are suffering from it now. . . .

The states of the Christian world have not merely reached, but in our day have gone beyond the limits reached by the states of the ancient world before they disintegrated. This is particularly evident from the fact that every technical advance today not only fails to contribute to the general welfare but, on the contrary, demonstrates more and more plainly that all these technical improvements can only increase men's miseries, not diminish them. We may keep on inventing new submarine, subterranean, aerial, and superaerial contraptions for transporting people from place to place with the utmost speed, and new devices for broadcasting their words and thoughts; but the people thus transported are unwilling, unqualified, and unable to do anything but evil, and their broadcast words and thoughts can do nothing but incite men to evil. As for the continual improvements in our means of exterminating each other which make it increasingly possible to commit murder without danger to oneself, they simply demonstrate more and more clearly that the career of the Christian nations cannot continue in its present direction.

The life of the Christian nations today is frightful. It is frightful, in particular, because of the absence of any sort of moral principle uniting these nations. It is frightful because of its irrationality, which reduces man, despite all his intellectual attainments, to a moral level lower than that of the animals. And it is frightful, above all, because of the complexity of the lie that has become established and that increasingly hides from men the whole calamity and cruelty of their lives. The lie feeds the cruelty of life, the cruelty requires a greater and greater lie, and like a snowball the two grow uncontrollably.

But everything comes to an end. And I believe that the end of this calamitous situation is now approaching.

The plight of men in the Christian world is frightful, but at the same time it is a plight which could not have been avoided, which was bound to be, and which inevitably must lead these nations to deliverance. The sufferings which the men of the Christian world have undergone, resulting from the absence of a religious outlook appropriate to our time, are necessary conditions of growth and will inevitably end when men adopt the religious outlook appropriate to their time.

The outlook appropriate to our time is that understanding of the meaning of human life and that rule of conduct flowing from it which were revealed by the Christian teaching in its true significance 1,900 years ago but have been concealed from men by arbitrary ecclesiastical distortion.

The whole true significance of the Christian doctrine, as it is being elucidated more and more in our time, consists in this: the essence of human life is the conscious, progressive manifestation of that principle or source of everything, the manifestation of which in us is signified by love; thus love is the essence of human life and the supreme law that should guide it.

That love is a necessary and valuable condition of human life was recognized by all the religious doctrines of antiquity. In all these doctrines—that of the Egyptian sages, the Brahmins, the Stoics, the Buddhists, the Taoists, and so on—friendliness, pity, mercy, charity, and, in general, love were recognized as among the principal virtues. The highest of these doctrines even carried this recognition to the point of extolling love toward everyone and even of returning good for evil, as was preached in particular by the Taoists and the Buddhists.

But not one of these doctrines made this virtue the foundation of life, the supreme law which had to be not merely the chief but the sole rule of human conduct, as has been done by the most recent of religious teachings, Christianity. In all pre-Christian doctrines love was recognized as one of the virtues, but not in the way in which it is recognized in the Christian doctrine: metaphysically, as the principle of everything, practically, as the supreme law of human life—i.e., in such a way as not to admit of exceptions in any case.

As compared with all the ancient doctrines, the Christian doctrine is not something new and peculiar: it is simply a clearer and more definite expression of the principle of human life which has been felt and vaguely preached by preceding religious doctrines. . . . What is expressed with particular clarity and precision in the Christian doctrine is that, since this law is the supreme law, its observance cannot admit of any exceptions, as former doctrines did; that the love defined by this law is love only when it does not admit of any exceptions and is directed equally to men of other countries and faiths and to enemies who hate us and do us evil. . . .

The explanation of why this law is the supreme law of life is expressed with particular clarity in the Epistles of John:

> Beloved, let us love one another: for love is of God; and everyone who loves is born of God, and knows God. He who does not love, has not known God, for God is love. No one has ever seen God; if we love one another, then God abides in us. God is love, and he who abides in love abides in God, and God in him. We know that we have passed from death to life, because we love our brothers; he who does not love his brother abides in death. (*First Epistle of John*, 4:7,8,12,16; 3:14)

The whole doctrine consists in this: what we call our self, our life, is a divine principle, limited in us by the body, which manifests itself in us as love, and for that reason the true life of every person, a life divine and free, is manifested in love.

As for the rule of conduct which follows from this understanding of the law of love and which does not admit of any exceptions, it is expressed in many places in the Gospels, and particularly exactly, clearly, and definitely in the fourth commandment of the Sermon on the Mount: "You have heard that it has been said: An eye for an eye and a tooth for a tooth (*Exodus*, 21:14), but I say to you: Resist not evil" (*Matthew* 5:38). And in verses 39 and 40, as if in anticipation of the exceptions that may seem necessary when the law of love is applied to life, it is clearly and definitely stated that there are not and cannot be any circumstances which would permit deviation from the simplest and first commandment of love: Do not do to others what you would not want them to do to you. It is said: "If someone strikes thee on thy right cheek, turn to him the other also, and if anyone wishes to sue thee and take away thy coat, give him thy cloak also." In other words, violence employed against you cannot give you the right to employ violence.

This inadmissibility of excusing deviations from the law of love by appealing to any actions of other men is expressed still more clearly and precisely in the last commandment of the Sermon on the Mount, which directly refers to those common, false interpretations of the law which would permit violation of it:

> You have heard that it has been said: Love thy neighbor and hate thine enemy (*Leviticus*, 19:17-18). But I say to you: Love your enemies, bless those who curse you, do good to those who hate you, and pray for those who offend you and persecute you, that you may be the children of your heavenly Father; for he makes his sun rise on the evil and on the good, and sends rain on the just and on the unjust. For if you love those who love you, what is the merit in that? Do not even the publicans do that? And if you salute only your brothers, what do you do more than others? Do not even the gentiles act thus? So, be perfect, as your heavenly Father is perfect. (*Matthew*, 5:43-46) . . .

Herein is both the principal difference between the Christian doctrine and previous doctrines, and the principle significance of the Christian doctrine in its true meaning; herein is the step forward it has made in the consciousness of mankind. This step consists in this: all previous religious and moral doctrines of love, recognizing—as, indeed, they could not help but do—the value of love for the life of mankind, at the same time allowed the possibility of there being circumstances under which the law of love need not be fulfilled, could be suspended. But as soon as the law of love has ceased to be the supreme, unalterable law of men's lives, all its value is destroyed and the doctrine of love is reduced to high-sounding precepts and phrases which do not commit one to anything, which leave men's lives just as they were before—i.e., founded on nothing but violence. Whereas the Christian teaching in its true sense, recognizing the law of love as supreme and its application to life as not admitting of any exceptions, destroys all violence by this recognition, and consequently cannot but reject every world order based on violence.

One would think it evident that if some men, despite acknowledging the value of love, can find it necessary to torture or murder people in the name of good future ends of some sort, then other men, who also acknowledge the value of love, are equally entitled to find it necessary to torture or murder other people in the name of future goods. Thus one would think it evident that the admission of any exceptions whatever to the law of love would destroy the whole significance, the whole meaning, the whole value of this law, which is the foundation of every moral as well as of every religious doctrine. One would think this so evident that he would blush to argue it, and yet the men of the Christian world—both those who regard themselves as believers and those who consider themselves nonbelievers but acknowledge a moral law—view the doctrine of love which rejects all violence, and in particular view the principle of non-resistance to evil by evil which follows from that doctrine, as something fantastic, impossible, and utterly inapplicable to life.

Understandably, the men who rule can say that without violence there can be no order or good life, meaning by "order" that arrangement whereby some profit excessively by the labors of others, and by "good" life the absence of obstacles to leading such a life. However unjust what they say, it is understandable that they say it, since the elimination of violence not only would deprive them of the opportunity to live as they do but would expose all the long-standing injustice and cruelty of their life.

But one would think that the working people would find

unnecessary the violence which, strange to say, they employ so vigorously against one another and from which they suffer so much. . . . One would think that they, who receive no benefit from the violence used against them, might finally perceive the lie in which they have become ensnared, and having seen it free themselves from it in the simplest and easiest way: by ceasing to participate in this violence, which can be used against them only by their participation.

One would think that nothing could be simpler and more natural than for the working people . . . and particularly for the agriculturalists, who in Russia as in all the countries of the world are the majority, to understand at last that their sufferings are self-imposed; that they themselves, as guards, policemen, and soldiers, protect the land owned by the idle proprietors, which is the chief source of their sufferings; that likewise they themselves collect all the taxes from themselves, both direct and indirect, in their capacities as village officials, tax collectors, and, again, policemen and soldiers. One would think that it would be so simple for the working people to understand this, and to say at last to those whom they consider their superiors: "Let us alone. If you emperors, presidents, generals, judges, bishops, professors, and learned men of every description need armies, navies, universities, ballets, synods, conservatories, prisons, gallows, guillotines—organize all these things yourselves. Collect money from each other, judge each other, imprison each other, execute people and murder them in wars, but do it yourselves and let us alone, because we need none of these things and do not wish to participate further in all these activities which are useless to us and, above all, are evil."

What more natural than this, one would think? Yet the working people, and especially the agriculturalists, who need none of these things, neither in Russia nor in any other country, fail to do this. Some, a majority, continue to torture themselves by carrying out the demands of the authorities to their own disadvantage and becoming policemen, tax collectors, and soldiers. Others, a minority, in order to free themselves from violence when they can, in time of revolution use violence

against the men from whose use of violence they suffer—
that is, they fight fire with fire, thereby only increasing the
use of violence against themselves.

Why do men act so irrationally?

Because, in consequence of the long existence of the lie,
they no longer see the connection between their oppression and
their participation in violence.

But why do they not see this connection?

Because of the same thing that is responsible for all the
miseries of men: because they have no faith. Without faith
men can be guided only by interest, and a man who is guided
only by interest can be nothing but a duper or a dupe.

It is precisely this that is the source of that seemingly surprising phenomenon, that the working people, despite the evident disadvantage to themselves of the use of violence, despite
the fact that the lie in which they have been ensnared is today
completely obvious, despite the clear disclosure of the injustice
from which they are suffering, despite all the revolutions aiming at eliminating violence—despite all this the working people,
the vast majority of people, not only continue to submit to
violence but support it, and, in opposition to common sense
and to their own advantage, employ violence against themselves.

So it has been for a long time, throughout the world, both
Christian and non-Christian. But I believe that now, precisely
now, after the pitiful, stupid Russian revolution and in particular after the horribly, insolently, senselessly cruel suppression
of that revolution, things are about to change. I believe that
the Russian people, who are less civilized than others—i.e., less
intellectually corrupted and still possessed of a dim conception
of the essence of the Christian teaching—that the Russian people,
and above all the agriculturalists, will understand at last where
the means of salvation lies, and will be the first to begin to
apply it.

"A frightful burden of evil hangs over men and crushes
them," I wrote fifteen years ago. "The men bearing this burden,

weighed down by it more and more, are seeking a means of deliverance from it.

"They know that by their joint efforts they can lift up this burden and cast it from themselves; but they cannot all agree to seize it together, and each of them sinks lower and lower, letting the burden fall on the shoulders of others. It crushes men more and more and would have crushed them completely long ago, had there not been some men who are guided in their actions not by considerations of external consequences but solely by the internal correspondence of an act with the voice of conscience. These men were and are Christians: for it is in this—in setting up, in place of an external goal, to attain which everyone's agreement is needed, an internal goal, to attain which no one's agreement is needed—that the essence of Christianity in its true meaning lies. And thus salvation from the enslavement in which men now find themselves is impossible for men of society, and has been effected and is being effected solely by Christianity, solely by the substitution of the law of love for the law of violence.

"The goal of social life cannot be fully known to you—says the Christian teaching to every man—and you think of it simply as a closer and closer approach to the welfare of all the world, to the Kingdom of God on earth. But the goal of personal life is known to you beyond all question, and consists in the realization in you of the highest perfection of love, which is essential for the realization of the Kingdom of God. And this goal is always known to you and is always attainable.

"You may be ignorant of the best particular external goals to pursue, and there may be obstacles to their realization. But the approach to internal perfection, the augmentation of love in yourself and in others, cannot be halted by anyone or in any way.

"And a man has only to set himself, in place of a false, external, social goal, this one true, indubitable, and attainable internal goal of life, for all those chains by which he seemed so permanently fettered instantly to burst and for him to feel perfectly free. . . .

"The Christian is freed from the law of the state by the

fact that he has no need of it either for himself or for others, considering human life better protected by the law of love which he professes than by a law sustained by violence. . . .

"The profession of Christianity in its true sense, including non-resistance to evil by violence, frees men from every external authority. But not only that—it makes it possible at the same time for them to achieve that betterment of life which they vainly seek through alteration of the external forms of life.

"Men think that their lot is improved by altering external forms, but such alteration is always simply a result of an alteration of consciousness, and only improves life to the extent that it *is* based on an alteration of consciousness. . . .

"Men can be saved from their abasement, enslavement, and ignorance not through revolutions, not through labor unions or world congresses but through the simplest means: everyone who is called upon to take part in violence against his brothers and against himself has only to recognize his true spiritual self and ask in bewilderment: 'Why should I do this?'

"It is not revolutions or the artful, brilliant, socialistic, communistic organization of unions or arbitrations or the like that will save mankind, but this spiritual consciousness, when it becomes general.

"Indeed man has only to come to his senses from the mesmerism that hides from him his true human calling, for him not only to reject the state's demands but to be astonished and indignant that such demands should be addressed to him.

"And this awakening can take place at any moment."

So I wrote fifteen years ago. This awakening is taking place, I boldly write now. I know that I, with my eighty years, shall never see it. But I know, just as surely as I know that winter yields to spring and night to day, that this time has come in the life of our Christian humanity.

"All this may be so, but for men to be able to free themselves from the life based on violence in which they are ensnared all men must be religious—i.e., must be prepared, in order to fulfill the law of God, to sacrifice their material, personal welfare and live not for the future but solely for the present, striving simply to fulfill in the present the will of God revealed to them in love. But the men of our world are not religious, and so cannot live like that."

So say the men of our time, as if supposing that religious consciousness in man is something exceptional, cultivated, affected.[1] But men can only think and speak thus who are, as a consequence of the present plight of the Christian world, temporarily deprived of the most necessary and natural condition of human life—faith. . . .

Just as labor is not something artificial, invented, and prescribed but something inevitable, essential, without which men could not live, so, too, is faith—i.e., a consciousness of one's relation to the infinite and of the rule of conduct which follows from that relation. Not only is such faith not something cultivated, artificial, exceptional—on the contrary it is a natural property of human nature, without which, like birds without wings, people never have lived and never can live.

If we now, in our Christian world, see people devoid of, or, to speak more correctly, not devoid of but with an obscured religious consciousness, this abnormal, unnatural condition is only temporary and accidental—the condition of a few, proceeding from those special circumstances in which the men of the Christian world have been living, a condition as exceptional as that of men who can and do live without laboring.

And thus for men who have lost it to experience again this feeling which is natural and indispensable to human life, they need not invent anything or organize anything. They need simply eliminate the lie which has temporarily obscured this feeling and concealed it from them.

If only the men of our world were freed from this lie—from the perversion of Christian doctrine by Church faith and from

1. One of Tolstoy's epigraphs to this chapter is the following passage written by himself: "The human soul is Christian in its nature. Christianity is always accepted by men as something forgotten which is suddenly remembered. Christianity raises man to a height from which there is revealed to him a joyous world subject to rational law. The feeling experienced by a man in recognizing the truth of Christianity is like that of a man who, locked in a dark, stifling tower, has climbed to its highest, open storey and sees a beautiful world unseen before."—TRANS.

the vindication and even exaltation of the state which is advanced on the basis of that faith, but which is incompatible with Christianity and is based on violence—then of itself there would be eliminated from the souls of all men, Christian and non-Christian, the chief obstacle to the religious recognition of the supreme law of love that tolerates no exceptions or violence. . . .

But when this law is recognized as the *supreme* law of life, of itself there will end that human plight, ruinous to morality, wherein the greatest injustices and cruelties which men inflict upon one another are considered natural and proper to human beings. Everything the socialistic and communistic builders of future societies now dream about and promise will be achieved—and in much greater measure. And it will be achieved by completely different means, and achieved only *because* the self-contradictory means of violence by which both governments and their opponents strive to achieve it, will not be employed. This emancipation from the evil which is tormenting and corrupting men will be attained not by strengthening or supporting the existing order—monarchy, republic, or what have you—and not by destroying the existing order and establishing a better socialistic or communistic one, and in general not by some men dreaming up a social order they consider best and imposing it upon other men by violence, but only by each person (the majority of men), without worrying about or considering the consequences of his action for himself or for others, acting in a certain way not for the sake of some social order but simply to fulfill for himself and for his own life the law of life acknowledged by him to be supreme—the law of love, which does not admit of violence under any circumstances.

"But how can we live without government, without authority? Men have never lived like that," it will be objected.

Men, living in states, have grown so accustomed to the institution of the state that it seems to them an inevitable, perpetual form of human life. But this only seems to be the case: people have lived and still live outside the state. All primitive peoples who have not reached what is called "civilization" are living in that way today; so are the men whose understanding of the meaning of life places them above civilization: in Europe, in America, and especially in Russia there are communities of Christians who reject the government, having no need of it and simply enduring its unavoidable interference.

The institution of the state is not a permanent but a temporary form of human life. Just as the life of an individual is not static but constantly changes, advances, improves—so, too, the life of all mankind ceaselessly changes, advances, improves, Each individual once nursed, played with toys, studied, worked, married, raised children, found release from his passions, grew wiser with age. Similarly nations grow wiser and improve, only not by years, as with an individual, but by centuries, by millennia. And just as the principal changes take place in the spiritual, invisible realm for the individual, so, too, for mankind the chief changes take place first and foremost in the invisible realm, in its religious consciousness. . . .

We do not know the hour when the child becomes a youth, but we know that the former child can no longer play with toys. Similarly we cannot name the year, or even the decade, in which the men of the Christian world outgrew their previous form of life and made the transition to another age determined by their religious consciousness, but we cannot avoid knowing and seeing that the men of the Christian world can no longer seriously play at conquests, at conferences of monarchs, at diplomatic stratagems, at constitutions with their Houses and Dumas, at social-revolutionary, democratic, and anarchistic parties and revolutions, and above all cannot base all these games on violence.

This is particularly evident now in Russia, given the external transformation which has been effected in our state system. In connection with all the new governmental institutions which have been introduced, serious-minded Russians today cannot help but feel something like adults who have been given a new toy which they did not have as children. However novel and interesting the toy, it is useless to them now and they can only view it with a smile. Thus it is in Russia both for all thinking men and for the great mass of people with respect to our Constitution, our Duma, and all the different revolutionary associations and parties.

The Russian people of our time—who, I think I am not mistaken in saying, already sense, if only vaguely, the essence of the true teaching of Christ—cannot seriously believe that man's mission in this world consists in using the brief interval allotted him between birth and death to make speeches in parliaments or at congresses of socialist comrades; to judge his neighbors in courts, seize them, lock them up, and murder them; or throw bombs at them; or take away their land; or worry about whether Finland, India, Poland, or Korea is annexed to what is called Russia, England, Prussia, or Japan, or about liberating these lands by violence and being prepared to murder one another wholesale in order to do it. A man of our time cannot help but recognize, in the depths of his heart, the utter madness of such activity. . . .

Even apart from the fact that there is no likelihood whatever that elimination of the use of violence by man against man, which is contrary to man's rational and loving nature, would worsen instead of improving men's lot—even apart from that, the present plight of society is so horribly bad that it is difficult to imagine a worse one. Consequently the question as to whether men can get along without government is not only not intimidating, as the defenders of the existing order would like to present it, it is simply ridiculous—as ridiculous as asking a man who is being tortured how he will get along when they stop torturing him.

The men whom the existing state order places in an exceptionally advantageous position imagine human life without state authority to be a supreme confusion, a war of all against all, as if they were speaking of a community not even of animals (animals live together peaceably without state force) but of horrible monsters of some sort whose actions are guided solely by hatred and madness. But they imagine men thus only because they attribute to them those qualities, repugnant to their nature, which have been instilled in them by that very state system which has formed them and which they continue to support despite the fact that it is manifestly useless and does nothing but harm.

And thus to the question of what life would be without authority and without government, there can be only one answer—namely, that there will certainly be none of that evil which government produces: there will be no property in land, no taxes to be used for things men do not need, no divisions among nations or enslavement of some by others, no devouring of the best energies of nations in preparation for war, no fear of bombs on the one hand and of gallows on the other, no senseless luxury for some and still more senseless penury for others. ⟹ *unrealistic*

"But still, what will their lives be like—these men who decide to live without government?" people ask, evidently supposing that men can always know what form their lives will take and will continue to have in the future, and that therefore the men who decide to live without government must also know this in advance.

But actually men have never known and cannot know what their lives will be like in the future. The conviction that they can know this, and can even prearrange their future lives, is merely a very gross if also a very old and widespread superstition. Whether they have submitted to governments or not, men equally have never known and cannot know what their future lives will be like. . . .

Thus the belief that some, a minority, can prearrange the future life of the majority—a belief which is considered the most indubitable truth, and in the name of which the greatest crimes are committed—is nothing but a superstition. As for the activity based on this superstition—the political activity of revolutionaries and rulers and their accomplices, which ordinarily is considered the most honorable and important work—it is in essence the most hollow and at the same time pernicious human activity, which more than any other has obstructed and continues to obstruct the true welfare of mankind. Rivers of blood have been spilled and are still being spilled in the name of this superstition, and incalculable sufferings have been borne and are still being borne by men on account of the stupid and pernicious activity which has sprung from this superstition. And worst of all, while these rivers of blood are being spilled in its name, it is precisely this superstition which, more than anything else, has obstructed the successful social accomplishment of the very improvements in life which are appropriate both to the time and to the present stage of development of human consciousness. This superstition is an obstacle to true progress principally because men bend all their efforts to influencing other men, in the name of the preservation and strengthening, or of the alteration and betterment, of the social order, thereby preventing themselves from engaging in that activity of inner improvement which alone can promote the transformation of the social order as a whole.

Human life in its totality advances and cannot but advance toward the eternal ideal of perfection solely through the approach of each individual to his personal and equally limitless perfection.

What a dreadful, ruinous superstition it is that makes men neglect inner cultivation, i.e., neglect the one thing actually needed for their own welfare and for the general welfare, and the one thing fully in man's power, and makes them bend all their efforts to ordering the lives of other men, which are outside their power, and for the attainment of this impossible goal makes them employ means that are unquestionably evil and harmful, to themselves and to others—i.e., the means of violence, which is the avenue most certain to lead them away from both their own personal perfection and the perfection of all!

"All this may be true, but to renounce violence will be rational only when all or a majority of people understand the disadvantage, the needlessness, and the irrationality of violence. So long as this is not the case, what are separate individuals to do? Shall we really not defend ourselves, shall we leave ourselves and the lives and fate of our loved ones to the arbitrary action of cruel and evil men?"

But actually the question as to what I should do to oppose acts of violence being performed before my eyes is based entirely on the gross superstition that it is possible for man not only to know the future but to prearrange it according to his will. For the man who is free from that superstition this question does not and cannot arise.

The villain raises a knife over his victim; I have a pistol in my hand and can kill him. But I really do not know, and cannot know, whether the upraised knife will effect its evil purpose. It may not, while I most likely *shall* accomplish my evil deed. And thus the only thing a man can and must do, in this as in all similar cases, is the same thing he must *always* do, in every case: he must do what he considers proper before God and his conscience. And a man's conscience may demand the sacrifice of his own life, not the life of another. The same may be said with regard to ways of opposing social evil.

Thus to the question of what a man is to do in the presence of villainies performed by one person or by many, only one answer can be given by the man who is free from the superstition that it is possible to know men's future situation and to prearrange this situation by violence: Do unto others as you would have them do unto you.

"But he steals and murders, whereas I do not. Let him observe the Golden Rule, and then observance of it can likewise be demanded of me," ordinarily say the men of our world, and with greater confidence the loftier the social eminence they occupy. "I do not steal or murder," says the ruler, the government minister, the general, the judge, the landowner, the merchant, the soldier, the policeman. The superstition that the social system justifies every variety of violence has clouded their consciousness to such a degree that they fail to see the continuous, uninterrupted robbery and murder in which they engage in the name of the superstition of the future world order, and see only those infrequent attempts at violence on the part of the so-called murderers and thieves who cannot excuse their use of violence by appealing to the general welfare.

"He is a thief, he is a murderer, he does not observe the Golden Rule," say—who? The very men who murder ceaselessly in wars and force people to prepare for murder, who plunder other nations and their own.

If the Golden Rule is ineffective against the men who in our society are called murderers and thieves, it is only because they belong to that vast majority who have been murdered and robbed ceaselessly for generations on end, by men who as a

consequence of their superstitions do not see the criminal nature
of their acts.

And thus to the question of how to act relative to those who
attempt to use violence of any sort against us there is one
answer: stop doing unto others what you do not wish them to
do unto you.

Not to mention the sheer injustice of applying the antiquated
law of retaliation to some uses of violence while leaving unpun-
ished the most horrible and cruel uses—uses by the state in the
name of the superstition of a future order—applying crude retaliation against the so-called robbers and thieves is furthermore
manifestly unreasonable, and leads directly to a result opposite
that intended. It leads to an opposite result because it destroys
that mightiest of forces, public opinion, which protects men from
every use of violence against one another a hundred times more
effectively than jails and gallows.

This reasoning applies with special force to international relations. "What are we to do when savage nations come to take
from us the fruits of our labors, our wives, our daughters?"
men say, thinking only of protecting themselves against the very
villainies and crimes they forget that they commit ceaselessly
against other nations. The whites say: "Yellow peril!" The
Hindus, the Chinese, and the Japanese say, with greater reason:
"White peril!" But one has only to free oneself from the
superstition that justifies violence to be horrified at all these
crimes which have been committed and are being committed
ceaselessly by some nations against others, and still more to be
horrified at the national moral stupidity resulting from that
superstition, according to which the English, the Russians, the
Germans, the French, and the Americans can talk—in the face
of the frightful crimes they have committed and are still com-
mitting in India, Indo-China, Poland, Manchuria, and Algeria—
can talk not only about the threats of violence confronting them,
but about the need to protect themselves against these threats.

Thus a man has but to free his mind, if only briefly, from the
horrible superstition that it is possible to know the future order
of society—a superstition that justifies the use of every sort of
violence in support of that order—and to look sincerely and

seriously at the present life of men, for him to realize that *the claim that it is necessary to resist evil by violence is nothing more than an excuse men give for their pet habitual vices: vengeance, avarice, envy, ambition, love of power, pride, cowardice, and spite.*

If every man would only understand that he lacks not only the right but the ability to order the lives of other men, that the task of each is only to order and guide his own life in accordance with that supreme religious law which has been revealed to him, then of itself that bestial mode of existence of the so-called Christian nations—an existence which is agonizing, clashes with our souls' demands, and is increasingly worsening—would be abolished.

Whoever you may be: sovereign, judge, farmer, factory worker, beggar—reflect on this; take pity on yourself, take pity on your soul. No matter how befogged and stupefied you may be by your crown, your authority, or your wealth, no matter how exhausted and embittered you may be by your need and by the wrongs that have been done you—you are the possessor or rather the manifester of that same Divine spirit which abides in us all and which in our time clearly and plainly says to you: Why do you torment yourself and all those with whom you come in contact in this world? Only understand who you are, and on the one hand how insignificant is that which you mistakenly call your self—identifying your self with your body—and on the other hand how boundlessly great is that of which you are truly conscious as your self—your spiritual nature. Only understand this and begin to live each hour of your life not for external goals but for the fulfillment of that true purpose of your life which is revealed to you by the wisdom of the entire world, by the teaching of Christ, and by your own consciousness. Begin to live by finding the goal and the good of your life in freeing your spirit more and more each day from the illusions of the flesh, or in perfecting yourself more and more in love—which is in essence the same thing. Only begin to do this, and from the first day and the first hour you will feel a new and joyous sense of complete freedom and well-being flow increasingly into your soul, and—what will strike you most of all—you will find that the very external conditions which so concerned you and which nonetheless remained so different from what you desired, will of themselves (whether you are left in the same external situation or taken out of it) cease to be obstacles and will only become greater and greater joys of your life.

And if you are unhappy—but I know that you are unhappy—reflect on this: what has been set before you here was not invented by me, but is the fruit of the spiritual efforts of all the highest and best minds and hearts of mankind, and in it lies the sole means of delivering you from your unhappiness and giving you the greatest good which man can attain in this life.

This is what I wanted to say to my brothers before I die.

2 July 1908
Yasnaya Polyana

FYODOR MIKHAILOVICH
DOSTOEVSKY
[1821–1881]

Today FYODOR DOSTOEVSKY requires no introduction—his books are translated and read the world over. It is only in terms of his place in the intellectual development of Russia in the nineteenth century that his work need be discussed.

Born in Moscow in 1821, the son of a military doctor of Ukrainian origin, Dostoevsky was brought up in a devoutly religious atmosphere. He went to the School of Military Engineering in Saint Petersburg and spent many of his free hours reading Schiller, Hugo, and other romantic poets. While he was there, his father was killed by the peasants of his country estate: it is said that it was upon receiving the news of his father's death that Dostoevsky had his first epileptic attack.[1]

Soon after his graduation in 1842, Dostoevsky retired from government service and began to write—and from that time to his death in 1881 he was constantly in financial difficulties. His first novel, *Poor Folk*, published in 1846, won him immediate literary acclaim, however, from both the general public and such critics as Belinsky and Nekrasov.

Dostoevsky's social interests are already evident in his first book. It is therefore not surprising that he joined the Petrashevsky Circle,[2] or even that on two occasions he read aloud to this group Belinsky's famous *Letter to Gogol* (1847).[3] When,

1. The history of Dostoevsky's epilepsy is obscure. The date of the first attack is open to question. It is clear that the attacks were frequent at times of grievous nervous strain and that they abated in the last ten years of his life.
2. See above, Vol. I, p. 244.
3. See above, Vol. I, pp. 312-320.

in 1849, government attention was directed to the Circle and its members were arrested, these readings formed part of the government's case against Dostoevsky.

In accordance with a method of punishment not uncommon in the reign of Nicholas I, Dostoevsky and his fellow prisoners were found guilty, condemned to death, taken to the place of execution, and, at the last moment, reprieved. They were then sent to penal servitude in Siberia. It was at this time—after facing execution and during his years in Siberia in the company of murderers and other criminals—that Dostoevsky suffered a spiritual crisis which was to change his outlook for the rest of his life.

Dostoevsky's literary interpretation of his experiences in Siberia is recorded in *Notes from the House of the Dead*. These experiences also provide material for much of his literary work.

Dostoevsky returned to European Russia in 1858. In 1861, he and his brother, Michael, started the periodical *Vremya* (Time). The aim of the journal, which expresses that of the *pochvenniki*,[4] was stated in its announcement: "We have at last persuaded ourselves that we too are a separate nationality, independent and original in the highest degree, and that our task is to create for ourselves an indigenous form native to *our own soil*. . . . We foresee that . . . the Russian idea may well be a synthesis of all the ideas that have developed in Europe."[5] The journal was suspended after two years because of an article which expressed liberal views on the "Polish question." Permission was granted in 1864 to resume publication under another name, *Epokha* (The Epoch), but this second effort was doomed because of financial difficulties.

In the early sixties, the intellectual liberalism Dostoevsky had known—and for which he was arrested—had developed into what was to become an active revolutionary movement. At this time it was still mostly in a theoretical stage, but its theory—Nihilism—was now clearly revolutionary. Dostoevsky, who had known and approved its stage of the forties, could not accept the form in which he found it after his return from Siberia. As the reader has noted, Turgenev, in *Fathers and Sons* (1861), was the first to recognize Nihilism for what it was. In reply

4. See above, pp. 203-204.
5. Quoted in Zenkovsky, *op. cit.*, p. 414.

to Turgenev, Chernyshevsky wrote the novel *What Is To Be Done?* (1863). In a brilliant attack, not on the man he liked personally but on Chernyshevsky's view—a view which he saw as a terrible perversion of the aspirations of mankind—Dostoevsky wrote *Notes from Underground* in 1864. In this novelette, Dostoevsky is particularly concerned to refute Nihilism's "scientific" materialistic basis. In *Crime and Punishment* (1866) Dostoevsky attacks Nihilism's ethics of "scientific egoism." In another major work, *The Devils* [6] (1871-1872), Dostoevsky attacks its practical consequences.

The view expressed in the selection from *Notes from Underground* given here is a coherent part of Dostoevsky's whole mature outlook. The spiritual crisis which he underwent was not one that led to a complete break with his earlier views. Dostoevsky's social concern never leaves him. His socialism, indeed, remains. But he has transcended its secularity and now appraises the problems of man from a spiritual standpoint. The idea of socialism has given way to that of *sobornost*.[7] And Dostoevsky sees the two viewpoints, the religious and secular utopias, opposed as good and evil, where evil is not the mere negation of good but is positively, actively antagonistic to it. This is made evident in the "Legend of the Grand Inquisitor" in *The Brothers Karamazov* (1880).

In the same novel, the spiritual point of view is expressed by *Starets* Zosima. Zosima points out that this world, in which the materialist finds inequality, injustice, and pain, is, for him who sees it in the proper light, the Kingdom of Heaven: "We do not understand that life is a paradise . . . we have only to wish to understand this and it will immediately appear before us in all its beauty." Dostoevsky is by no means, however, here denying the reality of evil; he is, rather, saying that evil is both the real cause and the real product of the rationalistic, scientific outlook. It is the logical conclusion of the logical approach, so evident in the West, and taken over by the radicals of the sixties.

And Dostoevsky knew the West. He made his first trip abroad in 1860; he returned to Europe frequently after that, staying mostly in Germany. In *Winter Notes on Summer Im-*

6. Also known in English as *The Possessed*.
7. See above, Vol. I, pp. 161-162.

pressions (1863), Dostoevsky records his reaction to Western Europe after his first visit. The reaction to France is reminiscent of Herzen's: Dostoevsky was disgusted by the French bourgeoisie. He describes, now with biting irony, now with buffoonery, the pettiness, false morality, materialism, and selfishness of the French bourgeoisie—these traits are repulsive to him both aesthetically and morally, and to them Dostoevsky contrasts love, brotherhood, *sobornost:*

> . . . the highest use a man can make of his individuality, of the completed development of his *I*, would be to destroy this *I*, to return it entirely to all and to each inseparably and supremely. And this is the greatest happiness. In this way the law of *I* merges with the law of humanity and both are one, and *I* and all (which appear to be two opposed extremes) are both mutually destroyed, while at the same time they attain the higher goal of their own individual development on this basis.
>
> This is the paradise of Christ. All history, both of humanity and of every separate part of it, is only the growth, the struggle, the yearning for, and the attainment of this goal.[8]

Dostoevsky's ideal society, then, is the society of the Church as conceived by Khomyakov, brotherhood in the free love of God. And it is this ideal which Dostoevsky himself recognizes as the basis of his Slavophilism. Russia has the mission of bringing about the "genuine unification of mankind as a whole in a new, brotherly, universal union whose inception is derived from the Slavic genius, pre-eminently from the spirit of the great Russian people who have suffered so long. . . ."[9] Shestov's interpretation to the contrary,[10] Dostoevsky's socialism has never been denied—like Berdyaev's, it has merely been de-secularized.

8. *Notebooks,* entry of April 16, 1864, quoted by N. O. Lossky in *Dostoyevsky and His Christian World View,* New York, 1953, p. 152; this passage translated by Jesse Zeldin from *Dostoyevsky i yevo khristianskoye miroponimaniye.*

9. *The Diary of a Writer,* trans. Boris Brasol, New York, 1954, p. 780.

10. *Dostojewski und Nietzsche,* trans. R. von Walter, Cologne, 1924, p. 7, quoted in Zenkovsky, *op. cit.,* p. 417.

SELECTED BIBLIOGRAPHY

Works:
All of Dostoevsky's major works and many minor ones are available in English, most of them in both paperback and hard-cover editions.

Secondary Sources:
N. Berdyaev, *Dostoevsky*, trans. Donald Attwater, New York, 1957.

R. Fülop-Miller, *Fyodor Dostoevsky: Insight, Faith, and Prophecy*, trans. Richard and Clara Winston, New York, 1950.

V. Ivanov, *Freedom and the Tragic Life: A Study in Dostoevsky*, trans. Norman Cameron, New York, 1960.

K. Mochulsky, *Dostoevsky: His Life and Work*, trans. Michael A. Minihan, Princeton, 1967.

G. Steiner, *Tolstoy or Dostoevsky: An Essay in the Old Criticism*, New York, 1959.

R. Wellek, *Dostoevsky: A Collection of Critical Essays*, New York, 1962.

A. Yarmolinsky, *Dostoevsky: His Life and Art*, New York, 1962.

[FYODOR DOSTOEVSKY]

Notes from Underground *

Oh, tell me, who was it first announced, who was it first proclaimed, that man only does nasty things because he does not
know his own interests; and that if he were enlightened, if his
eyes were opened to his real normal interests, man would at once
cease to do nasty things, would at once become good and
noble because, being enlightened and understanding his real
advantage, he would see his own advantage in the good and
nothing else, and we all know that not one man can, consciously,
act against his own interests, consequently, so to say, through
necessity, he would begin doing good? Oh, the babe! Oh, the
pure, innocent child! Why, in the first place, when in all these
thousands of years has there been a time when man has acted
only from his own interest? What is to be done with the millions of facts that bear witness that men, *consciously*, that is,
fully understanding their real interests, have left them in the
background and have rushed headlong on another path, to
meet peril and danger, compelled to this course by nobody and
by nothing, but, as it were, simply disliking the beaten track, and
have obstinately, willfully, struck out another difficult, absurd
way, seeking it almost in the darkness. So, I suppose, this obsti-
nacy and perversity were pleasanter to them than any advantage.
. . . Advantage! What is advantage?

  And will you take it upon yourself to define with perfect
accuracy in what the advantage of man consists? And what
if it so happens that a man's advantage, *sometimes*, not only
may, but even must, consist in his desiring in certain cases what
is harmful to himself and not advantageous. And if so, if there
can be such a case, the whole principle falls into dust. What do
you think—are there such cases? You laugh; laugh away, gentlemen, but only answer me: have man's advantages been reckoned
up with perfect certainty? Are there not some which not only

---

* From *Notes from Underground*, trans. Constance Garnett, Part I, Sections vii and viii.

have not been included but cannot possibly be included under any classification? You see, you gentlemen have, to the best of my knowledge, taken your whole register of human advantages from the averages of statistical figures and politico-economical formulas. Your advantages are prosperity, wealth, freedom, peace —and so on, and so on. So that the man who should, for instance, go openly and knowingly in opposition to all that list would, to your thinking, and indeed mine too, of course, be an obscurantist or an absolute madman: would he not? But, you know, this is what is surprising: why does it so happen that all these statisticians, sages and lovers of humanity, when they reckon up human advantages invariably leave out one? They don't even take it into their reckoning in the form in which it should be taken and the whole reckoning depends upon that. It would be no great matter, they would simply have to take it, this advantage, and add it to the list. But the trouble is, that this strange advantage does not fall under any classification and is not in place in any list. I have a friend for instance . . . Ech! gentlemen, but of course he is your friend, too; and indeed there is no one, no one, to whom he is not a friend!

When he prepares for any undertaking this gentleman immediately explains to you, elegantly and clearly, exactly how he must act in accordance with the laws of reason and truth. What is more, he will talk to you with excitement and passion of the true normal interests of man; with irony he will upbraid the shortsighted fools who do not understand their own interests, nor the true significance of virtue; and, within a quarter of an hour, without any sudden outside provocation, but simply through something inside him which is stronger than all his interests, he will go off on quite a different tack—that is, act in direct opposition to what he has just been saying about himself, in opposition to the laws of reason, in opposition to his own advantage—in fact, in opposition to everything. . . . I warn you that my friend is a compound personality, and therefore it is difficult to blame him as an individual. The fact is, gentlemen, it seems there must really exist something that is dearer to almost every man than his greatest advantages, or (not to be illogical) there is a most advantageous advantage (the very one omitted of which we spoke just now) which is more important and more advantageous than all other advantages, for the sake of which a man if necessary is ready to act in opposition to all laws; that is, in opposition to reason, honor, peace, prosperity—in fact, in opposition to all those excellent and useful things if only he can attain that fundamental, most advantageous advantage which is dearer to him than all. "Yes, but it's advantage all the same" you will retort. But excuse me, I'll make the point clear, and it is not a case of playing upon words. What matters is, that this advantage is remarkable from the very fact that it breaks down all our classifications, and continually shatters every system constructed by lovers of mankind for the benefit of mankind. In fact, it upsets everything. But before I mention this advantage to you, I want to compromise myself personally, and therefore I boldly declare that all these fine systems—all these theories for explaining to mankind their real normal interests, in order that inevitably striving to pursue these interests they may at once become good and noble—are, in my opinion, so far, mere logical exercises! Yes, logical exercises. Why, to maintain this theory of the regeneration of mankind by means of the pursuit of his own advantage is to my mind almost the same thing as . . . as to affirm, for instance, following Buckle, that through civilization mankind becomes softer, and consequently less bloodthirsty, and less fitted for warfare.

Logically it does seem to follow from his arguments. But man has such a predilection for systems and abstract deductions that he is ready to distort the truth intentionally, he is ready to deny the evidence of his senses only to justify his logic. I take this example because it is the most glaring instance of it. Only look about you: blood is being spilt in streams, and in the merriest way, as though it were champagne. Take the whole of the nineteenth century in which Buckle lived. Take Napoleon— the Great and also the present one. Take North America—the eternal union. Take the farce of Schleswig-Holstein. . . . And what is it that civilization softens in us? The only gain of civilization for mankind is the greater capacity for variety of sensations—and absolutely nothing more. And through the development of this many-sidedness man may come to finding enjoyment in bloodshed. In fact, this has already happened to him. Have you noticed that it is the most civilized gentlemen who have been the subtlest slaughterers, to whom the Attilas and Stenka Razins could not hold a candle, and if they are not so conspicuous as the Attilas and Stenka Razins it is simply because they are so often met with, are so ordinary and have become so familiar to us. In any case civilization has made mankind if not more bloodthirsty, at least more vilely, more loathsomely bloodthirsty. In old days he saw justice in bloodshed and with his conscience at peace exterminated those he thought proper. Now we do think bloodshed abominable and yet we engage in this abomination, and with more energy than ever. Which is worse? Decide that for yourselves.

They say that Cleopatra (excuse an instance from Roman history) was fond of sticking gold pins into her slave-girls' breasts and derived gratification from their screams and writhings. You will say that that was in the comparatively barbarous times; that these are barbarous times too, because also, comparatively speaking, pins are stuck in even now; that though man has now learned to see more clearly than in barbarous ages, he is still far from having learned to act as reason and science would dictate. But yet you are fully convinced that he will be sure to learn when he gets rid of certain old bad habits, and when common sense and science have completely re-educated human nature and turned it in a normal direction. You are confident that then man will cease from *intentional* error and will, so to say, be compelled not to want to set his will against his normal interests. That is not all; then, you say, science itself will teach man (though to my mind it's a superfluous luxury) that he never has really had any caprice or will of his own, and that he himself is something of the nature of a piano-key or the stop of an organ, and that there are, besides, things called the laws of nature; so that everything he does is not done by his willing it, but is done of itself, by the laws of nature. Consequently we have only to discover these laws of nature, and man will no longer have to answer for his actions and life will become exceedingly easy for him. All human actions will then, of course, be tabulated according to these laws, mathematically, like tables of logarithms up to 108,000, and entered in an index; or, better still, there would be published certain edifying works of the nature of encyclopaedic lexicons, in which everything will be so clearly calculated and explained that there will be no more incidents or adventures in the world.

Then—this is all what you say—new economic relations will be established, all ready-made and worked out with mathematical exactitude, so that every possible question will vanish in the twinkling of an eye, simply because every possible answer to it will be provided. Then the "Palace of Crystal" will be built. Then . . . In fact, those will be halcyon days. Of course there is no guaranteeing (this is my comment) that it will not be, for instance, frightfully dull then (for what will one have to do when everything will be calculated and tabulated?), but on the other hand everything will be extraordinarily rational. Of course boredom may lead you to anything. It is boredom sets one sticking golden pins into people, but all that would not matter. What is bad (this is my comment again) is that I dare say people will be thankful for the gold pins then. Man is stupid, you know, phenomenally stupid; or rather he is not at all stupid, but he is so ungrateful that you could not find another like him in all creation. I, for instance, would not be in the least surprised if all of a sudden, apropos of nothing, in the midst of general prosperity a gentleman with an ignoble, or rather with a reactionary and ironical, countenance were to arise and putting his arms akimbo, say to us all: "I say, gentlemen, hadn't we better kick over the whole show and scatter rationalism to the winds, simply to send these logarithms to the devil, and to enable us to live once more at our own sweet foolish will!" That again would not matter; but what is annoying is that he would be sure to find followers—such is the nature of man. And all that for the most foolish reason, which, one would think, was hardly worth mentioning: that is, that man everywhere and at all times, whoever he may be, has preferred to act as he chose and not in the least as his reason and advantage dictated. And one may choose what is contrary to one's own interests, and sometimes one *positively ought* (that is my idea). One's own free unfettered choice, one's own caprice—however wild it may be, one's own fancy worked up at times to frenzy—is that very "most advantageous advantage" which we have overlooked, which comes under no classification and against which all systems and theories are continually being shattered to atoms. And how do these wiseacres know that man wants a normal, a virtuous choice? What has made them conceive that man must want a rationally advantageous choice? What man wants is simply *independent* choice, whatever that independence may cost and wherever it may lead. And choice, of course, the devil only knows what choice. . . .

"Ha! ha! ha! But you know there is no such thing as choice in reality, say what you like," you will interpose with a chuckle. "Science has succeeded in so far analyzing man that we know already that choice and what is called freedom of will is nothing else than—"

Stay, gentlemen, I meant to begin with that myself. I confess, I was rather frightened. I was just going to say that the devil only knows what choice depends on, and that perhaps that was a very good thing, but I remembered the teaching of science . . . and pulled myself up. And here you have begun upon it. Indeed, if there really is some day discovered a formula for all our desires and caprices—that is, an explanation of what they depend upon, by what laws they arise, how they develop, what they are aiming at in one case and in another and so on, that is, a real mathematical formula—then, most likely, man will at once cease to feel desire, indeed, he will be certain to. For who would want to choose by rule? Besides, he will at once be transformed from a human being into an organ-stop or something of the sort; for what is a man without desires, without free will and without choice, if not a stop in an organ? What do you think? Let us reckon the chances—can such a thing happen or not?

"H'm!" you decide. "Our choice is usually mistaken from a false view of our advantage. We sometimes choose absolute nonsense because in our foolishness we see in that nonsense the easiest means for attaining a supposed advantage. But when all that is explained and worked out on paper (which is perfectly possible, for it is contemptible and senseless to suppose that some laws of nature man will never understand), then certainly so-called desires will no longer exist. For if a desire should come into conflict with reason we shall then reason and not desire, because it will be impossible retaining our reason to be *senseless* in our desires, and in that way knowingly act against reason and desire to injure ourselves. And as all choice and reasoning can be really calculated—because there will some day be discovered the laws of our so-called free will—so, joking apart, there may one day be something like a table constructed of them, so that we really shall choose in accordance with it. If, for instance, some day they calculate and prove to me that I made a coarse gesture at someone because I could not help doing so and that I had to use that particular finger, what *freedom* is left me, especially if I am a learned man and have taken my degree somewhere? Then I should be able to calculate my whole life for thirty years beforehand. In short, if this could be arranged there would be nothing left for us to do; anyway, we should have to understand that. And, in fact, we ought unwearyingly to repeat to ourselves that at such and such a time and in such and such circumstances nature does not ask our leave; that we have got to take her as she is and not fashion her to suit our fancy, and if we really aspire to formulas and tables of rules, and well, even . . . to the chemical retort, there's no help for it, we must accept the retort too, or else it will be accepted without our consent. . . ."

Yes, but here I come to a stop! Gentlemen, you must excuse me for being over-philosophical; it's the result of forty years underground! Allow me to indulge my fancy. You see, gentlemen, reason is an excellent thing, there's no disputing that, but reason is nothing but reason and satisfies only the rational side of man's nature, while will is a manifestation of the whole life, that is, of the whole human life including reason and all the impulses. And although our life, in this manifestation of it, is often worthless, yet it is life and not simply extracting square roots. Here I, for instance, quite naturally want to live, in order to satisfy all my capacities for life, and not simply my capacity for reasoning, that is, not simply one-twentieth of my capacity for life. What does reason know? Reason only knows what it has succeeded in learning (some things, perhaps, it will never learn; this is a poor comfort, but why not say so frankly?) and human nature acts as a whole, with everything that is in it, consciously or unconsciously, and, even if it goes wrong, it lives. I suspect, gentlemen, that you are looking at me with compassion; you tell me again that an enlightened and developed man, such, in short, as the future man will be, cannot consciously desire anything disadvantageous to himself, that that can be proved mathematically. I thoroughly agree, it can—by mathematics.

But I repeat for the hundredth time, there is one case, one only, when man may consciously, purposely, desire what is injurious to himself, what is stupid, very stupid—simply in order to have the right to desire for himself even what is very stupid and not to be bound by an obligation to desire only what is sensible. Of course, this very stupid thing, this caprice of ours, may be in reality, gentlemen, more advantageous for us than anything else on earth, especially in certain cases. And in particular it may be more advantageous than any advantage even when it does us obvious harm, and contradicts the soundest conclusions of our reason concerning our advantage—for in any circumstances it preserves for us what is most precious and most important—that is, our personality, our individuality. Some, you see, maintain that this really is the most precious thing for mankind; choice can, of course, if it chooses, be in agreement with reason; and especially if this be not abused but kept within bounds. It is profitable and sometimes even praiseworthy. But very often, and even most often, choice is utterly and stubbornly opposed to reason . . . and . . . and . . . do you know that that, too, is profitable, sometimes even praiseworthy? Gentlemen, let us suppose that man is not stupid. (Indeed one cannot refuse to suppose that, if only from the one consideration, that, if man is stupid, then who is wise?) But if he is not stupid, he is monstrously ungrateful! Phenomenally ungrateful. In fact, I believe that the best definition of man is the ungrateful biped. But that is not all, that is not his worst defect; his worst defect is his perpetual moral obliquity, perpetual—from the days of the Flood to the Schleswig-Holstein period.

Moral obliquity and consequently lack of good sense; for it has long been accepted that lack of good sense is due to no other cause than moral obliquity. Put it to the test and cast your eyes upon the history of mankind. What will you see? Is it a grand spectacle? Grand, if you like. Take the Colossus of Rhodes, for instance, that's worth something. With good reason Mr. Anaevsky testifies of it that some say that it is the work of man's hands, while others maintain that it has been created by nature herself. Is it many-colored? It may be it is many-colored, too: if one takes the dress uniforms, military and civilian, of all peoples in all ages—that alone is worth something, and if you take the undress uniforms you will never get to the end of it; no historian would be equal to the job. Is it monotonous? It may be it's monotonous, too: it's fighting and fighting; they are fighting now, they fought first and they fought last—you will admit that it is almost too monotonous. In short, one may say anything about the history of the world—anything that might enter the most disordered imagination. The only thing one can't say is that it's rational. The very word sticks in one's throat. And, indeed, this is the odd thing that is continually happening: there are continually turning up in life moral and rational persons, sages and lovers of humanity, who make it their object to live all their lives as morally and rationally as possible, to be, so to speak, a light to their neighbors simply in order to show them that it is possible to live morally and rationally in this world. And yet we all know that those very people sooner or later have been false to themselves, playing some queer trick, often a most unseemly one. Now I ask you: what can be expected of man since he is a being endowed with such strange qualities? Shower upon him every earthly blessing, drown him in a sea of happiness, so that nothing but bubbles of bliss can be seen on the surface; give him economic prosperity, such that he should have nothing else to do but sleep, eat cakes, and busy himself with the continuation of his species, and even then out of sheer ingratitude, sheer spite, man would play you some nasty trick. He would even risk his cakes and would deliberately desire the most fatal rubbish, the most uneconomical absurdity, simply to introduce into all this positive good sense his fatal fantastic element. It is just his fantastic dreams, his vulgar folly, that he will desire to retain, simply in order to prove to himself—as though that were so necessary—that men still are men and not the keys of a piano, which the laws of nature threaten to control so completely that soon one will be able to desire nothing but by the calendar. And that is not all: even if man really were nothing but a piano-key, even if this were proved to him by natural science and mathematics, even then he would not become reasonable, but would purposely do something perverse out of simple ingratitude, simply to gain his point. And if he does not find means he will contrive destruction and chaos, will contrive sufferings of all sorts, only to gain his point! He will launch a curse upon the world, and as only man can curse (it is his privilege, the primary distinction between him and other animals) it may be by his curse alone he will attain his object—that is, convince himself that he is a man and not a piano-key! If you say that all this, too, can be calculated and tabulated—chaos and darkness and curses, so that the mere possibility of calculating it all beforehand would stop it all, and reason would reassert itself—then man would purposely go mad in order to be rid of reason and gain his point! I believe in it, I answer for it, for the whole work of man really seems to consist in nothing but proving to himself every minute that he is a man and not a piano-key! It may be at the cost of his skin, it may be by cannibalism! And this being so, can one help being tempted to rejoice that it has not yet come off, and that desire still depends on something we don't know?

You will scream at me (that is, if you condescend to do so) that no one is touching my free will, that all they are concerned with is that my will should of itself, of its own free will, coincide with my own normal interests, with the laws of nature and arithmetic.

Good heavens, gentlemen, what sort of free will is left when we come to tabulation and arithmetic, when it will all be a case of twice two makes four? Twice two makes four without my will. As if free will meant that!

[FYODOR DOSTOEVSKY]

Summer Impressions *

Why does everyone here want to shrink back and shrivel and make out he is only small fry and remain as inconspicuous as is possible: "I don't exist, I don't exist at all; I am hiding, walk past, please, don't take any notice of me, pretend you don't see me: pass along, pass along!"

"But whom are you talking about? Who shrinks back?"

The bourgeois, of course.

"Come now, he is King, he is everything, *le tiers état c'est tout*, and you say he shrinks back!"

Oh yes, he does; Why otherwise, should he have hidden himself behind the Emperor Napoleon? Why has he forgotten the lofty language he used to love so much in the Chamber of Deputies? Why does he not want to remember anything and runs away from any reminders of the past? Why do his thoughts, his eyes, his speech betray so much worry whenever others dare express a wish for something in his presence? Why, whenever he foolishly forgets himself and expresses a wish for something, does he suddenly give a start and begin to deny his own words: "Good Heavens, what's the matter with me, really!" and for a long time after that he tries scrupulously to make amends for his behavior by conscientiousness and obedience? Why does he look and almost say: "Well, now, I'll do a bit of trade in my shop today, and, God willing, I'll do a bit of trade tomorrow too, and perhaps even the day after if the Lord lets me, in His great mercy . . . and then, then—oh, if only I could save just a teeny bit and . . . *après moi le déluge*." Why does he stick his poor out of the way somewhere and assure people that there aren't any? Why does he make do with official literature? Why does he so want to convince himself that his newspapers are not open to bribery? Why does he agree to give so much money for the maintenance of police spies? Why does he not

* From *Summer Impressions*, trans. Kyril Fitzlyon, London, 1955, pp. 70-75, 77-88, 90-92, 93-94.

dare breathe a word about the Mexican expedition? Why on the stage are husbands made out to be so very noble-minded and rich, while lovers are all so tattered, jobless and friendless, clerks or artists, so much trash? Why does he imagine that all wives without exception are faithful to the last extreme, that the home prospers, that the *pot-au-feu* is cooking on the most virtuous of hearths and that no horns disfigure his forehead? About the horns—this has been decided once and for all, agreed without further ado and taken for granted, and though cabs with drawn blinds constantly ply up and down the boulevard, though time and place can always be found for requirements of an interesting nature, and though wives very often dress more expensively than could be warranted by the husband's pocket, this has been agreed and ratified, and what more do you want? And why has it been agreed and ratified? The answer is quite obvious: otherwise people might perhaps think that an ideal state of things has not been reached yet, that Paris is not yet Heaven on Earth, that something could perhaps still be wished for, that, therefore, the bourgeois himself is not quite satisfied with the state of things which he supports and which he tries to force on everyone, that the cloth of society has rents which must be mended. This is precisely why the bourgeois smears holes in his shoes with ink lest, God forbid, people should notice anything! The wives, in the meantime, suck sweets, wear gloves of a kind to send Russian ladies in far-off Saint Petersburg into envious hysterics, show their little feet and lift their skirts on boulevards with all the grace in the world. What more is needed for perfect bliss? It follows that, circumstances being what they are, novels can no longer bear titles such as, for example, "Wife, Husband, and Lover," because there are no, and cannot be any, lovers. And even if in Paris they were as numerous as the sands of the sea (and maybe they are even more numerous there), there are none there all the same, and there cannot be any because it is thus agreed and ratified and because virtue shines everywhere. That is the way it should be: virtue must shine everywhere. The sight of the great courtyard of the Palais Royal in the evening and up to eleven o'clock at night is surely enough to make anyone shed a sentimental tear. Innumerable husbands stroll about arm-in-arm with their innumerable spouses, their sweet and well-behaved children gambol round them, a little fountain tinkles and its monotonous plash reminds you of something still and quiet, everlasting, permanent Heidelbergian. And it isn't as if there was only one little fountain in Paris tinkling in this way; there are many little fountains, and everywhere it is the same and one's heart rejoices at the sight of it all.

Paris has an unquenchable thirst for virtue. Nowadays the Frenchman is a serious and reliable man, often tender-hearted, so that I cannot understand why he is so afraid of something even now, and is afraid of it in spite of all the *gloire militaire* which flourishes in France and which Jacques Bonhomme pays so much for. The Parisian dearly loves to trade, but even as he trades and fleeces you in his shop, he fleeces you not for the sake of profit, as in the old days, but in the name of virtue, out of some sacred necessity. To amass a fortune and possess as many things as possible—this has become the Parisian's main moral code, to be equated with religious observance. The same thing happened in the old days too, but now—now it has assumed, so to speak, a sort of sacramental aspect. In the old days some value was attached to other things besides money, so that a man with no money but possessing other qualities could expect some kind of esteem; but now—nothing doing. Now you must make money and acquire as many things as possible and you will then be able to expect at least some sort of esteem, otherwise you cannot expect to have any *self*-esteem, let alone the esteem of other people. The Parisian has a very low opinion of himself if he feels his pockets are empty—and he holds this opinion consciously, and with great conviction.

You are allowed to do amazing things if only you have money. Poor Socrates is nothing but a stupid and obnoxious phrase-monger, and is esteemed, if anywhere, only in the theatre because the bourgeois still likes to show esteem for virtue in the theatre. A strange man, this bourgeois: he proclaims openly that the acquisition of money is the supreme virtue and human duty and yet dearly loves to play at supremely noble sentiments. All Frenchmen have an extraordinarily noble appearance. The meanest little Frenchman who would sell you his own father for six-pence, and add something into the bargain without so much as being asked for it, has at the same time, indeed at the very moment of selling you his own father, such an impressive bear-ing that you feel perplexed. . . .

But in spite of this, the bourgeois is passionately fond of unutterable high-mindedness. On the stage he must have nothing but people completely disinterested in money. Gustave must shine by the light of high-mindedness alone and the bourgeois sheds tears of tender emotion. Without unutterable high-minded-ness he will not even sleep quietly. And as to taking twelve thousand francs instead of fifteen hundred, this was his duty: he took it because he was virtuous. To steal is wicked and mean—that's what the galleys are for; the bourgeois is ready to forgive a great deal, but he will not forgive stealing even if you and your children should be dying of starvation. But should you steal for virtue's sake, then, oh then, everything is forgiven unto you. It means you want to *faire fortune* and amass many possessions, i.e., perform a natural and human duty. In other words, the legal code very clearly defines stealing for low motives, i.e., for the sake of a piece of bread, and stealing in the name of highest virtue. The latter is completely assured, encouraged, and is organized on an extraordinarily sound footing.

Why then—I am back at my old theme again—why then does the bourgeois look nervous and ill at ease? What causes him all this worry? The speechifiers? The phrase-mongers? But he can send them all to hell with one kick of his foot. Argu-ments of pure reason? But reason has proved bankrupt in face of reality, and besides, the rational people themselves, the phi-losophers and metaphysicians, are now beginning to teach that there are no arguments of pure reason, that pure reason does not even exist in this world, that abstract logic is not applicable to humanity, that there is such a thing as John's, Peter's or Gustave's reason, but there has never been any pure reason, that it is a baseless fiction of the eighteenth century.

Whom should he fear then? Workers? But workers are all of them capitalists too, in their heart of hearts: their one ideal is to become capitalists and amass as many things as possible; such is their nature. People don't get their nature for nothing. All this requires centuries of growth and upbringing. National characteristics cannot easily be altered: it is not easy to get away from centuries-old habits which have become ingrained in one's personality.

Peasants? But French peasants are capitalists *par excellence,* the blunt kind of capitalists, i.e., the very best and the most ideally perfect type of capitalist that can possibly be imagined. Communists? or perhaps Socialists? But these fellows have considerably compromised themselves in their day, and in his heart of hearts the bourgeois has a profound contempt for them; and yet, for all his contempt, he is afraid of them. In fact, these are the people he fears. But why should he fear them, really? For did not the Abbé Sieyès in his famous pamphlet predict that the bourgeois would be *everything?* "What is the *tiers état?* Nothing. What must it be? Everything." Well, now, things have turned out as he foretold them. Of all the words spoken at the time they were the only ones to have come true; the only ones to have remained. But the bourgeois still refuses to believe, somehow, despite the fact that all that has been said since Sieyès' words has collapsed and burst like a soap bubble.

Indeed, soon after him, was proclaimed the principle of *liberté, égalité, fraternité.* Excellent. What is *liberté?* Freedom. What freedom? Equal freedom for all to do anything one wants within the limits of the law. When can a man do anything he wants? When he has a million. Does freedom give everyone a million? No. What is a man without a million? A man without a million is not a man who does anything he wants, but a man with whom anything is done that anyone wants. And what follows? What follows is that besides freedom there is also equality, in fact equality before the law. There is only one thing to be said about this equality before the law—that the way in which it is now applied enables, indeed forces, every Frenchman to consider it as a personal insult.

What then remains of the formula? Fraternity, brotherhood. Now this is a most curious concept and, it must be admitted, constitutes the principal stumbling block in the West. The Western man speaks of brotherhood as of the great moving force of humanity, and does not realize that brotherhood cannot come about if it does not exist in fact. What is to be done? Brotherhood must be created at all costs. But it turns out that brotherhood cannot be created, because it creates itself, is given, exists in nature. It was, however, found to be absent in French and in Western nature generally; what was found to exist instead was the principle of individuality, the principle of iso-lation, of intensified self-preservation, of self-seeking, of self-determination within one's own personality or self, of contrast between this self, the whole of nature, and the rest of humanity; and this contrast was considered as an independent and separate principle completely equal and equivalent in value to all that existed apart from itself.

Now such a contrast could not produce brotherhood. Why? Because within brotherhood, true brotherhood, it is not the individual personality, not the self, that should lay claim to its right of equality in value and importance with all the *rest*, but all this *rest* should *itself* approach the individual, the separate self laying this claim, and should itself, without being asked, recognize the individual as its equal in value and rights, i.e., the equal of all else that exists in the world. Nay more, the individual who rebels and makes claims should much rather sacrifice both his personality and the whole of himself to society and not only not claim his rights, but on the contrary, hand them over unconditionally to society. But the Western individual is not used to this kind of procedure: he demands by force, he demands rights, he wants to *go shares*. And, naturally, no brotherhood results. There is, of course, the possibility of regen-eration. But such a regeneration takes thousands of years, for ideas of this kind must, first of all, become completely ingrained and assimilated in order to become reality. Well then, you will reply, must one lose one's individuality in order to be happy? Is salvation to be found in the absence of individuality? My reply is no, on the contrary, not only should one not lose one's individuality, but one should in fact become an individual to a degree far higher than has occurred in the West. You must understand me: a voluntary, absolutely conscious and completely unforced sacrifice of oneself for the sake of all is, I consider, a sign of the highest development of individual personality, its highest power, highest self-possession, and highest freedom of individual will. Voluntarily to lay down one's life for all, be crucified or burned at the stake for the sake of all is possible only at the point of the highest development of individual personality.

A strongly developed individual personality, completely sure of its right to be a personality and deprived of all fear for itself can, in fact, make nothing else out of its personality, can put it, that is, to no other use than to give away the whole of it to all, in order that others too may become personalities just as independent and happy. This is a law of nature; man, normally, tends toward it. Here, however, there is a hair, one very, very thin hair, but if it gets into the machine, all will immediately crack and collapse. It is the following: there must not be in this case the slightest motive of personal gain. For example: I offer myself as a total sacrifice for. all; and this is as it should be—I should sacrifice myself wholly and irrevocably, without consideration of gain, not thinking in the least that here I am, sacrificing my entire self to society and in exchange society will offer the whole of itself to me. One must, in fact, make one's sacrifice with the intention of giving away everything, and even wish that nothing be given to you in exchange and that no one should spend anything on you.

Now, how is this to be done? Surely, this is rather like trying not to think of a polar bear. Try and set yourself the problem of not thinking about a polar bear and you will see that the damned animal will be constantly in your thoughts. What can we do then? We can do nothing; *it must be done of itself*, the solution must *exist in nature;* must form an unconscious part of the nature of the whole race; what is needed, in short, is the principle of brotherhood and love—we must love. Man must instinctively and of his own accord be drawn toward brotherhood, fellowship, and concord and he must be drawn toward them despite immemorial sufferings of his nation, despite the barbarous brutality and ignorance which have become rooted in the nation, despite age-old slavery and foreign invasions. The need for brotherly fellowship must, in fact, have its being in the nature of man, he must be born with it or else have acquired the habit of it from time immemorial.

What would this brotherhood consist in if expressed in rational and conscious language? In each particular individual without constraint or gain to himself, saying to society: "We are strong only when we are all together, therefore take the whole of me if you need me, do not think of me when you pass your laws, do not worry in the slightest, I am handing all my rights over to you, and please dispose of me as you wish. It is the height of happiness for me to sacrifice everything to you and in such a way that you do not suffer any loss in consequence. I shall fade away and merge with the completely uniform mass, only let your brotherhood remain and flourish. . . ." And the brotherhood, on the other hand, must say: "You are giving us too much. We have no right to refuse what you have to give, since you yourself say that therein consists the whole of your happiness; but what can we do, since we, too, care unceasingly for your happiness? You too, then, must take everything from us. We shall always do all we can that you might have as much personal freedom and as much independence as possible. You need no longer fear any enemies, either men or nature. You have the support of all of us, we all guarantee your safety and have your interests at heart night and day because we are brothers, we are all brothers of yours and there are many of us and we are strong. Therefore, do not worry, be of good cheer, fear nothing and put your trust in us."

After this, there will be no necessity for sharing things out, they will all share themselves out automatically. Love one another and all these things will be added unto you. What a Utopia this is, really! It is all based on sentiment and on nature, and not on reason. Surely this is humiliating for reason. What do you think? Is this Utopia or not?

But then what can a socialist do if the principle of brotherhood is absent in Western man, who recognizes, on the contrary, the individual and personal principle which always insists on isolation and on demanding rights sword in hand? Because there is no brotherhood he wants to create it, to build it up. To make jugged hare you must begin by having a hare. But there is no

hare, there is, in other words, no nature capable of brotherhood, no nature with a belief in brotherhood or drawn toward
brotherhood! In desperation, the socialist begins to make and
define the future brotherhood, weighs and measures it, throws
out the bait of personal advantage, explains, teaches and tells
people how much advantage each person will obtain out of this
brotherhood, how much each will gain; he determines the utility
and cost of each individual, and works out in advance the bal-
ance of this world's blessings: how much each individual deserves
them and how much each individual must voluntarily contribute
to the community in exchange for them at the cost of his own
personality. But how can there possibly be any brotherhood if
it is preceded by a distribution of shares and by determining
how much each person has earned and what each must do?

However, a formula was proclaimed which said: "Each for all
and all for each." Nothing better than this could, naturally, be
thought up, particularly as the whole formula was lifted in its
entirety from a well-known book. But then the brethren began
to apply this formula in practice and about six months later
brought an action against the founder of the brotherhood,
Cabet. The Fourierists have, it is said, spent the last 900,000
francs of their capital, but are still trying to organize a brotherhood. The results are nil. Of course it is very tempting to live
according to purely rational, if not brotherly, principles, that
is, to live well, when you are guaranteed by everyone and
nothing is demanded of you except your consent and your work.
But here again there is a curious paradox. A man is offered full
security, promised food and drink, and found work, and as
against this he is merely required to give up a tiny grain of his
personal freedom for the sake of the common good—just a tiny,
tiny grain. But man does not want to live on these conditions,
he finds even the tiny grain too irksome. He thinks that he is
being put in jail, poor fool, and that he would be better off
by himself, because then he would have full freedom. And
when he is free he is knocked about and refused work, he
starves to death and has no real freedom. But all the same, the
strange fellow still prefers his own freedom. Naturally enough,

the socialist is simply forced to give him up and tell him that he is a fool, that he is not ready yet, not ripe enough to understand what is good for him; that a dumb little ant, a miserable ant is more intelligent than he is because everything is so lovely in an ant hill, so well ordered, no one goes hungry and all are happy, everyone knows what he has to do; in fact man has a long way to go before he can hope to reach the standards of an ant hill.

In other words, though socialism is possible it is possible anywhere but in France.

And so, in final despair, the socialist proclaims at last: *Liberté, égalité, fraternité ou la mort.*[1] Then there is no more to be said, and the bourgeois is completely triumphant.

And if the bourgeois is triumphant it means that Sieyès' formula has come true literally and to the last detail. And so the bourgeois is everything. Why then is he shy and retiring, what does he fear? Everyone has collapsed, none has proved capable of standing up to him. In the old days, at the time of Louis-Philippe, for example, the bourgeois was not as shy and timid, and yet he reigned then too. Indeed, he still fought then, sensed that he had an enemy, and finally defeated him on the June barricades with the aid of rifle and bayonet. But when the battle was over the bourgeois suddenly realized that he was alone in the world, that there was nothing better than himself, that he was the ideal and that instead of trying as hitherto to convince the whole of humanity that he was the ideal, all that was left for him to do was simply to pose with quiet dignity in the eyes of humanity as the last word in human beauty and perfection. A ticklish situation, say what you will. Salvation came from Napoleon III. For the bourgeois he was the gift of the gods, the only way out of the difficulty, the only possibility available at the time. From that moment on the bourgeois begins to prosper, pays a frightful lot for his prosperity and fears everything just because he has attained everything. When one attains everything

1. Based on the slogan proclaimed by Gracchus Babeuf (1760-1795). Some of the "decrees" he published for the benefit of his future communist republic bore the words: *"Egalité, Liberté, Bonheur Commun ou la Mort."*—TRANS.

it is hard *to lose* everything. Whence follows, my friends, that he who fears most prospers most. Don't laugh please. For what is a bourgeois these days? . . .

And why are there so many flunkeys among the bourgeois, and of such noble appearance at that? Please don't blame me and don't exclaim that I am exaggerating or being libelous or spiteful. What or whom is my spite directed against? Why should I be spiteful? The fact is simply that there are many flunkeys. Servility seeps increasingly into the very nature of the bourgeois and is increasingly taken for virtue. And that's how it should be in present circumstances. It is their natural consequence. But the main thing, ah, the main thing is that nature itself lends a hand. It isn't only that the bourgeois has a strong, innate propensity for spying, for instance. I am, in fact, convinced that the extraordinary development of police spying in France— and not just ordinary spying, but spying which is both a skill and a vocation, an art in itself—is due to their innate servility in that country. What ideally noble Gustave, provided only he has not yet accumulated any possessions, will not immediately hand over his ladylove's letters in exchange for ten thousand francs and will not betray his mistress to her husband? . . .

I remember once sitting in a hotel dining room—not in France that time, in Italy, but there were a number of Frenchmen at my table. At that time everyone was always talking of Garibaldi. This was about a fortnight before Aspromonte. Naturally people spoke somewhat enigmatically: some kept silent not wishing to make their meaning absolutely clear, others shook their heads. The general sense of the conversation was that Garibaldi had started a risky, indeed a rash, venture; but this opinion was never stated quite explicitly, because Garibaldi is a man of such different stature to other people that what could in the ordinary way be considered rash might well in his case prove to be reasonable. Gradually the discussion turned to the actual personality of Garibaldi. His qualities were enumerated and the final judgment was rather favorable for the Italian hero.

"Now, there is just one quality in him that amazes me," exclaimed a Frenchman loudly. He was a pleasant, impressive-looking man, aged about thirty and with that extraordinary nobility of expression in his face which verges on the impudent and which strikes you in all Frenchmen. "There is just one fact about him which amazes me most of all."

Everyone, of course, turned to the speaker, their curiosity aroused by his statement.

The quality discovered in Garibaldi was intended to interest everyone.

"For a short time in 1860 he enjoyed unlimited and completely uncontrolled power in Naples. In his hands he held the sum of twenty million francs of public money. He was accountable to no one for that sum. He could have appropriated for himself any amount of it and no one would have held him responsible. He appropriated nothing and handed it all back to the government to the last sou. This is almost incredible!!"

Even his eyes sparkled when he spoke of the twenty million francs.

You can, of course, say what you will about Garibaldi; but to put Garibaldi's name side by side with common embezzlers of public funds—that, obviously, only a Frenchman can do. . . .

And what indifference to everything, what short-lived, empty interests! I had occasion in Paris to visit some people whose house had in my day a constant stream of visitors. They seemed all to be afraid of beginning a conversation about anything unusual, anything which was not petty, any subjects of general interest, you know—social and political problems or something. It could not, in this case, it seems to me, be fear of spies, it was simply that people no longer knew how to think or how to speak on the more serious subjects.

There were people among them, however, who were terribly interested to know what impression Paris had made on me, how awe-struck I had been, how amazed, crushed, annihilated. The Frenchman still thinks himself capable of morally crushing and annihilating. This, too, is rather an amusing symptom. I remember particularly one very charming, very polite, very kind old man to whom I took a sincere liking. He kept his eyes glued on my face as he questioned me on my opinion of Paris, and was terribly hurt whenever I failed to express any particular enthusiasm. His kind face even reflected suffering—literally suffering, I am not exaggerating. Oh, dear Monsieur Le M—re! One can never convince a Frenchman, i.e., a Parisian (because at bottom all Frenchmen are Parisians) that he is not the greatest man in the whole wide world. As a matter of fact, he knows very little about the wide world, apart from Paris, and does not want to know, either. That's his national trait and a very characteristic one at that.

The Brothers Karamazov *

My brother asked the birds to forgive him; that sounds senseless, but it is right; for all is like an ocean, all is flowing and blending; a touch in one place sets up movement at the other end of the earth. It may be senseless to beg forgiveness of the birds, but birds would be happier at your side—a little happier, anyway—and children and all animals, if you yourself were nobler than you are now. It's all like an ocean, I tell you. Then you would pray to the birds too, consumed by an all-embracing love, in a sort of transport, and pray that they too will forgive you your sin. Treasure this ecstasy, however senseless it may seem to men. . . .

If you sin yourself and grieve even unto death for your sins or for your sudden sin, then rejoice for others, rejoice for the righteous man, rejoice that if you have sinned, he is righteous and has not sinned. . . .

When you are left alone, pray. Love to throw yourself on the earth and kiss it. Kiss the earth and love it with an unceasing, consuming love. Love all men, love everything. Seek that rapture and ecstasy. Water the earth with the tears of your joy and love those tears. Don't be ashamed of that ecstasy, prize it, for it is a gift of God and a great one; it is not given to many but only to the elect. . . .

Fathers and teachers, I ponder "What is hell?" I maintain that it is the suffering of being unable to love. Once in infinite existence, immeasurable in time and space, a spiritual creature was given, on his coming to earth, the power of saying, "I am and I love." Once, only once, there was given him a moment of active *living* love and for that was earthly life given him, and with it times and seasons. And that happy creature rejected the priceless gift, prized it and loved it not, scorned it and remained callous. Such a one, having left the earth, sees Abraham's bosom

* From *The Brothers Karamazov*, trans. Constance Garnett, New York, 1943, pp. 383-384, 386, 387-388.

and talks with Abraham as we are told in the parable of the rich man and Lazarus, and beholds heaven and can go up to the Lord. But that is just his torment, to rise up to the Lord without ever having loved, to be brought close to those who have loved when he has despised their love. For he sees clearly and says to himself, "Now I have understanding and though I now thirst to love, there will be nothing great, no sacrifice in my love, for my earthly life is over, and Abraham will not come even with a drop of living water (that is the gift of earthly, active life) to cool the fiery thirst of spiritual love which burns in me now, though I despised it on earth; there is no more life for me and will be no more time! Even though I would gladly give my life for others, it can never be, for that life is passed which can be sacrificed for love, and now there is a gulf fixed between that life and this existence."

They talk of hell-fire in the material sense. I don't go into that mystery and I shun it. But I think if there were fire in the material sense, they would be glad of it, for, I imagine, that in material agony, their still greater spiritual agony would be forgotten for a moment. Moreover, that spiritual agony cannot be taken from them, for that suffering is not external but within them. And if it could be taken from them, I think it would be bitterer still for the unhappy creatures. For even if the righteous in Paradise forgave them, beholding their torments, and called them up to heaven in their infinite love, they would only multiply their torments, for they would arouse in them still more keenly a flaming thirst for responsive, active, and grateful love which is now impossible. In the timidity of my heart I imagine, however, that the very recognition of this impossibility would serve at last to console them. For accepting the love of the righteous together with the impossibility of repaying it, by this submissiveness and the effect of this humility, they will attain at last, as it were, to a certain semblance of that active love which they scorned in life, to something like its outward expression. . . .

The Diary of a Writer *

In many respects I hold Slavophile convictions, even though I am not quite a Slavophile. In Russia, Slavophiles up to the present are conceived differently. To some people, even in our day, much as in the past—for instance, to Belinsky—the Slavophile doctrine signifies nothing but kvas and radish. *Actually* Belinsky did not go beyond this conception of it. To others (and let me note to a great many, almost to the majority of the Slavophiles themselves) it means the desire to liberate and unite all the Slavs under the sovereign rule of Russia—a rule which may not even be strictly political.

Finally, to others still, the Slavophile doctrine, in addition to that assimilation of the Slavs under the rule of Russia, signifies and comprises a spiritual union of all those who believe that our great Russia, at the head of the united Slavs, will utter to the world, to the whole of European mankind and to civilization, her new, sane, and as yet unheard-of word. That word will be uttered for the good and genuine unification of mankind as a whole in a new, brotherly, universal union whose inception is derived from the Slavic genius, pre-eminently from the spirit of the great Russian people who have suffered so long, who during so many centuries have been doomed to silence, but who have always possessed great powers for clarifying and settling many bitter and fatal misunderstandings of Western European civilization. Now, I belong to this group of the convinced and the believing. . . .

Europe—but it is a dreadful and sacred thing—Europe! Oh, do you know, gentlemen, how this very Europe, this "land of sacred miracles," is dear to us, Slavophile dreamers—according to you, haters of Europe! Do you know how these "miracles" are dear to us; how we love and revere, with a stronger than brotherly feeling, those great nations inhabiting her, all the great

* From *The Diary of a Writer*, trans. Boris Brasol, New York, 1954, pp. 779-780, 782-783.

and the beautiful which they have created! Do you know what tears we shed, what pangs of the heart we feel when we suffer and fret over the destinies of that dear and *kindred* land of ours; how the dark clouds, overcasting more and more its horizon, frighten us!—Never did you, gentlemen—our Europeans and Westerners—love Europe as strongly as we love her, we—Slavophile dreamers and, according to you—her inveterate enemies!

CONSTANTINE NIKOLAYEVICH LEONTYEV

[1831–1891]

bureaucratic

CONSTANTINE LEONTYEV was born in Kudinovo in Kaluga province on January 25, 1831, the son of a landowner. He was educated in a *gymnasium* and in the Faculty of Medicine at the University of Moscow, and left before completing his studies to serve as an army doctor in the 1850's during the Crimean War. Very early in life he began to write and became well known, particularly for his short stories. It was in order to find more time for his literary activities that, after his service in the Crimea was over, he took a post as the private physician to a noble household. But he soon gave this up and moved to Saint Petersburg to establish himself as a journalist and writer, relinquishing the practice of medicine altogether. At this time he married (1861), but his wife developed a mental illness from which she suffered throughout the rest of her life, becoming a chronic invalid.

In 1863, Leontyev entered the Russian diplomatic service and spent the next seven or eight years of his life as a consular official in various towns of Turkey. He came to know Turkey well and fell in love with the East *as such*—as opposed to the West. As a young boy he had been brought up by his mother as a loyal son of the Russian Orthodox Church, but during the early part of his life his attention to Orthodoxy had been primarily "aesthetic" and "ritual"—an attachment to the sensuous richness of the "forms" of Orthodoxy. Now, toward the end of his diplomatic service, he underwent an intense spiritual crisis which resulted in what he called a "personal" conversion to

Christianity in its (only authentic) Byzantine form. He resigned his diplomatic post and, before returning to Russia, spent a year living on Mount Athos (1870-1871) where he absorbed the ascetic view of Christianity and the monastic spirituality which prevailed there.

After his return to Russia, Leontyev continued his journalistic career in various Russian cities but largely renounced the "aestheticism" of his earlier period in favor of political, historical, and literary criticism. His talents as a *destructive* critic were unparalleled, but the extremes to which he went to gain a point or to show up an adversary cost him many friends, and we are told that he lived a lonely life. He also served for a time as an official censor of literature in Moscow. Toward the end of his life (1887) he renounced the secular world altogether, was officially divorced from his wife, and went to live in the monastery of Optina Pustin where the *Starets* Ambrose (renowned at the time for his virtue and knowledge) became his chief spiritual mentor. During the last year of his life Leontyev secretly became a monk, taking the name Clement, and died a monk on November 24, 1891.

Leontyev's was a tormented and divided personality, torn between an amoral and quasi-pagan aestheticism, an "exquisite immorality" as he put it, which took delight in the fullness of life and sensuous experience, and the extreme desire for "salvation," for the safety of his soul which could only be guaranteed in an "absolute" and "positive" Christian life. It was the latter need which, after his conversion, won out—but not without inner doubts and great psychological struggle. Leontyev viewed Christianity as something necessarily hostile to culture, as the absolute, ascetic renunciation of the world, and he located this Christianity exclusively in the institutions of Russian Orthodoxy (particularly monasticism) and the divine, autocratic power of the Tsar as the representative of God. His view of Christianity was harsh. He ridiculed the "rose-colored Christianity" of such writers as Tolstoy, Dostoevsky, and even Solovyov, because they attempted to introduce "humanistic" and "philanthropic" elements into their religious views. They viewed God as the God of Love; Leontyev's God was a God of Fear.

"bouncing ball"

Leontyev was a religious extremist—a kind of "nihilist" in reverse
—who was led by his desire and need for an uncompromising,
pure Christian life to a "philosophical hatred" of contemporary
culture.[1]

His philosophical importance lies chiefly in his criticism of
the cultural institutions of his time, those of Russia and especially
those of Western Europe. One of his most remarkable essays
in this connection in his *Byzantinism and Slavdom*, which appears
in his collection of studies entitled *Russia, the East, and the Slavs*
(1885-1886).[2] Another is the essay from which excerpts are
given below. In these and other writings Leontyev represents
perhaps the most extreme literary form of religious and political
"reactionism" of nineteenth-century thought, more radical in his
denunciation of the West than any of the senior Slavophiles, more
literal and extreme in his other-worldly view of Christianity
than any other writer of his time. He developed a rather simple-
minded "biological" theory of the evolution of political, social,
and cultural institutions according to which a period of *childhood*, in which a primitive simplicity prevails, is followed by a
period of *adulthood*, when the primitive energies of childhood
proliferate to achieve a complex and highly differentiated organization, and which finally leads to a period of *old age* when,
through a process of disintegration, a new monochromatic, un-
differentiated simplicity results.

According to Leontyev, Western Europe has passed through
its childhood (the period of the barbarian invasions), its prime
(the hierarchized society of the High Middle Ages), and is now
entering its final period of disintegration and decay—as is seen
in the leveling of all class distinctions, in the progressive democ-
ratization of all social institutions, in the bourgeois, Philistine,
"utilitarian," mass culture of the "average man." Even more
serious, since the time of Peter the Great "Westernism" has
also been infecting Russia. The only salvation of Russia lies in
arresting this steady decay, in defending the institutions of Russia's
prime, namely the Autocracy and Orthodoxy. Leontyev does not
hesitate to lend his pen in support of the most extreme forms of

1. Zenkovsky, *op. cit.*, p. 444.
2. Cf. an appraisal of these essays in Mirsky, *op. cit.*, pp. 343 ff.

censorship and political repression in order to achieve this retardation of the democratizing and socializing process which has already begun in Russia.[3] In all, his message is one of gloom and pessimism.

Leontyev was a complex, brilliant, sensitive thinker who was unable to dominate or fully understand the internal psychological forces which lay behind his literary and philosophical production. His *positive* contribution to philosophy is minor, but, as a critic of the social and cultural institutions and values of his day, he was possessed of an almost demonic clarity of vision and insight. The following selection from his article, "The Average European as an Ideal and Instrument of Universal Destruction," is typical both of his style and of the major themes of his criticism of nineteenth-century culture and philosophy.

SELECTED BIBLIOGRAPHY

Works:
Sobranie sochineni, 9 vols., Moscow, 1912-1914.

Secondary Sources:
Nicholas Berdyaev, *Leontiev,* London, 1940.
Iwan Kologriwof, *Von Hellas zum Mönchtum. Leben und Denken Konstantin Leontjews,* Regensburg, 1948.
V. V. Zenkovsky, *A History of Russian Philosophy,* trans. George L. Kline, 2 vols., London and New York, 1953, pp. 434-453.

3. Thomas G. Masaryk, *The Spirit of Russia,* trans. E. and C. Paul, New York, 1955, II, 210-211.

[CONSTANTINE LEONTYEV]

The Average European as an
Ideal and Instrument of Universal
Destruction *

If there is so little inspiration in that which belongs exclusively
or primarily to the nineteenth century (machines, teachers, professors and lawyers, the chemical laboratories, bourgeois luxury
and bourgeois depravity, bourgeois moderation and bourgeois
morality, the polka tremblante, the frock coat, top hat, and
trousers), then the same must be expected of art in an era
which, as About [1] would have it, would see neither kings, nor
priests, nor generals, nor great statesmen. Then, of course, there
would be no artists either. . . .

Herzen, as a great aesthete of the 1840's was sickened first of
all by the very image of this average European in top hat and
trousers, trivially dignified, persistent, hard-working, smug, and,
in his own mind, stoical and in many cases quite honest, yet
having no other ideal than that of fashioning all men after himself, a model unrivaled in prosiness since the time of the Stone
Age. . . .

Herzen and Proudhon at first moved along together, but their
ways quickly and radically parted.

Herzen is the perfect antithesis of Proudhon.

Proudhon has no concern whatever for the aesthetics of life;
for Herzen the aesthetics of life is everything.

As soon as Herzen realized that even the French worker for
whom he had at first felt so much compassion, and in whom he
had placed so much hope (for the awakening of new aesthetic
currents in history), wanted nothing more than to become a

---

* Translated for this volume by William Shafer and George L. Kline,
from the unfinished work, "Sredny yevropeyets kak ideal i orudiye vsemir-
novo razrusheniya," *Sochineniya* (1911), VI, pp. 9-10, 28, 29, 30-31, 34, 37-38,
42, 43, 44, 45, 47-48, 50-51, 52, 58-60, 61, 63, 64, 65, 68-69.

1. Cf. Edmond About, *Le Progrès*, Paris, 1864.—TRANS.

petit bourgeois à la Proudhon as rapidly as possible, that there was absolutely nothing in the soul of this enigmatic worker, that there was nothing original or really *new* in his vision of the world—Herzen cooled toward the worker and turned away from him, even as he turned away from Europe, and came thenceforth to believe more in Russia and in her own non-European and non-bourgeois future. . . .

After Cabet, Proudhon, and Herzen we turn to the Englishman, John Stuart Mill, who bases his hopes on the *peculiarity* and *diversity* of human nature, correctly supposing that the diversity and depth of human nature renders creations of the mind as well as human actions profound and powerful. His essay, "On Liberty," was written with precisely this end in view; it should not be called "On Liberty," but rather "On Diversity."

Mill called his work "On Liberty" either out of caution, supposing that this simpler and more ordinary title would be more appealing to routine minds, or else he was mistaken in considering complete *political* freedom and complete freedom in *everyday life* a necessary condition for the diversified development of human nature. He identifies these freedoms with the removal of all possible restraints on the part of society and the state. Being an Englishman, he has no fear of the state; but he attacks the despotism of public opinion and the tendency of contemporary society to "make all men the same."

"Those whose opinions go by the name of public opinion," Mill says, "are not always the same sort of public: in America they are the whole *white* population; in England, chiefly the middle class. But they are always a mass, that is to say, collective mediocrity." [2] . . .

Is it possible for thinkers to be original and heterogeneous in their thought where the [socio-political] "ground" is already homogeneous and well established? Mill proved by his own ex-

2. Cf. John Stuart Mill, "On Liberty," e.g., in *English Philosophers from Bacon to Mill*, ed. E. A. Burtt, New York, 1939, pp. 1000-1001. Italics added by Leontyev, who quotes Mill in his own Russian rendering of a French translation (he refers parenthetically to *"mediocrité collective"*). As a result of this double translation, Mill's style, though not his substance, is noticeably altered.—TRANS.

ample that it is not possible, for, while seeming to be extremely
original as the negator of that part of progress which displeased
. him, namely the notion of an *intermingling simplification* of nations, classes, and individuals, he himself becomes very ordinary
when he tries to offer something positive in the way of ideals.
In his essay "Representative Government," he is a very ordinary
constitutionalist. He suggests certain insignificant new shadings
which, as a matter of fact, have a leveling effect (e.g., that the
minority as well as the majority should influence affairs, etc.).
He cannot bear the *idea* of autocracy; like Buckle, he defames
the great age of Louis XIV. He has no patience with the democratic crudeness of younger nations such as America and Greece,
whose representatives have not yet been choked by the public
opinion of average gentlemen and therefore sometimes fight in
the halls of congress. In other words, Mill accepts the most ordinary and proper *juste-milieu*.

In the essay "The Subjection of Women," we see him as a
very ordinary man; he wants the woman to be a less *original*
creature than she has been up to now, wants her to become less
feminine and thus be more like the man. He wants to *simplify*
and equalize even the picture of the family—only not in a
sternly bourgeois fashion as Proudhon would do, but giving it
a somewhat nihilistic, undisciplined character. He has a cold and
often hostile attitude toward religion in general, forgetting that
neither a constitution, nor the family, nor even communism could
endure without religion; for the English and American constitutions were wrought primarily out of religious beliefs and conflicts,
and the family, without an ikon in the corner, without the
Penates over the hearth, without the verses of the Koran over
the door, offers nothing but a terribly dull routine and even
"penal servitude," as Herzen put it. . . .

Mill proposes an impossible and unworkable compromise—he
wants individual peculiarity and diversity in European thought
without individual peculiarity and diversity in European life. . . .

When the new cultural worlds of Byzantium and Western
Europe were raised on the ruins of Rome and Hellas, (1) a new
mystical religion lay at their base; (2) as a forerunner to this
there was a mighty tribal movement (a migration of whole

nations)—a lesser one in the East for the founding of Byzantium
and a greater one in the West; and (3) there was the formation
of a new cultural center—Byzantium on the Bosphorus. Christianity was the new religion for all—for East and West. In the
West the old center was renewed by the influx of foreign tribes;
in the East the old Greek tribe, much less renewed by the
migrations, was refreshed, so to speak, by a long stagnation of
ideas, and found a completely new center in Byzantium.

There is nothing similar in Western Europe and for the present
it cannot be anticipated. . . .

We have said that in France the church, the gentry, the king
and the middle class ruled by turns; today it is the *worker* who
wishes to rule. But what would he rule in a communist republic,
assuming that such an ideal could be realized, even for a short
time? Why, he would be ruling *himself;* everybody would be
more or less a worker. There would be no church, no gentry,
no sovereign, not even large-scale capital. All men rule all; or,
as has been said more than once: *each is subject to the will of all.*

What could be simpler, if such a thing could endure? Guizot,[3]
we have said, desired no such simplification. He was neither a
democrat in his politics nor a realist in his philosophy. In politics
he was an aristocrat, and in his sentiments he was a Christian.
Moreover, Guizot was endowed with a fine classical (i.e., Graeco-
Latin) education. He supported the bourgeoisie and private capital only from necessity, because in France no better conservative
principle was at hand. He envied England because she still had
her lords. Thus, although he wrote nothing *directly* about
[leveling] interfusion and made no mention of it openly, nevertheless his writings and his very political role confirm our opinion
that through such interfusion France and, following her, all of
Europe, has been debased. . . .

That a complexity and diversity which are reconciled in something higher form the essence and apex of development (and
consequently of civilization as well) is evident, among other
things, from the fact that, after comparing ancient Graeco-
Roman culture with European culture, Guizot concludes that the

3. Cf. François Guizot, *Histoire de la civilisation en France*, Paris, 1830.—
TRANS.

former (the Graeco-Roman) was *simpler,* more homogeneous, and the latter incomparably more *complex.* Of course, while giving due respect to the classical world, he nevertheless considers the European civilization to be the *higher* one. This means that he understands the word "development" properly in the sense of a complication of principles and forms, and not in the sense of a striving for prosperity and simplicity. . . .

It is difficult for us *today* to admit that an experienced and intelligent man could believe in the limitation of the power of the sovereign by a council of elected lawyers, capitalists, and professors, as if it were something durable and an end in itself. The Russian liberals, who are, I think, not without talent, are not so naive in this respect as even the brilliant Guizot could be in the 1830's. . . .

Mill and Guizot, from the point of view of the political-cultural statics [4] of which I am speaking, mutually supplement one another. The former treats the vitally important question of human diversity and individuality in a more lucid and comprehensive way; the latter turns our attention more decidedly toward the principle of Christian, or generally speaking, religious *unity,* which is necessary to the preservation of those political-cultural types which issued directly from, or in antagonistic opposition to, such unity—even their antagonism furthering the general stability.

If these two writers (or to phrase it more correctly—the two works of which I am speaking) supplement one another, Riehl [5] confirms their opinions from another quarter. Mill is concerned with the *strength* and *diversity* of human characters and situations. Guizot deals more specifically with the Christian *unity* that is necessary to maintain all this social and individual diversity within definite limits. Riehl shows that in order to have a variety of individuals with strongly developed characters, there must be *separation,* a division of society into groups and strata. The more sharply separated these groups and strata are, one from the other—whether by nature (mountains, the steppe, the forest, the

4. Leontyev uses the term in the sense of Herbert Spencer's "social statics."—TRANS.

5. Cf. Wilhelm Riehl, *Land und Leute,* 4th ed., Stuttgart, 1857.—TRANS.

sea, etc.) or by laws, customs, and the structure of their life—the richer will be the moral and even the intellectual fruits of a given social stratum. They will not be richer *in spite of* the uneven diffusion of knowledge, but precisely *because of it*—because of the diversity of attitudes, customs, tastes, and needs.

Once again, as I have said before: knowledge and ignorance are *equally* important conditions for the development of societies, individuals, states, art forms, and even systematic knowledge; for the scientists and scholars too must have a variety of elements from which to build up their disciplines. . . .

To bring history to an end, having destroyed mankind! To make human life on this globe quite impossible through the diffusion of universal equality and the dissemination of universal freedom! . . .

. . . the rebels are an acute disease which has aroused a saving reaction. But those who would destroy the *village commune,* naively imagining that everything rests in the *enrichment of the individual,* are destroying the last support, the last remnants of the former alignment, stratification, serfdom, and immobility, i.e., they are annihilating one of the main conditions of both our state unity and our national-cultural isolation, and to some extent of our heterogeneous internal development as well. That is to say, at a single stroke they are depriving us of our individual peculiarity, our diversity, and our unity. Yes, even *unity,* for a democratic constitution (the highest degree of *capitalism* and a sort of sluggish and impotent mobility) is a weakening of *central power.* And a democratic constitution is tightly bound up with egalitarian individualism carried to its extreme. It creeps up on one unexpectedly. Give us a constitution—and straight off the capitalists will destroy the village commune; destroy the commune—and the rapid disintegration will lead us to the ultimate liberal idiocy, a house of representatives, i.e., the rule of bankers, lawyers, and landowners—not as *gentry* (this is still nothing), but rather as representatives of an *immobile force* which could be easily set in motion as they saw fit, needing no one's consent and meeting no opposition.

Salvation lies not in furthering this mobility, but in somehow checking it. If it were possible to find a law or some other means for stabilizing the estates of the gentry, this would be fine. We should not undo the corporation, but rather turn our attention to the fact that everywhere the former more or less coercive (immobile) *corporations* have been converted into all-too-free (mobile) *associations*, and that this degeneration is ruinous. We should worry not about freeing the peasants from bondage to their small communal plots, but rather about forcibly attaching the gentry themselves in some way (if we wish to conserve this class for cultural reasons) to their large personal properties. . . .

Not considering myself bound to read every new book and article in the world, finding this to be not only useless but extremely harmful, I even have the barbaric temerity to hope that in time mankind will, through rational and scientific means, reach that end which the Caliph Omar is supposed to have reached empirically and mystically, i.e., the burning of the majority of colorless and unoriginal books. I flatter myself with the hope that new societies will be established for the purification of the intellectual air, a philosophical and aesthetic censorship which will be more ready to pass the most shocking book (while strictly limiting its distribution) than a book that is colorless and without character. . . .

Today, in the nineteenth century, more or less everywhere among the Christian states, capitalism (or the accumulation of mobile wealth) has reached its height. And almost simultaneously with its attainment of a position of dominance, at the end of the eighteenth century and the beginning of our own, there appeared its most powerful antithesis—the first communist upheavals, Babeuf's Manifesto, etc. Since then communism has grown; it grows and will inevitably continue to grow until it reaches the limit set for it by social statics, i.e., until long-term restrictions are put, both by direct legislation and by all possible supplementary means, on the excessive freedom of growth of mobile capital as well as the excessive freedom of action with respect to the chief fixed property—land; in other words, on the freedom which almost everyone has today to buy and sell, to amass and divide up holdings in land. Communism, which counts on attaining full equality and complete immobility by means of preliminary destruction, must inevitably, through its own struggle with capital and its alternating victories and defeats, lead on the one hand to a significant decrease in economic inequality, to an *economic equalization* which is substantial compared to today's, and on the other hand, to a *juridical inequality* much greater than today's. The whole history of the nineteenth century, seen in this light, has consisted precisely in an increase of economic inequality, corresponding to the increase of civil, juridical, and political equality. The more the impoverished of our age become conscious of their civil rights, the more loudly do they protest against the purely *de facto* power of *capital*, a power justified neither by tradition nor by any mystical principle. Communism, in its violent striving for an ideal of *fixed equality*, must, through a series of combinations with other principles, gradually lead, on the one hand, to a decreased mobility of capital and property, and, on the other, to a new juridical inequality, to new privileges, to restrictions on individual freedom, and to *compulsory* corporate groups, clearly defined by laws—probably even to new forms of personal slavery or serfdom (although indirect, and called by another name . . . Monks).

Today's *anarchistic* communism is on the one hand nothing but an egalitarian liberalism of the kind which has enslaved so many moderate and law-abiding people of the nineteenth century, and at the same time a demand for absolutely unlimited personal rights, an individualism that has led to absurdity and crime, to lawlessness and villainy. On the other hand, precisely because this communism, by its undoubted success, makes further egalitarian liberalizing unpopular and even impossible, it is a necessary fatal push toward, and ground for, the building of a *new* kind of state that is neither liberal nor egalitarian. When we say it is not liberal, we inevitably mean by this not capitalistic, less mobile in the realm of economic development. The most immobile, most alienated form of proprietorship is unquestionably the wealthy commune that controls large land holdings and denies equality of rights to its members.[6] . . .

But if the anarchists and liberal communists, in striving for their

6. For example, Mt. Athos. (Mt. Athos, on the shores of Greece, was and is the site of a number of celebrated Greek Orthodox monasteries.— TRANS.)

communism a pipe dream?

own ideal of extreme equality (an impossibility) through their own methods of unbridled freedom from personal encroachments, must bring us, through a series of antitheses, to societies which have yet to live and develop, to great immobility and a highly significant inequality, then it is possible to assert in general that socialism, properly understood, is nothing but a new feudalism belonging to an already imminent future. We understand the word "feudalism," of course, not in the narrow and special sense of "Romano-Germanic knighthood" or the social structure of the age of chivalry, but in its broadest sense, i.e., in the sense of an inequality of rights among classes and groups, in the sense of a heterogeneous decentralization and grouping of social forces that are united in a kind of living spiritual or political center. "Feudalism" means a *new enslavement* of individuals by other individuals and institutions, the subjugation of some communes by other communes which are incomparably more powerful, or have some special claim to nobility (such, for example, as the way the village workers were bound to the monasteries in our country in days long past).

. . . they all consider the ideal of the future to be something like themselves, i.e., to these authors [7] it is rather like the European bourgeoisie. Something *average;* neither a peasant nor a gentleman, neither a soldier nor a priest, neither a man from Bretagne nor a Basque, neither a Tyrolian nor a Circassian, neither a Trappist in a hair shirt nor a prelate in brocade. No, they all are indeed satisfied by that petty and average cultural type to which they all belong, by virtue of their position in society and their manner of life, and in which, for the sake of a general and unpretentious dignity, they would like once and for all to enfold the upper and lower extremes of the [social] world. . . .

The aesthetic criterion is the most trustworthy and general, for it is uniquely applicable to all societies, to all religions, and to all epochs. What is *beneficial* to all of them—we do not know and never shall know. What is beautiful and elegant and lofty in all of them—it is high time we found out! . . .

. . . in history precisely those epochs are distinguished by the

7. I.e., About, Guizot, Mill, and Riehl.—TRANS.

greatest development of the state, by force, and the best social statics in which the social structure was marked by the greatest diversity in the strongest unity; and the sorts of human nature produced in these epochs were stronger and more diverse, whether they were one-sidedly expressed or most splendidly many-sided. Such eras were those of Louis XIV, Charles V, Elizabeth and George III of England, Catherine II and Nicholas I of our own country. . . .

[I conclude]: (1) that there began in the past [i.e., eighteenth] century a process of secondary interfusion in the social organisms of the Romano-Germanic world which resulted in homogeneity; (2) that the homogeneity of individuals, institutions, fashions, cities, and in general of cultured ideals and forms is spreading more and more, reducing everybody and everything to the very simple, average, so-called "bourgeois" type of the Western European; and (3) that the interfusion or mixing of homogeneous component parts (to a greater extent than heretofore) leads not to greater solidarity but to ruin and death (of states, of culture).

. . . but universal uniform law, universal equality, universal love, universal justice, and universal prosperity have neither psychological, nor historical, nor social, nor organic, nor cosmic plausibility. These universal goods do not even have moral plausibility; for the highest morality is known only in deprivation, in conflict, and in danger. Deny a man the possibility of a lofty personal moral conflict, and you deny morals to all mankind; you deny mankind the moral element of life. The highest degree of social material prosperity and the highest degree of universal political justice would be the highest degree of a-morality.[8] (I separate the particle "a" on purpose so that the word will not be understood in the usual sense of depravity and foul play; I suggest that there would then be neither depravity nor virtue: the first would not be permitted, and the second would not be necessary. Since all men would be equal, all men would be identical.)

8. In Russian: *bez-nravstvennost.*—TRANS.

VASILY VASILYEVICH ROZANOV
[1856–1919]

Vasily rozanov was born on April 20, 1856, of a poor provincial family in the town of Vetluga in Kostroma province. His father died when he was very young and he suffered through an extremely unhappy childhood living in great poverty. His elder brothers mistreated him and his overworked mother gave him little affection. He says that his only reaction to the death of his mother was the realization that now he could smoke cigarettes openly.

Rozanov attended the *gymnasium* at Simbirsk and later Novgorod, after which he entered the Faculty of History and Philology at the University of Moscow. He was not a conscientious student; he considered most of his professors as so much dead wood and found the academic environment stultifying. In later years he frequently boasted that he had "slept through" his entire university course. Nevertheless he did stay on to graduation and, as he had no other possible means of support, became a secondary-school history teacher in the provinces. He worked for five years on his first book, *On Understanding*, a volume of 737 pages published in 1886. It included an anti-academic diatribe directed chiefly at the University of Moscow. Though only about six hundred copies were printed, very few were sold and the paper from most of the copies which Rozanov did not keep to distribute himself was used by his publisher for wrapping novels. This was his only technically philosophical book and, by common consent, it holds little but historical interest today.

One of the most *positive* elements in Rozanov's intellectual development was his lifelong admiration for Dostoevsky; his first important work was a study of Dostoevsky entitled *The Legend of the Grand Inquisitor* (1894). The book was printed at Rozanov's expense but it brought him considerable attention and marked the beginning of his rise to fame. As a university student in 1880, at the age of twenty-four, he had married Dostoevsky's former mistress, the "infernal woman," Apollinaria Suslova; he had known her since adolescence and married her partly to establish a personal link to the great man whom he had never been able to meet in person. The marriage was a mistake, for Apollinaria Suslova treated Rozanov in the same way she had treated Dostoevsky and left him after six years, though he was unable ever to get her to consent to a divorce. Thus in 1889 he formed a liaison with Barbara Rudneva, whom he had met while teaching in Elets, and she became his common-law wife. They had five children and their union was quite happy; Rozanov frequently refers to her in his later writings with great affection.[1]

After thirteen years of teaching in provincial schools (he is said to have been an ineffectual teacher), during which time he wrote five books and numerous articles, Rozanov procured a job in the Department of State Inspection and Control in Saint Petersburg in 1893. As early as 1886, Nicholas Strakhov had urged him to come to Saint Petersburg to write for the conservative press. Once established in the capital, Rozanov expanded his journalistic efforts (most of his books are collections of articles previously published in journals and reviews) and by 1899 became a regular contributor to the ultra-conservative *Novoye Vremya* (New Times). His financial condition improved greatly and he even traveled briefly in the West (Italy, France, Germany), mainly to obtain material for his articles.

Rozanov's literary output during this period presents us with many problems. Apparently with complete cynicism he wrote numerous articles flattering government officials and upholding the most obscurantist policies of the Autocracy. He wrote several rabidly anti-Semitic pieces (for which he was eventually expelled from the "Petersburg Religious and Philosophical

1. Rozanov's marital experiences were one of the sources of his concern for the subject of divorce, illegitimacy, and related topics which he took up in his book *The Family Problem in Russia* (1903).

Society" in 1913), he publicly approved of Tolstoy's excommunication by the Holy Synod, and he carried on venomous polemics
with such "leftist" writers as Mikhailovsky. Yet at the same
time he was writing polemical articles against the Church and
criticizing Russian mores, and, using the pseudonym Varvarin, he
wrote a series of scornful and bitter criticisms of the Tsarist
regime for the leftist journal, *Russkoye Slovo* (The Russian
Word).[2] And despite his many services to chauvinism, his book,
In the World of the Obscure and of the Uncertain (1901), was
suppressed by the Church and the government as "pornographic."
We learn from Strakhov that, though most of Rozanov's collaborators of this period admired his outstanding intellectual abilities and his extraordinary gifts as a writer, they considered him
"psychologically unstable."

The final period of Rozanov's literary activity began in 1912
with the publication of *Solitaria*. This work, together with
Fallen Leaves (1913-1915) and finally *The Apocalypse of Our
Times* (1918-1919), represent Rozanov's major contributions; it is
because of them that his earlier, more strictly journalistic, pieces
are still remembered. With these works Rozanov achieves his
final, aphoristic, "Nietzschean" style and, with it, the courage to
write *for himself*, fearlessly to give his final critique of Russian
society, of Christianity (and Orthodoxy in particular), and to
elaborate his "metaphysics of sex" in its fullest form. These last
works were not written as books but consist of jottings and ideas
put down at random, as they occurred to him; they are unified
only by the particular themes which concerned Rozanov at
the time.

From 1913 onward Rozanov's fortunes began to decline; he
was an outspoken enemy both of Tsardom and the socialist revolution, and he gradually found himself more and more ostracized
from the society which he condemned. When the Bolshevik
Revolution began he took refuge, in a state of extreme poverty,

2. Some of these writings appeared in book form, *Kogda nachalstvo
ushlo* (1909). Since there is no collected edition of Rozanov's works in
Russian and very few of them have been translated into English, or any
Western language, the reader is referred to the bibliography in Renato
Poggioli, *Rozanov*, New York, 1962, pp. 101-104.

isolation, and physical distress, in the home of the theologian Fr. Paul Florensky near the Trinity Monastery of Saint Sergius outside Moscow. There, after finishing his most scathing attack on Christianity, *The Apocalypse of Our Times*, he calmly requested and received the last sacraments of the Church and died on January 23, 1919.

The following selections are taken from this last work, which is widely regarded as his masterpiece and the most eloquent presentation of his critique of Christianity on the one hand and his mysticism of sex on the other. These themes—Christianity and sex—are, indeed, common to much of his earlier writing; they constitute the two poles of his thought and are closely interrelated. But in this book they receive their final, most frenetic expression. The book consists of a series of nine fascicles which Rozanov wrote for his friends and distributed privately during the last months of his life. The modest proceeds from these little pamphlets helped keep him alive during this period. It is obvious, however, that they were not written primarily to make money, but out of Rozanov's inner necessity to have his final say on the topics which had obsessed him throughout his life. Ironically, this attack on Christianity *and* the Revolution could be published only because all laws of ecclesiastical censorship had been abolished by the revolutionary government, and because Rozanov was being sheltered during this period by the monks of the Trinity Monastery. The paradoxical personality of Rozanov is thus present both in their content and in the circumstances of their production.

The two major themes of this work are the condemnation of Christianity and the glorification of the powers of sex. Sexuality, for Rozanov, is not some abstract or mystical force, a Platonic Eros; it is the genitals, the physical act of coitus, childbirth, and child care which he calls "holy." His chief criticism of Christianity is that it has suppressed the ancient fertility religions (both of the Jews of the Old Testament and of the pagans), and has thus destroyed the "holiness" of the primary biological processes and created a culture of "phantom men." Rozanov— like Nietzsche, but in a different sense—demands a "return to the earth," a worship of the vital forces which Christianity has weakened and "emaciated." He contrasts the Father of the Old Testament and the "Sun" of the fertility cults with the "impotent" Son of the New Testament who came to "castrate" the universe and turn it away from the wholesome "works of the flesh" to other-worldly and imaginary "works of the spirit."

On all these themes it is best to let Rozanov speak for himself. His message is essentially that the "religion of the Father" and the "religion of the Son" are at odds, and that salvation (not of the "soul" but of *life*) lies in a return to the earth. In order to proclaim this "truth" he adopts an "apocalyptic" style, based on his own reading of the New Testament *Apocalypse,* and addressed to the generation which is living through the dissolution of Christianity in "our times."

SELECTED BIBLIOGRAPHY

Works:
V. V. Rozanov, *Fallen Leaves,* London, 1929.
——————, *Solitaria,* with an abridged Account of the Author's life by E. Gollerbach, other biographical material, and matter from *The Apocalypse of Our Times,* trans. S. S. Koteliansky, London, 1927.
——————, *La face sombre du Christ,* trans. Nathalie Reznikoff, Paris, 1964.
——————, *Izbrannoye,* ed. George Ivask, New York, 1956.

Secondary Sources:
Renato Poggioli, *Rozanov,* New York, 1962. (This book has a good bibliographical section.)
John Cournos, "V. V. Rozanov—A Balaam of Our Times," *Reflex,* vol. 2, No. 3, New York, 1928, pp. 82-87.
E. Gollerbach, "Rozanov: a Critical and Biographical Account," *Calendar,* vol. 3, London, 1927, pp. 271-296.

[VASILY ROZANOV]

The Apocalypse of Our Times *

The Last Days[1]

Have we said enough of our stinking Revolution and of our thoroughly rotten Empire? One is as bad as the other. Let us rather return to a harmonious period, to a crucial epoch, to a terrible epoch. . . .

Here is the *Apocalypse*. . . . A mysterious book which burns your tongue as you read it. The heart can no longer breathe; the whole man dies, dies and is reborn. . . . From the first lines it reveals itself as a *judgment on the Christian Churches,* churches situated in Asia Minor, at Laodicea, at Smyrna, at Thyatira, at Pergamum, and in other cities. It is obvious that neither Laodicea nor Pergamum, today in ruins, will have any importance in "the last days" about which the writer of this strange book is speaking. But he looked at the tree planted by Christ, and he grasped, more deeply than he himself or his own epoch knew, that it was *not* the Tree of Life. And he predicted their fate at a time when the churches were only beginning to be born.

The *Apocalypse* is not a Christian book. It is an anti-Christian book—no doubt about it. The "Christ," with the "sword issuing from his mouth" and with feet "like gems of jasper and sardonyx" of whom it speaks (very little, as a matter of fact), has nothing in common with the Christ of the Gospels. The

---

* The first two parts of this selection, "The Last Days" and "Truth and Lies," were translated for this volume by James M. Edie, from V. Rozanov, *L'Apocalypse de notre temps précédé de Esseulement,* trans. Vladimir Pozner and Boris De Schloezer (Paris, 1930), pp. 190-200, 212-221. This English translation was collated by James P. Scanlan with the original Russian in V. Rozanov, *Apokalipsis nashevo vremeni* (Sergiyev Posad, 1917), pp. 21-32, 47-57. The third part, "On the Passions of the World," is reprinted with the permission of the publisher from V. V. Rozanov, *Solitaria . . . and matter from The Apocalypse of Our Times,* trans. S. S. Koteliansky (London, 1927), pp. 159-166. These selections are whole and complete; the suspension points in the text are Rozanov's.

1. From the second fascicle of *The Apocalypse of Our Times.*—TRANS.

arrangement of Heaven has nothing in common with any Christian conceptions. "Everything is new." The Contemplator of mysteries himself,[2] by his own will and by that of God who backs him, pulls down the stars, destroys the earth, piles everything up in ruins, annihilates everything. He annihilates Christianity which, strangely enough, "weeps and laments" but remains impotent. No one comes to its aid. As *consolation*, as "dried tears," as "*white* garments" he creates something new; he creates the joy of living on earth—*specifically on earth*—a joy which surpasses all the joys which humanity had experienced in the course of its history.

If we look at the overall composition of the *Apocalypse* and if we ask: "What is it about? what is the *mystery* of the judgment on the churches? whence come *the anger, the wrath*, the roaring of the *Apocalypse*?" (for it is a roaring, groaning book), we are brought back to our own epoch: Yes, it is about the *impotence* of Christianity to organize human life, to gives us an "earthly life"—specifically earthly, difficult and sad. This has become apparent now, just in our time . . . when we can say with cynicism and vulgarity: "It is not Christ who brings bread but the railroads." Everybody has suddenly forgotten Christianity, in a moment—the muzhiks, the soldiers—because it is of *no help*, because it has suppressed neither war nor famine. It just keeps on singing and singing. Like a light chanteuse. "We have heard you, we have heard. And we have had enough."

But it is more horrible than one thinks. It is not the human heart which has corrupted Christianity; it is Christianity which has corrupted the human heart. That is what the roaring of the *Apocalypse* means. Otherwise there would not have been a "new earth" or a "new heaven." Otherwise there would not have been an *Apocalypse* at all.

The *Apocalypse* demands, calls for, and prescribes a new religion. That is its essence. But what has happened? What has, in fact, happened?

2. This is Rozanov's name for the author of this final book of the New Testament, traditionally ascribed to John, the author of the fourth Gospel, and believed to have been composed on the island of Patmos.—TRANS.

What is terribly apocalyptic ("mysterious"), terribly strange, is that men, peoples, humanity *are going through the apocalyptic crisis,* but that Christianity itself is unaffected by it. This is so evident, it is written so clearly in the *Apocalypse* itself, "in these very lines," that it is astonishing that no one of its readers or innumerable commentators has noticed it. The peoples "sing a new song," are consoled, put on white garments and go toward the "tree of life," toward the "sources of living water." Places toward which the popes and priests of old never led anyone.

Prostitutes lament. High-priests weep. Kings wail. Peoples writhe in torment. Still a *remnant of the people* is saved and obtains a supreme consolation, which however contains no element of Christianity, nothing Christian or ecclesiastical.

But then what is it? Why does the Contemplator of mysteries say in such a clear and irrefutable way that *humanity will outlive* "its Christianity" and will *still live a long time after it?* To judge from his description, which is left unfinished, this time will be indefinitely long, "eternal."

Let us make some comparisons:

The Gospel paints a picture.

The *Apocalypse* moves masses and monoliths, it creates.

With images which surpass the tableaux of the Gospels in power, and which are no less beautiful, with poignant images which cry and shout in the face of heaven and earth, the *Apocalypse* recounts that the little churches still isolated in the villages of Asia Minor—the first Christian communities—will spread out over the universe, over all the earth. And at the moment when Christianity will be completely, and apparently definitively, triumphant, when "the Gospel will have been preached to every creature," it will collapse completely at a single blow, with all its kingdoms, "with the kings who aided it," and "its high-priests will break into lamentations." And amid the general wreckage there will arise something absolutely "new," while the "stars fall from heaven" and "heaven rolls up like a scroll." "Heaven will pass away"; "earth will pass away," and everything will become "new" and completely *different* from what formerly existed. To have been able to say this two thousand years in advance, to have been able to predict through the whole history of Christianity, down to their exact details, what is happening today—piercing in a single thrust through the thickness of time and the immensity of events—is a thing so strange, so incredible that, in truth, no human words are comparable to it. The *Apocalypse* is a happening; it is not a word. We are tempted to believe that the Universe vomited it forth as soon as the other Master of the same Universe had pronounced his prophetical and menacing words which also spoke for the first time of a "judgment of this world."

Thus there are two judgments: one comes from Jerusalem and is addressed to Jerusalem itself, especially to Jerusalem. The other comes from the island of Patmos and is addressed to the whole world, which the other Master had taught.

Is there not a difference in the very structure of these two texts? And though it is strange to pose such questions with respect to these word-happenings, does not *the style of the writing reveal something to the soul* in these two different accounts?

The Gospel tells us a human story, the history of God and man, of the "Divine-human process" and of their "alliance."

The *Apocalypse*, one would say, rejects this "alliance between God and man" as a useless and worn-out object.

But the basis? The reason for all this? But why? Why?

The Apocalypse reveals its essence precisely in the structure of power, in a language charged with such fearsome images that, by contrast, the *Book of Job* itself seems to be weak and empty, and the story of the "Creation of the world and of man" in Genesis seems insipid and dull, pale and bloodless. One could say that it roars "at the end of time," for "the end of time," for "mankind's last day": "*Impotence!*"

The end of the world and of humanity will occur because the Gospel is a book marked by exhaustion.

For there are: *power* and *impotence*.

And Christ suffered and died out of *impotence* . . . even though he was in *the truth* totally and absolutely.

Christianity is not the truth and it is impotent.

The image of Christ, as it is traced in the Gospels, exactly as it is shown to us, in all its details, with its miracles, its appearances, and so on, reveals nothing but *impotence* and *exhaustion* . . .

The *Apocalypse* seems to say: Yes, Christ could describe "the beauty of the lilies of the field," he could call "Mary, the sister of Lazarus" to harken to him, but he did not plant a single tree, did not engender the smallest plant. In general, he lacks "earthly *seed*," *semen, ova;* he is not vegetal; he is not animal. Ultimately he is not a being but a phantom, a shadow who passed by some sort of miracle over the earth. Shadow, appearance, vacuity, non-being—such is the essence of Christ. As if it were only a Name, a "tale." If "the last days" seem so terrible, of an unimaginable terror, so merciless, so cruelly "ravenous," if men transform themselves into "scorpions who sting themselves and one another," it is because, more generally, "nothing has happened" and because human beings with empty bellies and flaccid flesh, whose ribs we can count—have mysteriously become the "shadows of men," "phantom-men," and to a certain extent are no longer men "except in name."

Oh, oh, oh.

Behold, behold, behold . . .

Do we not recognize *ourselves* here? The *Apocalypse* could not help but roar, and surround the Heavenly Throne with animals—with the stomachs, with the bellies of the strongest animals, who also roar, shriek, and howl: the lion, the ox, the eagle, and the virgin.[3] Everything is flight and force. Why is there no hummingbird, no "lilies of the fields"? A little bird is as valuable as a large one, "lilies" are as beautiful as baobabs. Yet suddenly the *Apocalypse* cries:

More meat! . . .

More howls! . . .

More groans! . . .

—The world has become emaciated; it is sick . . . A mysterious Shadow has spread sickness over the world . . .

—The world has fallen silent . . .

3. From the Scriptural account, we would expect Rozanov to name here the "young man" who was the final attendant at the Heavenly Throne. Cf. *Revelation*, 4:6-8.—TRANS.

—The world is without life . . .

—Quick, quick, before it is too late . . . While the final moments last. "Turn everything back," "a new heaven," "new stars" . . .

The abundance of "the waters of life," "the Tree of Life"! . . .

The sun was lighted before Christianity. And it will not be put out if Christianity disappears. Christianity has its limit, against which neither "liturgies" nor "funeral services" will prevail. And with regard to liturgies—many have been celebrated, but human existence has not been alleviated.

Christianity is not of this world; "grass does not grow in it." It does not contribute to the reproduction of cattle, to the multiplication of herds. Yet men cannot live without grass, without cattle. Therefore, "despite all the beauty of Christianity" man cannot "live solely on Christianity." The monastery is perfect. "There reigns integral Christianity," and yet *it is the neighboring village that feeds the monastery.* Without this village the monks would all die of hunger. It is necessary to take that into consideration, and to reflect on this perfectly "apocalyptic thought" that *alone* and *of itself* Christianity collapses, that it has no "being," that it is tainted, that it is hungry, that it is thirsty, that it "nourishes" itself with *non-Christianity,* with non-Christian grains and plants. And for this reason Christianity in itself, in its most pure, most ecstatic form, requires, demands, and desires "*non-Christianity.*"

It is stupefying, but it is so. The words of the Saviour to the five thousand people were very pretty. But the evening came and the people cried: "Master, *give us bread!*"

Christ gave them bread. It is one of the greatest of the miracles. Don't doubt it. Oh, not at all, not for an instant. But then what should we think of the sun which gives bread to countless multitudes of men, which thus acts "officially," doing its "duty," almost as if it were to receive a pension? It gives and *can* give. It gives and, consequently, *wants* to give.

Does the sun have a will and . . . *a power of desire?*

But then . . . is it the "Baal-sun"? The Baal-sun of the Phoenicians?

In this case, "should we worship it"? It, and its immense *power?*

Yes, unquestionably. It, and its great, *noble, philanthropic desire?* . . . It is unimaginable. Yet the Pope himself does not deny that "the sun is more powerful than Christ." As to whether it desires the happiness of humanity more than Christ does we are still in doubt, although Vladimir Solovyov, who had studied the whole "Divine-human process" and who constructed a "theurgy of the Old Testament" and a "domestic economy of the Old Testament" (or "theocracy"), was unable to find any objection against it.

The rest of us turn to Phoenicia: "You were in God's paradise . . . You scintillated with multicolored fire . . ." "You were My firstborn, My firstborn from the creation of the world," said Ezekiel, Isaiah, or someone in the Old Testament, addressing himself to a city where Baal was worshiped and not Jehovah.

Who does not see, across my leaden words, that ·"the Divine-human process of the Incarnation of Christ" is collapsing? It collapses in storms and lightning . . . It collapses in the "famines of humanity" which are being prepared and which are already coming upon us . . . In the lamentations of peoples. "We have cried forth to Christ, and He has not come to our aid." "He is powerless." "Let us pray to the Sun; it has greater power. It nourishes not only five thousand men but immense hordes. We did not pay It sufficient attention. We did not suspect Its power."

—"Christ, give us meat!"

—"To cover our ribs, to fill our bellies, for us and for our children!"

Jesus is silent. Is he not? And if so, is he not a Shadow? A Mysterious Shadow which has emaciated the whole earth.

Truth and Lies [4]

"Deprived of *sin*, man would be unable to live. He could live only too well without *holiness*." It is in this above all that the a-cosmical character of Christianity is evident.

Not only: "Whether I read the Gospel from the beginning to

4. From the fourth fascicle of *The Apocalypse of Our Times.*—TRANS.

the end or from the end to the beginning," I understand absolutely nothing of this: "*How* is the world organized? and *why?*"

Thus Jesus Christ has taught us nothing about creation. But also—and this is the most important point—he proclaimed that the "works of the flesh" were sin, but that the "works of the spirit" were holy. Now I, I believe that the "works of the flesh" are the essential thing, whereas the "works of the spirit" are, how shall I put it, only talk . . .

The "works of the flesh"—there is cosmogony. The "works of the spirit" are more or less a matter of fantasy.

Christ, who occupied himself with the "works of the spirit," was occupied with accessory, secondary, partial, private things. He concerned himself with adverbs rather than with verbs. That is to say, he forsook the *predicate* of the proposition, which constitutes universal history and human life, for *adverbial* accessories, for shadowy, shady words.

The *predicate*—that means eating, drinking, copulating. Jesus called all this "sinful" and said that the "works of the flesh lead into temptation." If they "did not lead into temptation," man and humanity would die. But since—"Blessed be God!"—they do lead into temptation, then—"Blessed be God!"—men continue to live.

Permit me to ask, how can we "thank God" if man (humanity) dies?

How could He say: "I am the way and the life?" He is nothing of the sort. Nothing even approaching it. "Adverbs."

Man in Paradise makes us understand why "stars and beauty" exist. He is already beautiful by himself and is the "morning star." I mean to say that God gave the morning star to man in paradise, and by the mysterious creation of Eden He expressed the whole plan of creating something wonderful, splendid, unique, inimitable. Everything aspires to this: "Better," "Better," "Better." There are measures and the measurable. It is as if God had announced: "I am immeasurable and everything which I have created aspires to the immeasurable, to the infinite, to the eternal." This can be understood. "There we find onyx and bdellium" (in Paradise). On the contrary, when we read the Gospel, what do we understand of the immeasurable? And not only of the immeasurable! In general, we understand nothing, exactly nothing of the universe.

And a great portent appeared in heaven, a woman clothed with the sun, with the moon under her feet, and on her head a crown of twelve stars.

She was with child and she cried out in her pangs of birth, in anguish for delivery.

Apocalypse 12:1-2.

Here we understand that childbirth, and specifically human childbirth, is at the center of cosmogony.

The Bible is infinite.

Jesus said: There are eunuchs who have been so from birth, and there are eunuchs who have been made eunuchs by men, and there are eunuchs who have made themselves eunuchs for the sake of the kingdom of heaven. He who is able to understand this, let him understand.

Matthew 19:12.

Here we understand absolutely nothing, except that it is useless.

The Gospel is a blind alley.

And now "sin" and "holiness," the "cosmic" and the "a-cosmical." It seems to me that if holiness exists, it is in the "predicate" of the world and not in the "adverbial modifiers." What aestheticism! The magnificence of the Gospel is striking: by speaking of the "works of the spirit" and opposing them to the "works of the flesh," Christ proves precisely in this way that "I and the Father are not one." The "Father" is truly a father. Look at the Old Testament, what don't you find there? The Father does not disdain to occupy himself with the smallest discomforts of his child, even when it is only a matter of caprices or acts of mischief. Thus we find "everything" in the Old Testament. Passions boil; no circumstance, however unlikely, is left out. The "Father" takes his child in his arms; he bathes it and cleans it, wipes its wet bottom. See what is said of the healing of sicknesses, of scabs, of scurf! In the desert he covers his people with a *shade* (cloud, heat) during the day; at night he goes before them in the form of a pillar of fire *to light their way*. They had stolen some golden objects from the Egyptians. This is not even dissimulated, for it is such a natural, such a simple thing: actually they had worked for them in slavery, worked without pay. This mysterious and profound solicitude which covers and envelops man is what distinguishes the "paternal testament" from that of the Son.

The Son, specifically, is "not one" with the Father. The ways of physiology are the cosmic ways, and "childbirth" takes place before "the sun, the moon, and the stars." Here also we have an *explanation* which is absolutely lacking in the Gospel. In fact, the vision of the *Apocalypse* shows that the moon, the stars, and the sun were made in order to facilitate "childbirth." *Life is placed above everything.* And human life above all. The pyramid is revealed clearly from its base to its summit. But the Gospel ends in a blind alley—in castration. "No need." No need even of childbirth. But then what good are the sun and the moon and the stars? The Gospel answers with a strange aestheticism: "They are for ornamentation." For the production of life they are useless. Just as "the sun, the moon, and the stars" ultimately exist for nothing, in the same way the Gospel has "no need" for childbirth, and the universe loses all meaning. "Everything is comprehensible" in the Bible; in the Gospel "one understands nothing."

Behold the throne of the *Apocalypse*, surrounded by animals. What, then, is this image of heaven? Still in what way is the cow who calves inferior to the woman who gives birth? These are the "divine ways." It is precisely in the "universal justification" undertaken by the *Apocalypse* that we rediscover the Divine and Paternal justification—with the sores, the scabs, the diarrheas, the constipations of his baby-man. What a wonder! Oh, how good it is! Great and glorious are Your ways, Lord! Glorious in sickness and in healing! The *Apocalypse* seems to set forth the truth of the Universe, the truth of Everything, as opposed to the *narrow* "evangelical truth" which leads, in a strange way, not to the riches, to the joy and the fullness of the world, but to the impasse, to the silence and the non-being of castration. In truth "the foundations of the earth are shaken." Christ came mysteriously to "shake all the foundations" of the Universe "said to have been created by his Father." And when Copernicus answered the question of the sun and the earth by "the squares of distances," this was a perfectly Christian answer. This is precisely an "adverbial modifier." As to knowing "why it is thus," we do not know and are not even interested.

In a mysterious way Christianity came little by little to content itself with "trifles." It answered the question of the earth and the moon by "the squares of distances." It resolved the caterpillar-cocoon-butterfly problem in an even less satisfactory manner by saying: "That's the way it is!" "Christian science" was ultimately reduced to twaddle, to positivism, to absurdity. "I have seen, I have heard, but I do not understand." "I see but I grasp nothing," and even "I have no opinion about it." Now the caterpillar, the cocoon, and the butterfly have an explanation, not in physiology but in cosmogony. Physiologically they are inexplicable, i.e., *inexpressible*. However, from the point of view of cosmogony, they are perfectly intelligible. Every living thing, absolutely everything which lives, participates thus in life, death, and resurrection.

The stages of the life of the insect represent the phases of universal *life*. The caterpillar: "We crawl, we eat, we are lifeless and immobile." "The cocoon" is the tomb and death, the tomb and vegetative life, the tomb and the *promise*. The butterfly is the "soul" plunged into the cosmic ether, flying, knowing only the sun and nectar, and nourishing itself only by plunging into the immense corollas of flowers. Christ said: "In the *future life* there will be no desire, neither will men give or be given in marriage." Yet the "butterfly" is the "future life" of the caterpillar, a life in which there is not only marriage but in which—in spite of the Gospel, in spite of the relative awkwardness of the caterpillar and the apparent death of the cocoon—the butterfly, which is wholly spiritualized and gives up eating entirely (it is stupefying! not only is its papilla not designed to eat with but it does not even have an intestine, at least in certain species), strange to say is in contact exclusively *with the sexual organs* of certain "beings which are strangers to it"—with the Tree of Life itself, so to speak, with incomprehensible, mysterious plants. This *je ne sais quoi* which appears to each butterfly is enormous, unfathomable. It is a forest, a garden. What does this mean? In a mysterious fashion the life of the butterfly shows us or predicts that our souls, too, beyond the cocoon-tomb, will taste of the nectar of two or of both divinities. For it is said that the Universe was created by Elo*him* (the dual form of the divine Name cited in the Biblical story of the Creation of the world) and not by Elo*ah* (singular). Thus there are *two* divinities and not *one:* "In the *image* and *likeness* of whom *God created man in the forms of man and woman.*"

The butterfly is the soul of the caterpillar. The soul alone, without extraneous elements. But this proves that the "soul" is not immaterial. It is tangible, visible; it *exists*, but *differently than in earthly existence.* How then? Oh, our dreams and our nocturnal visions are sometimes more real than our waking thoughts. The caterpillar and the butterfly demonstrate that on earth we do nothing but "eat," while "in the beyond" everything will be flight, movement, myrrh and incense.

The life *beyond the tomb* will be made of light and perfume. Precisely of something perceptible to the senses, physically odoriferous, of what gives off scent in a carnal and not in an incorporeal manner. We cannot say the words "temptations *of this world*" with a straight face. It is precisely in them that "the life of the future age" circulates, as flowing from the soul of things, from their entelechy. And that part of our face which was created to taste and to smell and which is, generally, the most beautiful and "celestial" part of our face, is beautiful only through the contours of the lips, the mouth and the nose. "What a monster is the man who has no lips or nose," or on whom they are mutilated or simply misshapen or ugly. What is most apocalyptic in us is our smile. The smile is the most apocalyptic of all.

Joy, you are the *spark of heaven, you are divine.*

Girl of the *Elysian fields* . . .

This is no allegory; it is a real, or more exactly a noumenal, truth. "It is good to be seduced" and "it is good to let oneself be tempted." He is good who "enters the world through temptation." He brings the edge of heaven to earth, which is rather dull by itself. A mysterious thing, the Gospel does not once mention scent, nothing odoriferous, aromatic, as if to emphasize its divergence from the flower of the Bible, the *Song of Songs*, that song of which a *starets* of the East once said: "The whole world is not worth the day which saw the creation of the *Song of Songs*." Thus the Gospel represents "this life" and the "future life" completely backward. The "ways" of life insofar as they are *physiological ways* are *the essential, the celestial* (the Throne of the *Apocalypse*); this is the "subject" which is "predicated."

As to the other "way of life," the "way of the *spirit*," this is an "adverb," the way of laziness, of aesthetics, of conversations . . .

⁓And *long has it languished in the world.*

It is the terrestrial life of the caterpillar who crawls and eats . . .

Filled with a marvelous desire.

It is the butterfly which bathes in ether, in the sun's rays. In the rays of the same Sun which is there only to envelop, "with the stars and the moon," "the woman with child."

> The tiresome songs of the earth
> Cannot, for her, replace the songs of love.[5]

No "hell or gnashing of teeth" *there*, but nectar taken from flowers. After having borne the sufferings, the mud, the dung, and the "geophagy" of the caterpillar, the tomb and the semblance, but only the *semblance*, of death, in the cocoon, the soul will rise from the coffin, and every soul, innocent or sinful, will live its ineffable "song of songs." It will be rendered unto each man according to his soul and his desire. Amen.

On the Passions of the World [6]

The earthly life here already contains the roots of life unearthly. As the poet says:

> There is exhilaration in *fight*. . . .

These are Mars and Ares, the deities of Mars and Ares; they are like gods. . . .

5. From a poem by Lermontov, *The Angel.*—TRANS.
6. From the eighth and ninth fascicles of *The Apocalypse of Our Times.*—TRANS.

And on the verge of the dark abyss,
And in the roaring of the hurricane,
And in the wafting of the plague . . .
The pledge may be of immortality. (Pushkin)

What a thought, what a thought flashed, *intuitively*, through Pushkin's mind! Just so, "the pledge of immortality and life eternal." This is the Hades and Eleusis of antiquity: and how can we help not believing in them and in their *reality*, if the thought of Pushkin, the Christian, of Pushkin, the poet—who at the moment of writing his poem was not thinking of the ancients— suddenly and unexpectedly, suddenly and unconsciously, suddenly and irresistibly approached the Greeks, the Romans, Tartarus, the ideas of Hesiod and of Homer. . . .

Similarly I thought of nothing when looking at a caterpillar, a chrysalis, and a butterfly, which I saw, on one hand, with one part of my being; but on the other hand I saw them as clearly, as distinctly, and not with *one* part of my being only.

Then, coming in to my friends who were staying with me, Professor Kapterev, the naturalist, and Florensky, the priest, I asked them:

"I say, in a caterpillar, chrysalis, and butterfly—which is the 'I'?"

I.e., the "I," as it were one letter, one scintillation, one ray.

Kapterev was silent; but Florensky, having thought for a moment, said: "Surely, the butterfly is the entelechy of the caterpillar and chrysalis."

"Entelechy" is an Aristotelian term, and one of the most famous terms which he himself thought out and composed philologically. A certain medieval schoolman sold his soul to the devil so that the latter might even in a dream explain to him what precisely Aristotle meant by "entelechy." But among other sayings, there is also this of Aristotle's: "The soul in the entelechy of the body." Then it became suddenly clear to me—from Florensky's answer (and what else could Florensky have said, if not this?)—that the "butterfly" is *really*, mysteriously, and metaphysically, the soul of the caterpillar and chrysalis.

Thus happened this cosmogonically overwhelming discovery. It may be said that the three of us *discovered* the soul of insects before it was discovered and *proved* in man.

Now let us see "what is it doing"?

"It gathers nectar," "it rummages among flowers." This is rather suspicious and *reprehensible*. But, actually, a butterfly has no *mouth*, nothing to drink with or to take in solid food. Kapterev, as a naturalist, said then: "They (he did not say *all of them*) have no intestines." Does it mean then that they have *not a stomach either?* Certainly! What a strange . . . being, existence? "It does not eat." Do they live for a long time? There are flies—*ephemerides*. And at any rate they, and beyond any doubt all of them, *copulate*. It means then the "world of the future age" is pre-eminently determined by "copulation"; and then light is thrown on its irresistibility, on its insatiability, and —"alas!" or "not alas!"—on its "sacredness," and that it is a "mystery" (the mystery of marriage). The further, the more discoveries. But it is obvious that in insects, cows, everywhere in the animal and vegetable world, and not only in man alone, it is a "mystery, heavenly and sacred." And, indeed, it is so, in its central point, *in copulation*. Then we understand "the shame that attaches to sexual organs": it is the "life of the future age," through which we enter into "life beyond the grave," into "life of the future age."

And, strangely, then becomes understandable also the *joy*. "Eden, bliss." Yet, more than this: let us examine the "nectar of flowers." Indeed, this particularly is amazing that insects (not butterflies only, but scarabs, beetles, ladybirds, etc.) rummage in the huge—as compared with their own size—sexual organs of trees, and particularly of bushes, roses, etc., oleanders and such like, orchids. *How do flowers appear to the butterflies?* This is what we must understand, and the *understanding of which is noumenally essential*. It is not impossible that to each insect there appears a "tree and flower." A garden and flowers are imagined as "paradise.". . . And so indeed it is: "summer, warmth, and the sun, into the rays of which they fly; and from the flowers they 'gather nectar.'" Then we can't help seeing the association of "nectar and the soul," and that the soul is for the nectar, and the nectar for the soul. Again, there is the myth: "the gods on

Olympus feed on nectar and ambrosia." But previous to the myth and parallel to it: what a flood of light is poured on "why do flowers smell," and why the flowers of plants are so huge that a whole insect can "enter into them." It is perfectly evident that the bigness of the flowers is just designed to allow the insect to enter *entire*. Then we can accept the idea that "plants hear and think" (as in the tales of antiquity), and that they "have a soul"!! Oh, what a soul! . . . But what is still more interesting that a "garden," any garden generally, "ours and earthly" is yet somehow not "ours" and not "earthly," but also of the future, of "life beyond the grave.". . . Then we can understand "*winter* and summer," since *out of the winter and through the winter*, having lain in the earth throughout the winter, the "seed rises from the grave." Essentially, in accordance with the same law, as does the "chrysalis" of the butterfly.

Thus "our fields" are "fields beyond the grave," "meadows of the life to come."

> When the yellowing field is stirring . . .
> Then in the skies I see God. . . .[7]

We understand then the peculiar and agitating feeling, experienced by man in a garden, experienced by us in a field, experienced by us in a forest—which, from a rationalist point of view, is *utterly inexplicable*. We understand why Antaeus, in touching mother-earth, recovers his former strength. A great many stories of "antiquity" become quite clear; as well as Dostoevsky's phrase, a phrase overwhelming, worthy of the *whole* Goethe, the pagan: "God has taken seeds *from other worlds* and planted them in the earth. And all that could grow, grew. *But everything on earth lives through the mysterious contact with the other worlds.*" Herein is the whole of paganism. As, for instance, the whole of Egypt, whose temples were just groves, pillars—trees, invariably trees with "flower-shaped capitals." And even a garden of ours is a mysterious temple, and not only does "sitting in the garden give health," but "sitting there turns one to prayer." Then we can understand the "sacred groves of antiquity," "the stillness of the night in the woods,"

7. Verses from Lermontov.—TRANS.

and Nature as sacred, not only "sacred theology alone." But let us return once more to the passions and to fire.

Through the passions and "orgies" we get an insight, mysterious yet real, into "the life of the future age." Just look how suspiciously and *reprehensibly* butterflies caress flowers! Yes, you can't help blaming them. But . . . there's "the life of the future age"; and, well, what's to be done? It becomes clear then, wherefrom and wherefore sprang the "orgies of antiquity," and that "without orgies there were no ancient religions." Remember the "nectar and ambrosia" of Olympus; and how in my *Oriental Motifs* I explained the Egyptian mysteries by means of drawings, *not daring to do it with words.* . . . Examining now collections of coins—coins of various countries with identical images—I already look at them with a feeling of kinship and with mute understanding. Without articulation and without words, just as I did in *Oriental Motifs,* the ancients conveyed through them their beloved mysteries, *all* of which they knew and knew *completely;* but no one has dropped a single word about "the life of the future age," of which life *in this earthly life silence must for ever be preserved.*

But . . . it is *thence* that "our passions" arise!!?? These are, indeed, "protuberances of the sun" (torches, eruptions from the body of the sun). And the sun itself, is not it subject to "passions"? Verily, "there are spots even on the sun." Christ alone is spotless. But our lovely sun is a bit of a "sinner": it burns and warms, it burns and heats; it burns—and in springtime when it "grows bigger," when it not only warms, but begins to excite the blood, all animals start conceiving. The strength of the sun, the "sin" of the sun, passes into animals. Everything grows stout, all bellies grow big. The earth itself wants seed. . . . There is Demeter, there is Gea, there again is the "stirring field heaving its breasts in prayer." Now, shall we say with Christianity that all this is "a lie"? And that theology can be found only in seminaries? But surely there is much more theology in a bull jumping on a cow. . . . And generally:

> Spring is coming, spring is coming
> And the green noise is rising, rising . . .

this is paganism which is true; this is Apis and Serapis.

Kapterev mused for a while and said: Observations show that in a caterpillar wrapped up in a cocoon and appearing as though dead, there actually begins after this a reconstruction of the tissues of the body. So that it does not only appear dead, but actually dies. . . . Only instead of the dead caterpillar there begins to emerge a something else, but just out of this definite caterpillar, as it were out of the caterpillar-personality, with as it were a Christian and family name. Since out of any caterpillar placed there will come *that butterfly there*. And if you were to pierce the caterpillar, say, with a pin, then no butterfly will come out of it, nothing will come out of it, and the grave will remain a grave, and the body will not "come to life again." At that moment, just then, it became clear to me why the fellahin (the descendants of the ancient Egyptians who have evidently preserved their whole faith) cried and fired their guns on the Europeans, when the latter carried away the mummies, removed from the pyramids and from the royal graves. They, those European nihilists, dead whilst alive and tainted, understanding neither life nor death, had violated the wholeness of their (fellahin's) ancestors, and thereby had deprived them of "resurrection." As Kapterev said, they as it were "broke the mummies in two," or "pierced the chrysalis with a pin," after which it *passes into the grave without being*. And, then, the idea that "the butterfly is the soul of the caterpillar," "the entelechy of the caterpillar" (according to Florensky) became still more confirmed in me; and above all it became clear and *proved* to me that the Egyptians in their thinking and in their discoveries of "life beyond the grave" had proceeded in the same way as I did; that is, through the "butterfly" and its "phases." That to them, too, it was a way of discoveries and revelations, and that it was altogether *true*. Then I clearly understood the sarcophagi-mummies. Who that has seen them on the ground floor of the Hermitage in Petersburg could help being struck first of all by their *size*? Why such a *large*, huge sarcophagus for a mummy of a dead person, which itself is not at all large? But surely this is the "cocoon" of the chrysalis-man; and the sarcophagus was invariably constructed on the model of a cocoon. Just as oblong and smooth as any cocoon which a caterpillar invariably builds was the sarcophagus which the

Egyptians made for the body "becoming a cocoon." And the body was put in winding-sheets, was wrapped, as the caterpillar of a silkworm, just letting out silk threads and, as it were, making a "silk shirt" for itself.

And a rough brown shell over it. That is the sarcophagus—always of a uniform brown tone. I think that even in its material it is identical with the shell of a chrysalis. Altogether the burial ritual of the Egyptians sprang from imitating the phases of the caterpillar. And hence chiefly comes the scarabeus, the insect as a symbol of transition into future life, into life after death. This is the most famous of Egyptian deities—one might say their greatest deity. Why an insect then? But there was there just the same way of reasoning, as in my case. The supreme, the highest that the Egyptians discovered, was "the insect-like future life." And they immortalized their discovery through the insect, the scarabeus. It is the noblest memory, i.e., the recollection and grateful memory of their own history and of the significance for which their history chiefly stood. Hence a multitude of explanations; as, for instance, why at "feasts" and particularly at "domestic feasts" they loved to carry mummies about. This is not sorrow, nor fear, nor a menace. Not the "Christian menace of death" which can cut short any joy. On the contrary: it is joy of the promise of eternal life, and *the joy of this life, of its limpidity and of its glory.* "We are now enjoying ourselves, but not yet perfectly," "we are at a feast, but not yet at a perfect one." Only when everything is over shall we participate in perfect love, in a perfect feast, with perfect food and drink. And our wine will be inexhaustible, and our drinks sweeter than all which we have here, for it will be pure love, and although material and concrete, yet already formed as it were out of the very rays of the sun, out of the light and scent and essence of flowers supernal. For if there are flowers, indeed they must be *supernal.*

Heavenly roses! Heavenly roses!! And the Egyptians carried about a mummy.

Index

This is one of three volumes of RUSSIAN PHILOSOPHY.

VOLUME I

The Beginnings of Russian Philosophy
The Slavophiles
The Westernizers

VOLUME II

The Nihilists
The Populists
Critics of Religion and Culture

VOLUME III

Pre-Revolutionary Philosophy and Theology
Philosophers in Exile
Marxists and Communists

The University of Tennessee Press